CBEST
California Basic Educational Skills Test

CBEST
California Basic Educational Skills Test

2nd Edition

NEW YORK

Copyright © 2002 LearningExpress, LLC.

All rights reserved under International and Pan-American Copyright Conventions.
Published in the United States by LearningExpress, LLC, New York.

Library of Congress Cataloging-in-Publication Data:
CBEST : California Basic Educational Skills Test.—2nd ed.
    p. cm.
   ISBN 1-57685-429-9 (pbk.)
  1. California Basic Educational Skills Test—Study Guides. I. Title:
California Basic Educational Skills Test. II. LearningExpress (Organization)
   LB3060.33.C34 C24 2002
   370'.76—dc21

                                                  2002011019

Printed in the United States of America
9 8 7 6 5 4 3 2 1
Second Edition

ISBN 1-57685-429-9

For more information or to place an order, contact LearningExpress at:
  900 Broadway
  Suite 604
  New York, NY 10003

Or visit us at:
  www.learnatest.com

Contents

INTRODUCTION:	How to Use This Book	vii
CHAPTER 1:	What is the CBEST?	1
CHAPTER 2:	LearningExpress Test Preparation System	7
CHAPTER 3:	Diagnostic CBEST Exam	25
CHAPTER 4:	CBEST Mini-Course	63
CHAPTER 5:	CBEST Practice Exam 1	155
CHAPTER 6:	CBEST Practice Exam 2	195
APPENDIX:	How to Use the CD-ROM	235

How to Use This Book

CHAPTER SUMMARY
So you have to take the CBEST, and you're wondering if this book can help you. The answer is YES! Read on to see how . . .

This book is designed to help you pass the California Basic Educational Skills Test (CBEST®). It contains all the information you'll need to help you improve your chances of achieving a good score—in the shortest amount of time possible. There are three components to your success on the CBEST: this book, a sample CBEST CD-ROM, and most importantly, *you* yourself.

▶ The Book

As you will discover in subsequent chapters, one of the most important skills for a test-taker to have is that of being a good reader. Good readers often begin with an overview of the text they are about to read. So, if you haven't done so yet, you may want to look at the Table of Contents. By doing this, you will know what to expect. Since time is of the essence, knowing what to expect offers you the freedom and opportunity to focus on what you think is most relevant to your goals.

After having browsed the Table of Contents, you can then turn to Chapter 1, "What is the CBEST?" This chapter tells you what the CBEST is; it provides you with the *Who, What, When, Where,* and *How,* those

HOW TO USE THIS BOOK

all-important details such as who must take the test, what it's like, when and where it's given, how it's scored, and how to register.

Once you know this basic information, you can skip right to Chapter 2, our innovative *LearningExpress Test Preparation System*. It is packed full of test-taking tips and advice developed by leading test experts exclusively for LearningExpress. This chapter shows you how to get prepared—physically, emotionally, and mentally—to take the CBEST. It also shows you how to use this book to set up your own study plan.

Chapter 3 is the first of three sample CBEST exams in this book. You can take this first exam as a diagnostic exercise to see where your strong and weak points are. Remember, in conjunction with this, you have access to a CD-ROM—that you can take and score at any time—to give you additional test-taking experience.

Next is Chapter 4, the "CBEST Mini-Course." This Mini-Course—successfully used for CBEST test prep classes in California—reviews everything you need to know to pass the CBEST. Conveniently divided into 24 lessons, you can cover it effortlessly in just half-hour pieces. The first pages of Chapter 4 give you an outline of the topics covered in each of the 24 lessons. You can work through the whole Mini-Course from start to finish, or you can pick out the areas that you need to work on most and just concentrate on those. If you're still having trouble after working through the lessons in a given area, check out the last section of Chapter 4, "More Help with Reading, Writing, and Math." This section lists other books you can turn to for more in-depth advice.

Then, in Chapters 5 and 6, you have two complete, three-section, sample CBEST exams, to help you practice your test-taking skills. Once finished with your practice test, you will be able to self-evaluate your progress with the answer and scoring explanations included at the end of each of these two chapters. Answer explanations are written in a friendly, informative, yet conversational tone, so you can quickly diagnose your weakest areas and see where you might need more work.

There's nothing like having a lot of practice under your belt to make you feel confident when you go in to take the real exam!

▶ The CD-ROM

The CD-ROM that comes free with this book includes hundreds of practice questions. You may choose to take one or more of your practice exams using your computer rather than writing the exam on paper. (You should take at least one practice exam on paper, though, since that's the format you will have to use when you take the real exam.) Or you may simply want to try some practice questions in Reading, Math, or Writing. You can do it either way; the CD-ROM gives you the option to take a complete test or select as many practice questions as you want. The CD-ROM will score your practice test or practice questions and let you know how you did. It will also, if you choose, show you the correct answer for each question and tell you why the answer is correct.

You have the option, when using the CD-ROM, of writing your essay either on paper or on the computer using a pop-up word processor. Either way, you should take your essay to a teacher or other professional you know to help you score it, using the scoring criteria the CD-ROM will distribute for you. (Unfortunately, computers aren't yet smart enough to grade a written piece!)

HOW TO USE THIS BOOK

▶ You

The most important factor in your success on the CBEST is *you*. You can't put this book under your pillow at night and expect to improve your score. But you can use this book, and the test scores from the CD-ROM, to find out where you need to improve and what you need to know. If you carefully follow all the steps in the *LearningExpress Test Preparation System*, you'll be fully prepared for the CBEST, and you will go into the exam knowing how to conquer this all-important test.

CBEST
California Basic **Educational** Skills Test

CHAPTER 1

What is the CBEST?

CHAPTER SUMMARY
This chapter provides the *Who, What, When, Where, and How* of the CBEST—those all-important details such as: who has to take it, what it's used for and what it's like, when and where it's given, how it's scored, and how to register.

California Education Code (Section 44252) requires that teachers, administrators, and other school practitioners demonstrate adequate proficiency, in English, of three basic skills: reading, mathematics, and writing. Administered by National Evaluation Systems, Inc. (NES®), the California Basic Educational Skills Test (CBEST®) was created to assess and verify these skills. The CBEST is not a measurement of teaching abilities or skills, but is rather a tool for measuring proficiency in the more basic, necessary skills as indicated above—skills employed by all school practitioners at the elementary, secondary, and adult education levels.

By law, the CBEST provides separate scores in each of these three areas, and acceptable scores must be achieved in each area to meet the requirements of this code relative to credentialing and employment in California—and Oregon.

In July 1984, the CBEST guideline was adopted by the Oregon Teacher Standards and Practices Commission (TSPC). Within six months, satisfactory CBEST scores were made mandatory for initial licensure in Oregon as a teacher, personnel specialist, or administrator. The CBEST test requirement is additional to other licensing requirements as set forth in the Oregon Revised Statutes (ORS, Chapter 342), and the Oregon Rules for

WHAT IS THE CBEST?

Licensure of Teachers, Personnel Specialists, and Administrators (OAR, Chapter 584).

▶ Who Must Take the CBEST?

California

In California, you are required to take the CBEST if any one of the following provisions applies to you:

- You are applying for a teaching or service credential for the first time.
- You are applying for issuance or renewal of an Emergency Permit unless you already hold a valid California teaching credential for which a bachelor's degree is required.
- If you have not taught during the 39 months prior to new employment, the CBEST may also be a condition of employment under CEC Section 44830. If you are uncertain whether the CBEST is required in the school district where you are considering employment, contact them for the necessary information.
- You are applying for admission to either a teacher-preparation or service-credential program approved by the California Commission on Teacher Credentialing (CCTC), unless you already hold a valid California teaching credential for which a bachelor's degree is required.

Oregon

Oregon requires passing CBEST scores prior to initial credentialing as a teacher, personnel specialist, or administrator, unless one of the following provisions is met:

- You can document five years of full-time, licensed employment in public schools in another state.
- You already hold one type of Oregon license and are a first-time applicant for a license of a different type. For example, an Oregon-licensed teacher who applies for an initial personnel specialist license does not need CBEST scores.
- You give evidence of passing scores on Praxis I, or the NTE Core Battery Test of Communication Skills and General Knowledge.

▶ Who is Exempt from the CBEST?

California

In California, you are exempt from taking the CBEST for the following kinds of employment:

- Instructor of adults in an apprenticeship program
- Teacher in a children's center or a development center
- Teacher in any subject for which a bachelor's degree is not required
- Provider of health services, unless you are also required to teach
- Student Teacher status, which requires a Certificate of Clearance
- Educational Specialist in Deaf and Hearing Impaired, or School Counseling Services, where the individual seeking employment is prelingually deaf. Service under this option is limited to state special schools or to classes for students who are deaf or hearing impaired. However, those who choose this option are required to complete a job-related assessment in lieu of the CBEST
- Any position where a valid, non-emergency California teaching credential is held which requires a bachelor's degree, and for which CBEST is not required for renewal
- Any position that requires the renewal or reissuance of a clear, or professional clear, credential

NOTE: CBEST states that candidates wishing to obtain an Exchange Credential, a Sojourn Credential, or a credential based upon the completion of a teacher-preparation program outside of California may obtain an initial teaching credential without meeting the CBEST requirement. All such candidates must pass the CBEST, however, during the first year of validity of the initial credential.

Oregon

In Oregon, you may be granted a two-year (24-month) exemption from the CBEST requirement if you have not yet passed the CBEST, but are otherwise qualified for licensure.

The CBEST waiver is only granted upon request of the employing school superintendent or school board in the event that (1) attempts were made to hire a properly licensed educator, but were unsuccessful, and that (2) the position is necessary for the school to operate normally. However, exemption can be granted without district request to candidates from states with reciprocral agreements in Oregon—such an exemption is nonrenewable. For further licensure, passing scores on the CBEST must be presented by the candidate.

▶ What is the CBEST Like?

What Sorts of Questions Does the CBEST Ask?

The CBEST exam is comprised of three separate sections: (1) Reading, which consists of 50 multiple-choice questions; (2) Mathematics, consisting of 50 multiple-choice questions; and (3) Writing, which consists of two essay subjects.

Questions in the Reading section are derived from two important skill areas: critical thinking/argument analysis, and research/comprehension. Drawn from a variety of fields, such as humanities, the social sciences, consumer affairs, or health, CBEST questions are based on passages that vary in degree of difficulty and complexity, and are designed to assess the test-taker's ability to evaluate and comprehend the information presented. Some passages are longer (200 words or more); some are shorter (about 100 words). Some may be statements of one or two sentences, while others may even be tables or graphs. Every question is based on a particular passage, table, or graph. None require outside knowledge, and all of the questions can be answered on the basis of the analysis and comprehension of the information provided.

The Mathematics section is mostly comprised of questions—presented as word problems—that evaluate the test-taker's ability to solve mathematical problems. The questions asked are designed to assess three major skill areas: estimation, measurement, and statistical principles; computation and problem solving; and numerical and graphic relationships.

The Writing section is comprised of two essay subjects—both of which the test-taker must respond to—and are designed to assess your ability to write coherently, authoritatively, and persuasively. In one of the essays, you will be asked to analyze a situation or statement, while the other requires a written response relating to a personal experience. Your essays must be written in your own words, and you must write only on the topics presented. All points in both essays must address the assigned topic, and should be aimed at a specific audience. Essay responses must support any assertions with specific, relevant details and examples. The key to success here is to stay specific—do not digress! For more detailed information on what it takes to write a fantastic essay, see the section on Writing in the CBEST Mini-Course (Chapter 4). The criteria for scoring the CBEST essays is found at the end of Chapter 5; many tips for successfully writing a "4" (Pass) essay are also found there.

How Long Does the CBEST Take?

When you take the CBEST, you have a total of four hours in which to complete the three separate sections.

You do not need to complete all three sections in one four-hour sitting. (The exception to this rule is the CBEST Writing section. The essays cannot be split up; both essays in the section must be completed at one sitting. They cannot be administered separately.) You may choose to concentrate on one or two sections at any given test administration, reregister, and then work solely on a third section at a later date. If you choose this latter option, take note that regardless of the number of sections you are taking at any given sitting—even just *one*—the *entire test fee* is required, and you will be required to reregister each time.

If you choose to do the whole test in one four-hour sitting, be aware that you don't have to do the sections in any particular order. The test is not timed according to individual sections, so you may want to get the hardest sections out of the way while you are fresh and still have your wits about you. You may want to do the essays first, because you can guess on the other sections if you run out of time. This may work to your advantage, since no points are deducted—there is no penalty—for guessing.

Doing the practice tests in this book, or taking advantage of the practice questions on the CD-ROM—which has the advantage of ease of use, and automatic, immediate test scores—will help you decide what is the best course of action for you.

What Should I Bring to the Test Site?

Because of test security, few materials are allowed in the test-taking room. You will need to bring the following materials:

- Your admission ticket
- Several sharpened #2 pencils with erasers
- A current, government-issued photo ID with signature

Some other materials NOT permitted in the testing room (unless previously authorized or provided by NES®) include:

- Scratch paper
- Calculators
- Dictionaries
- Cellular phones or other communication devices
- Alarm watches
- Visitors

Bringing any prohibited materials to a test administration may result in your score(s) being voided. If you have questions or require more detailed information on the day of the test, call CBEST at (916) 928-4001, from 7:30 A.M. to 3:30 P.M. PST (Pacific standard time).

What is a Passing Score?

To pass the CBEST, you must pass all three sections of the CBEST. Raw scores can range from 1–50, which are then converted to scaled scores ranging from 20–80. The passing scaled score on each section of the test is 41. You must achieve a minimum total score of 123 for the three sections to pass (the sum of the Reading, Writing, and Mathematics scaled scores).

It is possible to pass the CBEST even if your scaled score in one or two sections is as low as 37, providing your total scaled score is 123 or higher. (Take note that regardless of how high your total scaled score might be, you will *not* pass the CBEST if, in any section, you get a scaled score *lower* than 37.)

▶ What Do My Scores Mean?

You should receive your scores four to six weeks after the test date. For each section—Reading, Math, and Writing—your scores will announce whether or not you passed the section and will suggest areas within each section that you may need to study. The score report will also include the highest score you have obtained so far in that section. A passing score on any part of the test means that you will not have to take that part of the CBEST again!

Retaking the Test

What happens if you fail, or fail to finish, one or more sections of the CBEST? Don't worry. You don't need to pass all three sections at the same time, nor is there a limit to the number of times you can retake any or all sections of the CBEST to achieve a passing score. Once a section is passed, you need never take that section again. However, you may wish to repeat a section already passed to achieve a higher score, if that higher score can help you reach the total score required to pass the entire CBEST.

Once the entire CBEST has been passed, you will never have to take it again. You only need to pass the entire CBEST once to qualify for the initial issuance or future renewal of any teaching credential.

▶ How Do I Register for the CBEST?

When is the Test Given?

The CBEST is offered six times a year, once every two months, at various locations throughout California and Oregon. It is usually given on the first or second Saturday of the months of February, April, June, August, October, and December.

How Do I Register?

There are three periods of registration: Regular, Late, and Emergency; and three registration options: mail, phone, and Internet.

For Regular Registration, you should register at least one month prior to the applicable test date. You can register either by mail or the Internet; phone registration is not available for this option. If registering by mail, applications must be postmarked by the Regular Registration deadline, or received by the Late Registration deadline. If registering online, applications should be completed by 5:00 P.M. PST on the Regular Registration deadline.

For Late Registration (up to approximately two weeks prior to the test date), a late fee applies, and registration is granted on a space-available basis only. You may register by mail, phone, or Internet. If registering by mail, your completed materials must be received on or before the Late Registration deadline. If you register by phone, you must call before 5:00 P.M. PST on the Late Registration deadline. If registering online, your application must be finished by 5:00 P.M. PST on the Late Registration deadline.

For Emergency Registration (up to four days prior to the test), an additional late fee is charged, and registration is granted on a space-available basis only. You can register either by phone or Internet; mail registration is not available for this option. If you register by phone, you must call before 5:00 P.M. PST on the Emergency Registration deadline. If registering online, your application must be finished by 5:00 P.M. PST on the Emergency Registration deadline. Emergency Registration is limited to ten test areas in California, and one in Oregon.

Alternative testing arrangements can be made for either religious reasons or for special needs accommodations. All requests for alternative testing arrangements must be postmarked by the Regular Registration deadline for the test date applied for. Be advised that registration deadlines are *strictly enforced*—and there are NO exceptions!

Whom Do I Contact with Questions?

For any questions, or more detailed information regarding registration procedures, test dates, or locations, contact:

WHAT IS THE CBEST?

CBEST PROGRAM
National Evaluation Systems, Inc.
P.O. Box 340880
Sacramento, CA 95834-0880
916-928-4001
Telephones are open 9:00 A.M.–5:00 P.M. PST
  Monday–Friday, excluding holidays; Saturday test dates only: 7:30 A.M.–3:30 P.M. PST
Facsimile: 916-928-6110 (note: Registration forms are not accepted by fax)
Automated Information System is available 24 hours daily: 800-262-5080
CBEST website: www.cbest.nesinc.com
Telecommunications Device for the Deaf (TDD): 916-928-4191
Telephones are open from 9:00 A.M.–5:00 P.M. PST, Monday–Friday, excluding holidays; 7:30 A.M.–3:30 P.M. PST, Saturday test dates only.
For Late and Emergency Registration services: 916-928-4001
During phone-in registration periods, telephones are open from 9:00 A.M.–5:00 P.M. PST, Monday–Friday, excluding holidays.

For more detailed information about CBEST policies in general, contact:

CALIFORNIA COMMISSION ON TEACHER CREDENTIALING (CCTC)
Attention: CBEST Project Officer
P.O. Box 944270
Sacramento, CA 94244-2700
916-445-7254; If outside the 916 area code, call toll free: 888-921-2682.
Telephones are open 8:00 A.M.–5:00 P.M. PST, Monday–Friday, excluding holidays. (Automated Information System is available 24 hours daily.)
CCTC website: www.ctc.ca.gov
(Please include postal address in any e-mail messages.)

OR

Oregon Teacher Standards and Practices Commission
465 Commercial Street NE
Salem, OR 97310
503-378-3586

For more detailed information about CBEST test requirements in California and Oregon, or other questions:

- For college or university program admission in California, you can contact the department or school of education that you are interested in.
- For employment in California, you can contact the county school district's credentialing department, or office of education.
- For employment, or college or university Commission-approved program admission in Oregon, call the personnel office, or the Education Service District, of the school district you are interested in, the Dean of Teacher Education at the university or college you are interested in, or the Oregon Teacher Standards and Practices Commission.

▶ Don't Panic

The CBEST probably will not be the hardest test you will be faced with in your life. For many, it will require some careful and thoughtful preparation. If you have completed four years of college, you will be able to pass the CBEST. Some of you may need extensive review first, and some of you may need private tutoring. If you are willing to put forth the effort, passing is possible!

CHAPTER

LearningExpress Test Preparation System

CHAPTER SUMMARY

Taking the CBEST can be difficult. If you want to achieve a good score, it demands a lot of preparation. And you need that good score if you want to be certified! The LearningExpress Test Preparation System, developed exclusively for LearningExpress by leading test experts, gives you the attitude and discipline you need to be successful.

First, the bad news: Taking the CBEST is no picnic, and neither is getting ready for it. Your future career as a teacher depends on a good score, and there are all sorts of pitfalls that can keep you from doing your best on this all-important exam. Here are some of the obstacles that can stand in the way of your success:

- Being unfamiliar with the format of the exam
- Being paralyzed by test anxiety
- Leaving your preparation to the last minute
- Not preparing at all
- Not knowing vital test-taking skills: how to pace yourself through the exam, how to use the process of elimination, and when to guess
- Not being in tip-top mental and physical shape
- Arriving late at the test site, having to work on an empty stomach, or shivering through the exam because the room is cold

LEARNINGEXPRESS TEST PREPARATION SYSTEM

What's the common denominator in all these test-taking pitfalls? One word: control. Who's in control, you or the exam?

Now the good news: The LearningExpress Test Preparation System puts *you* in control. You only have to pass the CBEST *once*, and in nine easy-to-follow steps, you will learn everything you need to know to make sure that you do. Why? Because *you* will be in charge of your preparation and and your performance on the exam. *Other* test-takers may let the test get the better of them; *other* test-takers may be unprepared or out of shape, but not *you*. *You* will have taken all the steps you need to take to get a good score on the CBEST.

Here's how the LearningExpress Test Preparation System works: Nine easy steps lead you through everything you need to know and do to get ready to master your exam. Each of the steps listed below includes both reading about the step and one or more activities. It's important that you do the activities along with the reading, or you won't be getting the full benefit of the system. Each step tells you approximately how much time that step will take you to complete.

We estimate that working through the entire system will take you approximately three hours, though it's perfectly ok if you work faster or slower than the time estimates assume. If you can take a whole afternoon or evening, you can work through the whole LearningExpress Test Preparation System in one sitting. Otherwise, you can break it up, and do just one or two steps a day for the next several days. It's up to you—remember, *you're* in control.

▶ Step 1: Get Information

Time to complete: 60 minutes
Activities: Use the suggestions listed here to find out about the content of your exam.

Knowledge is power. The first step in the LearningExpress Test Preparation System is finding out everything you can about the CBEST. Once you have your information, the next steps in the LearningExpress Test Preparation System will show you what to do with it.

Part A: Straight Talk About the CBEST

Why do you have to take this exam? The states of California and Oregon require the CBEST for all applicants for a first-time teaching or service credential. Unless the applicant already has a California teaching credential or is exempted, he or she must take the CBEST in order to be issued—or obtain renewal of—an Emergency Permit. (This latter requirement does

Step 1. Get Information	60 minutes
Step 2. Conquer Test Anxiety	20 minutes
Step 3. Make a Plan	25 minutes
Step 4. Learn to Manage Your Time	10 minutes
Step 5. Learn to Use the Process of Elimination	20 minutes
Step 6. Know When to Guess	20 minutes
Step 7. Reach Your Peak Performance Zone	10 minutes
Step 8. Get Your Act Together	10 minutes
Step 9. Do It!	5 minutes
Total	**3 hours**

not apply to Oregon applicants.) The CBEST might also be required for applicants who have not taught for 39 months or more, and for students applying for admission to a California Commission on Teacher Credentialing (CCTC) approved teacher-preparation program.

But why reading, writing, and math? Why don't they test professional knowledge instead? Simply because the states of California and Oregon want to know that every teacher has the basic skills necessary both to communicate clearly to students, parents, and colleagues and to impart their knowledge of the English language and math to their students. Basically, the states just want to know that you *did* learn what you should have learned in high school and college.

Of course, there are all sorts of things a written exam like this can't test. So keep some perspective when you take this exam. Don't make the mistake of thinking that your score determines who you are or how smart you are or whether you'll make a good teacher. However, your chances of being certified depend on your getting a passing score. And that's why you're here—using the LearningExpress Test Preparation System to achieve control over your exam.

Part B: What's on the Test

If you haven't already done so, stop here and read the first chapter of this book, which gives you vital information on the CBEST. The CBEST is given six times a year at selected schools in California and Oregon; you can go to the placement office at your school or check the CBEST website, at the Web address listed in Chapter 1, to find out when and where to take the exam.

The CBEST tests the skills reflected in the practice exams in this book:

- **Reading comprehension:** demonstrating skills in criticism, understanding literal meaning, and making inferences
- **Writing:** demonstrating insight, logical thinking, and the ability to write clearly and coherently for a specific audience
- **Mathematics:** demonstrating skills in arithmetic, algebra, measurement, and geometry

▶ Step 2: Conquer Test Anxiety

Time to complete: 20 minutes
Activity: Take the Test Stress Test

Having complete information about the exam is the first step in getting control of the exam. Next, you have to overcome one of the biggest obstacles to test success: *test anxiety*. Test anxiety can not only impair your perfomance on the exam itself, but can even keep you from preparing! Having complete information about the exam is the first step in getting control of the exam, and with the LearningExpress Test Preparation System, you'll learn stress management techniques that will help you succeed on your exam. Learn these strategies now, and practice them as you work through the exams in this book, so they'll be second nature to you by exam day.

Combating Test Anxiety

The first thing you need to know is that a little test anxiety is a good thing. Everyone gets nervous before a big exam—and if that nervousness motivates you to prepare thoroughly, so much the better. It's said that Sir Laurence Olivier, one of the foremost British actors of this century, threw up before every performance. But his stage fright didn't impair his performance. In fact, it probably gave him a little extra edge—just the kind of edge you'll need to do well in the CBEST examination room.

Test Stress Test

You only need to worry about test anxiety if it is extreme enough to impair your performance. The following questionnaire will provide a diagnosis of your level of test anxiety. In the blank before each statement, write the number that most accurately describes your experience.

0 = Never
1 = Once or twice
2 = Sometimes
3 = Often

___ I have gotten so nervous before an exam that I simply put down the books and didn't study for it.
___ I have experienced disabling physical symptoms such as vomiting and severe headaches because I was nervous about an exam.
___ I have simply not showed up for an exam because I was scared to take it.
___ I have experienced dizziness and disorientation while taking an exam.
___ I have had trouble filling in the little circles because my hands were shaking too hard.
___ I have failed an exam because I was too nervous to complete it.
___ **Total:** Add up the numbers in the blanks above.

Your Test Anxiety Score

Here are the steps you should take, depending on your score. If you scored:

- **Below 3**, your level of test anxiety is nothing to worry about; it is probably just enough to give you that little extra edge.
- **Between 3 and 6**, your test anxiety may be enough to impair your performance, and you should practice the stress management techniques listed in this section to try to bring your test anxiety down to manageable levels.
- **Above 6**, your level of test anxiety is a serious concern. In addition to practicing the stress management techniques listed in this section, you may want to seek additional, personal help. Call your local high school or community college and ask for the academic counselor. Tell the counselor that you have a level of test anxiety that sometimes keeps you from being able to take an exam. The counselor may be willing to help you or may suggest someone else you should talk to.

On the previous page is the Test Stress Test. Stop here and answer the questions on that page, to find out whether your level of test anxiety is something you will need to manage.

Stress Management Before the Test

If you feel your level of anxiety getting the best of you in the weeks before the test, here is what you need to do to bring the level down again:

- **Get prepared.** There's nothing like knowing what to expect and being prepared for it to put you in control of test anxiety. That's why you're reading this book. Use it faithfully, and remind yourself that you're better prepared than most of the people taking the test.
- **Practice self-confidence.** A positive attitude is a great way to combat test anxiety. This is no time to be humble or shy. Stand in front of the mirror and say to your reflection, "I'm prepared. I'm full of self-confidence. I'm going to ace this test. I know I can do it." Say it into a tape recorder and play it back once a day. Memorize the words. If you hear it often enough, you'll believe it.
- **Fight negative messages.** Every time someone starts telling you how hard the exam is or how it's almost impossible to get a good score, start telling them the self-confidence messages you have been practicing. If the person with the negative messages is you, telling yourself you don't do well on exams, you just can't do this, don't listen. Turn on your tape recorder and listen to your self-confidence messages.
- **Visualize.** Imagine yourself standing in front of your class or chatting with a student. Think of yourself coming home with your first paycheck as a teacher and taking your family or friends out to celebrate. Visualizing success can help make it happen—and it reminds you of why you're going through all this work in preparing for the exam.
- **Exercise.** Physical activity helps calm your body down and focus your mind. Besides, being in good physical shape can actually help you do well on the exam. Go for a run, lift weights, go swimming—and do it regularly.

Stress Management on Test Day

There are several ways you can bring down your level of test anxiety on test day. Practice them in the weeks before the test; they'll be effective only if you know which ones work best for you.

- **Deep breathing.** Take a deep breath while you count to five. Hold it for a count of one, then let it out on a count of five. Repeat several times.
- **Move your body.** Try rolling your head in a circle. Rotate your shoulders. Shake your hands from the wrist. Many people find these movements very relaxing.
- **Visualize again.** Think of the place where you are most relaxed: perhaps lying on the beach in the sun or walking through the park. Now close your eyes and imagine you're actually there. If you practice in advance, you'll find that you only need a few seconds of this exercise to experience a significant increase in your sense of well-being.

When anxiety threatens to overwhelm you right there during the exam, there are still things you can do to manage the stress level:

- **Repeat your self-confidence messages.** You should have them memorized by now. Say them quietly to yourself, and believe them!
- **Visualize one more time.** This time, visualize yourself moving smoothly and quickly through the test, answering every question right and

finishing with time to spare. Like most visualization techniques, this one works best if you've practiced it ahead of time.
- **Find an easy question.** Skim over the test until you find an easy question, and answer it. Getting even one circle filled in gets you into the test-taking groove.
- **Take a mental break.** Everyone loses concentration once in a while, so don't worry about it. Instead, accept what has happened. Say to yourself, "Hey, I lost it there for a minute. My brain is taking a break." Put down your pencil, close your eyes, and do some deep breathing for a few seconds. Then you're ready to go back to work.

Use these tried and true techniques ahead of time, and see if they don't work for you!

▶ Step 3: Make a Plan

Maybe the most important thing you can do to manage anxiety and get control of your exam is to make a study plan. Too many people fail their test simply because they don't allot enough study time for test preparation! Spending hours cramming on the day before the test, poring over sample test questions, not only raises the level of your test anxiety, but there is simply no substitute for careful preparation and practice over time!

So DON'T fall into the cram trap. Take control of your preparation time by mapping out a study schedule. In fact, all the instructional material you'll need to study for the CBEST is in Chapter 4, the "CBEST Mini-Course." The "Mini-Course" is conveniently divided into 24 half-hour lessons, so a study schedule has already been provided for you, built right into the LearningExpress Test Preparation System. The best way to devise your own personal study plan is to first do the sample CBEST Diagnostic Exam in Chapter 3 of this book. Your study plan will be based on your own personalized scores from each of the individual sections—with this knowledge, you can then concentrate on the areas that give you the most difficulty.

On the following pages, we have provided sample schedules of "what" you should do "when," based on how much time you have before you take the exam. If you have months before the exam—lucky you! REMEMBER: You can't improve your reading, writing, and math skills overnight! So...

- DON'T PUT OFF YOUR STUDY UNTIL THE WEEK BEFORE THE EXAM!
- START NOW!

You have to set aside some time **every** day for study and practice. Try for at least thirty (30) minutes a day—but even a few minutes a day, with a half-hour or more on weekends, can make a big difference in your score—and in your chances of landing that plum teaching job!

▶ Schedule A: The Leisure Plan

If you have six months or more in which to prepare, you're lucky! Make the most of your time.

▶ Schedule B: The Just-Enough-Time Plan

If you have three to five months before the exam, you still have enough time to prepare for the written test. This schedule assumes four months; stretch it out or compress it if you have more or less time.

Schedule A: The Leisure Plan

Time	Preparation
Exam minus 6 months	Take the CBEST Diagnostic in Chapter 3 and skim the 24 lessons in the Mini-Course. Based on your scores on the individual sections of the diagnostic exam, divide up the next 5 months into segments of time which you estimate each lesson will take. Be sure to schedule in more time on those skills that give you problems.
Exam minus 6 months to 2 months	Work steadily and calmly through each lesson, sticking to your schedule and being sure to do the practice exercises. Besides doing the lessons, be sure to read more during these months than you are accustomed to—novels, non-fiction books, magazines, newspapers; it is very important for the CBEST that your reading skills be honed. Also, look at the "More Help" section of the Mini-Course. Choose one or two books from the area that gives you the most trouble, and use them to help you improve your weak area.
Exam minus 2 months	Take the first practice exam, CBEST Practice Exam 1. Use your score to help you decide where to concentrate your efforts. Review the relevant lessons of the Mini-Course and get the help of a friend or teacher. If necessary, choose additional resources from the "More Help" section of the Mini-Course to help you.
Exam minus 2 weeks	Take the second practice test, CBEST Practice Exam 2, to see how much you've improved, and then, again, review the areas that give you the most trouble.
Exam minus 1 day	Relax. Do something unrelated to the exam. Eat a good meal and go to bed at your usual time.

Schedule B: The Just-Enough-Time Plan

Time	Preparation
Exam minus 4 months	Take the CBEST diagnostic in Chapter 3 and skim the 24 lessons in the Mini-Course. Based on your scores on the individual sections of the diagnostic exam, divide up the next 4 months into segments of time which you estimate each lesson will take. Be sure to schedule in more time on those skills that give you problems.
Exam minus 4 months to 1 month	Work steadily and calmly through each lesson, sticking to your schedule and being sure to do the practice exercises. Besides doing the lessons, schedule in more reading during these months than you're used to doing—novels, non-fiction books, magazines, newspapers; it is very important for the CBEST that your reading skills be in top shape. If you fall behind in your schedule, remember that *you're* in control—it's your schedule. Don't shrug your shoulders and moan, "I'll never make it!" Just take a look at the schedule, see where you went off track, revise the schedule for the time you have left, and continue.
Exam minus 2 months	Take the first practice exam, CBEST Practice Exam 1. Use your score to help you decide where to concentrate your efforts. Review the relevant lessons of the Mini-Course and get the help of a friend or teacher. If you need more help, choose additional resources.
Exam minus 2 weeks	Take the second practice test, CBEST Practice Exam 2, to see how much you've improved, and then, again, review the areas that give you the most trouble.
Exam minus 1 day	Relax. Do something unrelated to the exam. Eat a good meal and go to bed at your usual time.

Schedule C: More Study in Less Time

Time	Preparation
Exam minus 2 months	Take the CBEST diagnostic in Chapter 3 and skim the 24 lessons in the Mini-Course. Based on your scores on the individual sections of the diagnostic exam, divide up the next month into segments of time which you estimate each lesson will take. Be sure to schedule in more time on those skills that give you problems.
Exam minus 2 months to 1 month	Work quickly, but steadily and calmly, through each lesson, sticking to your schedule and being sure to do the practice exercises. Besides doing the lessons, schedule in more reading than you usually do—novels, non-fiction books, magazines, newspapers; it is crucial for the CBEST that your reading skills be their sharpest. If you fall behind in your schedule, remember that *you* are the one who devised the schedule, and you're in control. Don't take to your bed lamenting, "I can't, I can't!" Just peruse your schedule, see where you went astray, revise the schedule for the time you have left, and forge ahead.
Exam minus 2 weeks	Take the first practice exam, CBEST Practice Exam 1. Use your score to help you decide where to concentrate your efforts. Review the relevant lessons of the Mini-Course and get the help of a friend or teacher. If necessary, get more help.
Exam minus 1 week	Take the second practice test, CBEST Practice Exam 2, to see how much you've improved, and then, again, review the areas that give you the most trouble.
Exam minus 1 day	Relax. Do something unrelated to the exam. Eat a good meal and go to bed at your usual time.

Schedule D: The Cram Plan

Time	Preparation
Exam minus 3 weeks	Take the CBEST diagnostic in Chapter 3 and skim the 24 lessons in the Mini-Course. Based on your score, choose one area to concentrate on this week: reading, writing, or math. Spend an hour a day working on that area.
Exam minus 2 weeks	First, skim over the CBEST Mini-Course lessons on the areas you didn't study last week. Choose 6 lessons to do in the first three days of this week. For the rest of the days, go back to the one area you need the most work on, and review the lessons that were most difficult for you.
Exam minus 1 week	Take the first practice exam, CBEST Practice Exam 1. Use your score to help you decide where to concentrate your efforts. Review the relevant lessons and get the help of a friend or teacher on those areas.
Exam minus 3 days	Take the second practice test, CBEST Practice Exam 2, to see how much you've improved, and then, again, review the areas that give you the most trouble.
Exam minus 1 day	Relax. Do something unrelated to the exam. Eat a good meal and go to bed at your usual time.

LEARNINGEXPRESS TEST PREPARATION SYSTEM

▶ Schedule C: More Study in Less Time

If you have one to three months before the exam, you still have enough time for some concentrated study that will help you improve your score. This schedule is built around a two-month time frame. If you have only one month, spend an extra couple of hours a week to get all these steps in. If you have three months, take some of the steps from Schedule B and fit them in.

▶ Schedule D: The Cram Plan

If you have three weeks or less before the exam, you really have your work cut out for you. Carve a half-hour out of your day, every day, for study. This schedule assumes you have the whole three weeks to prepare; if you have less time, you'll have to compress the schedule accordingly.

▶ Step 4: Learn to Manage Your Time

Time to complete: 10 minutes to read, many hours of practice!
Activities: Practice these strategies as you take the sample tests in this book
Steps 4, 5, and 6 of the LearningExpress Test Preparation System put you in charge of your exam by showing you test-taking strategies that work. Practice these strategies as you take the sample tests in this book, and then you'll be ready to use them on test day.

First, you'll take control of your time on the exam. The CBEST has a time limit of four hours, which may give you more than enough time to complete all the questions—or may not. It's a terrible feeling to hear the examiner say, "Five minutes left," when you're only three-quarters of the way through the test.

Here are some tips to keep that from happening to you.

- **Follow directions.** If the directions are given orally, listen to them. If they're written on the exam booklet, read them carefully. Ask questions before the exam begins if there's anything you don't understand. In your exam booklet, write down the beginning time and the ending time of the exam.
- **Pace yourself.** Glance at your watch every ten or fifteen minutes, and compare the time to how far you've gotten in the exam. When one-quarter of the time has elapsed, you should be a quarter of the way through the exam, and so on. If you're falling behind, pick up the pace a bit.
- **Keep moving.** Don't waste time on one question. If you don't know the answer, skip the question and move on. Circle the number of the question in your test booklet in case you have time to come back to it later.
- **Keep track of your place on the answer sheet.** If you skip a question, make sure you skip the corresponding bubble on the answer sheet too. Check yourself every 5–10 questions to make sure the question number and the answer sheet number are still the same.
- **Don't rush.** Though you should keep moving, rushing won't help. Try to keep calm. Work methodically and quickly.

▶ Step 5: Learn to Use the Process of Elimination

Time to complete: 20 minutes
Activity: Complete worksheet on Using the Process of Elimination
After time management, your next most important tool for taking control of your exam is using the

process of elimination wisely. It's standard test-taking wisdom that you should always read all the answer choices before choosing your answer. This helps you find the right answer by eliminating wrong answer choices. And, sure enough, that standard wisdom applies to your exam, too.

Let's say you're facing a reading comprehension question that goes like this:

13. According to the passage above, "Biology uses a <u>binomial</u> system of classification." In the context of the passage, the word <u>binomial</u> most nearly means
    a. understanding the law.
    b. having two names.
    c. scientifically sound.
    d. having a double meaning.

If you happen to know what *binomial* means, of course, you don't need to use the process of elimination, but let's assume that you don't. So you look at the answer choices. "Understanding the law" doesn't sound likely for something having to do with biology. So you eliminate choice **a**—and now you only have three answer choices to deal with. Mark an X next to choice **a** so you never have to read it again.

On to the other answer choices. If you know that the prefix *bi-* means *two*, as in *bicycle*, you'll flag answer **b** as a possible answer. Mark a check mark beside it, meaning "good answer, I might use this one."

Choice **c**, "scientifically sound," is a possibility. At least it's about science, not law. It could work here, though, when you think about it, having a "scientifically sound" classification system in a scientific field is kind of redundant. You remember the *bi* thing in *binomial*, and probably continue to like answer **b** better. But you're not sure, so you put a question mark next to **c**, meaning "well, maybe."

Now, choice **d**, "having a double meaning." You're still keeping in mind that *bi-* means *two*, so this one looks possible at first. But then you look again at the sentence the word belongs in, and you think, "Why would biology want a system of classification that has two meanings? That wouldn't work very well!" If you're really taken with the idea that *bi* means *two*, you might put a question mark here. But if you're feeling a little more confident, you'll put an X. You've already got a better answer picked out.

Now your question looks like this:

13. According to the passage above, "Biology uses a binomial system of classification." In the context of the passage, the word binomial most nearly means
    X a. understanding the law.
    ✓ b. having two names.
    ? c. scientifically sound.
    ? d. having a double meaning.

You've got just one check mark, for a good answer. If you're pressed for time, you should simply mark answer **b** on your answer sheet. If you've got the time to be extra careful, you could compare your check-mark answer to your question-mark answers to make sure that it's better. (It is: the *binomial* system in biology is the one that gives a two-part genus and species name like *homo sapiens*.)

It's good to have a system for marking good, bad, and maybe answers. We're recommending this one:

X = bad
✓ = good
? = maybe

If you don't like these marks, devise your own system. Just make sure you do it long before test day—while you're working through the practice exams in this book—so you won't have to worry about it during the test.

Using the Process of Elimination

Use the process of elimination to answer the following questions.

1. Ilsa is as old as Meghan will be in five years. The difference between Ed's age and Meghan's age is twice the difference between Ilsa's age and Meghan's age. Ed is 29. How old is Ilsa?
   a. 4
   b. 10
   c. 19
   d. 24

2. "All drivers of commercial vehicles must carry a valid commercial driver's license whenever operating a commercial vehicle."
   According to this sentence, which of the following people need **NOT** carry a commercial driver's license?
   a. a truck driver idling his engine while waiting to be directed to a loading dock
   b. a bus operator backing her bus out of the way of another bus in the bus lot
   c. a taxi driver driving his personal car to the grocery store
   d. a limousine driver taking the limousine to her home after dropping off her last passenger of the evening

3. Smoking tobacco has been linked to
   a. increased risk of stroke and heart attack.
   b. all forms of respiratory disease.
   c. increasing mortality rates over the past ten years.
   d. juvenile delinquency.

4. Which of the following words is spelled correctly?
   a. incorrigible
   b. outragous
   c. domestickated
   d. understandible

Answers

Here are the answers, as well as some suggestions as to how you might have used the process of elimination to find them.

1. **d.** You should have eliminated answer **a** immediately. Ilsa can't be four years old if Meghan is going to be Ilsa's age in five years. The best way to eliminate other answer choices is to try plugging them in to the information given in the problem. For instance, for answer **b**, if Ilsa is 10, then Meghan must be 5. The difference in their ages is 5. The difference between Ed's age, 29, and Meghan's age, 5, is 24. Is 24 two times 5? No. Then answer **b** is wrong. You could eliminate answer **c** in the same way and be left with answer **d**.

2. **c.** Note the word *not* in the question, and go through the answers one by one. Is the truck driver in choice **a** "operating a commercial vehicle?" Yes, idling counts as "operating," so he needs to have a commercial driver's license. Likewise, the bus operator in answer **b** is operating a commercial vehicle; the question doesn't say the operator has to be on the street. The limo driver in choice **d** is operating a commercial vehicle, even if it doesn't have a passenger in it. However, the cabbie in answer **c** is not operating a commercial vehicle, but his own private car.

Using the Process of Elimination (continued)

3. a. You could eliminate answer **b** simply because of the presence of the word *all*. Such absolutes hardly ever appear in correct answer choices. Choice **c** looks attractive until you think a little about what you know—aren't fewer people smoking these days, rather than more? So how could smoking be responsible for a higher mortality rate? (If you didn't know that mortality rate means the rate at which people die, you might keep this choice as a possibility, but you would still be able to eliminate two answers and have only two to choose from.) And choice **d** is plain silly, so you could eliminate that one, too. You are left with the correct choice, **a**.

4. a. How you used the process of elimination here depends on which words you recognized as being spelled incorrectly. If you knew that the correct spellings were outrageous, domesticated, and understandable, then you were home free.

Even when you think you're absolutely clueless about a question, you can often use the process-of-elimination technique to get rid of one answer choice. If so, you're better prepared to make an educated guess, as you'll see in Step 6. More often, the process of elimination allows you to get down to only two possibly right answers. Then you're in a stronger position to guess. And sometimes, even though you don't know the right answer, you find it simply by getting rid of the wrong ones, as you did in the example above.

Try using your powers of elimination on the questions in the Using the Process of Elimination worksheet on the next page. The answer explanations there show one possible way you might use the process to arrive at the right answer.

The process of elimination is your tool for the next step, which is knowing when to guess.

▶ Step 6: Know When to Guess

Time to complete: 20 minutes
Activity: Complete worksheet on Your Guessing Ability
Armed with the Process of Elimination, you're ready to take control of one of the big questions in test-taking: Should I guess? The first and main answer is "Yes." Unless an exam has a so-called "guessing penalty," you have nothing to lose and everything to gain from guessing. The more complicated answer depends on you—your personality and your "guessing intuition."

The CBEST doesn't have a guessing penalty. The number of questions you answer correctly yields your score, and there's no penalty for wrong answers. So simply go ahead and guess. But try not to guess wildly unless you absolutely have to. Remember to read the question carefully. You may know more about the subject than you think. Use the process of elimination as outlined in Step 5.

"Yes," you might say, "but the whole idea of guessing makes me nervous. I'm not good at guessing." Maybe, maybe not. Maybe you're not much of a risk-taker, so you don't like to guess. But remember, nothing bad can happen to you if you're wrong.

But maybe you really think you have lousy intuition. It seems like, when you have to guess, you *always* guess wrong! Test out your assumption about your guessing ability. Complete the Your Guessing Ability worksheet to get an idea of how good or bad your intuition really is.

Remember, nothing can happen to you if you're wrong.

Your Guessing Ability

The following are ten really hard questions. You're not supposed to know the answers. Rather, this is an assessment of your ability to guess when you don't have a clue. Read each question carefully, just as if you did expect to answer it. If you have any knowledge at all of the subject of the question, use that knowledge to help you eliminate wrong answer choices. Use this answer grid to fill in your answers to the questions.

1. September 7 is Independence Day in
   a. India.
   b. Costa Rica.
   c. Brazil.
   d. Australia.

2. Which of the following is the formula for determining the momentum of an object?
   a. p = MV
   b. F = ma
   c. P = IV
   d. $E = mc^2$

3. Because of the expansion of the universe, the stars and other celestial bodies are all moving away from each other. This phenomenon is known as
   a. Newton's first law.
   b. the big bang.
   c. gravitational collapse.
   d. Hubble flow.

4. American author Gertrude Stein was born in
   a. 1713.
   b. 1830.
   c. 1874.
   d. 1901.

5. Which of the following is **NOT** one of the Five Classics attributed to Confucius?
   a. the I Ching
   b. the Book of Holiness
   c. the Spring and Autumn Annals
   d. the Book of History

6. The religious and philosophical doctrine that holds that the universe is constantly in a struggle between good and evil is known as
   a. Pelagianism.
   b. Manichaeanism.
   c. neo-Hegelianism.
   d. Epicureanism.

7. The third Chief Justice of the U.S. Supreme Court was
   a. John Blair.
   b. William Cushing.
   c. James Wilson.
   d. John Jay.

8. Which of the following is the poisonous portion of a daffodil?
   a. the bulb
   b. the leaves
   c. the stem
   d. the flowers

9. The winner of the Masters golf tournament in 1953 was
   a. Sam Snead.
   b. Cary Middlecoff.
   c. Arnold Palmer.
   d. Ben Hogan.

10. The state with the highest per capita personal income in 1980 was
    a. Alaska.
    b. Connecticut.
    c. New York.
    d. Texas.

Your Guessing Ability (continued)

Answers
Check your answers against the correct answers below.
1. c.
2. a.
3. d.
4. c.
5. b.
6. b.
7. b.
8. a.
9. d.
10. a.

How Did You Do?
You may have simply gotten lucky and actually known the answer to one or two questions. In addition, your guessing was more successful if you were able to use the process of elimination on any of the questions. Maybe you didn't know who the third Chief Justice was (question 7), but you knew that John Jay was the first. In that case, you would have eliminated answer **d** and therefore improved your odds of guessing right from one in four to one in three.

According to probability, you should get $2\frac{1}{2}$ answers correct, so getting either two or three right would be average. If you got four or more right, you may be a really terrific guesser. If you got one or none right, your guessing may need some improvement.

Keep in mind, though, that this is only a small sample. You should continue to keep track of your guessing ability as you work through the sample questions in this book. Circle the numbers of questions you guess on as you make your guess. Or, if you don't have time while you take the practice tests, go back afterward and try to remember which questions you guessed at. Remember, on a test with five answer choices, your chances of getting a right answer are one in five, so keep a separate "guessing" score for each exam. How many questions did you guess on? How many did you get right? If the number you got right is at least one-fifth of the number of questions you guessed on, you are at least an average guesser, maybe better—and you should always go ahead and guess on the real exam. If the number you got right is significantly lower than one-fifth of the number you guessed on, maybe you're not such a good guesser. Since there's no guessing penalty, you would be safe in guessing anyway, but maybe you'd feel more comfortable if you guessed only selectively, when you can eliminate a wrong answer or at least have a good feeling about one of the answer choices.

▶ Step 7: Reach Your Peak Performance Zone

Time to complete: 10 minutes to read; weeks to complete!
Activity: Complete the Physical Preparation Checklist
To get ready for a challenge like a big exam, you have to take control of your physical, as well as your mental, state. Exercise, proper diet, and rest will ensure that your body works with, rather than against, your mind on test day, as well as during your preparation.

Exercise
If you don't already have a regular exercise program going, the time during which you're preparing for an exam is actually an excellent time to start one. And if you're already keeping fit—or trying to get that way—don't let the pressure of preparing for an exam fool you into quitting now. Exercise helps reduce stress by pumping wonderful good-feeling hormones called endorphins into your system. It also increases the oxygen supply throughout your body, including your brain, so you'll be at peak performance on test day.

Physical Preparation Checklist

Physical Preparation Checklist
For the week before the test, write down (1) what physical exercise you engaged in and for how long and (2) what you ate for each meal. Remember, you're trying for at least half an hour of exercise every other day (preferably every day) and a balanced diet that's light on junk food.

Exam minus 7 days
Exercise: _____ for _____ minutes
Breakfast: _____
Lunch: _____
Dinner: _____
Snacks: _____

Exam minus 6 days
Exercise: _____ for _____ minutes
Breakfast: _____
Lunch: _____
Dinner: _____
Snacks: _____

Exam minus 5 days
Exercise: _____ for _____ minutes
Breakfast: _____
Lunch: _____
Dinner: _____
Snacks: _____

Exam minus 4 days
Exercise: _____ for _____ minutes
Breakfast: _____
Lunch: _____
Dinner: _____
Snacks: _____

Exam minus 3 days
Exercise: _____ for _____ minutes
Breakfast: _____
Lunch: _____
Dinner: _____
Snacks: _____

Exam minus 2 days
Exercise: _____ for _____ minutes
Breakfast: _____
Lunch: _____
Dinner: _____
Snacks: _____

Exam minus 1 day
Exercise: _____ for _____ minutes
Breakfast: _____
Lunch: _____
Dinner: _____
Snacks: _____

A half hour of vigorous activity—enough to raise a sweat—every day should be your aim. If you're really pressed for time, every other day is OK. Choose an activity you like and get out there and do it. Jogging with a friend or listening to music always makes the time go faster.

But don't overdo it. You don't want to exhaust yourself. Moderation is the key.

Diet

First of all, cut out all the junk food. Go easy on caffeine and nicotine, and eliminate alcohol from your system at least two weeks before the exam. Promise yourself a binge the night after the exam, if need be.

What your body needs for peak performance is simply a balanced diet. Eat plenty of fruits and vegetables, along with protein and carbohydrates. Foods that

LEARNINGEXPRESS TEST PREPARATION SYSTEM

are high in lecithin (an amino acid), such as fish and beans, are especially good "brain foods."

The night before the exam, you might "carbo-load" the way athletes do before a contest. Eat a big plate of spaghetti, rice and beans, or whatever your favorite carbohydrate is.

Rest

You probably know how much sleep you need every night to be at your best, even if you don't always get it. Make sure you do get that much sleep, though, for at least a week before the exam. Moderation is important here, too. Extra sleep will just make you groggy.

If you're not a morning person and your exam will be given in the morning, you should reset your internal clock so that your body doesn't think you're taking an exam at 3 A.M. You have to start this process well before the exam. Try to get up a half hour earlier each morning, and then go to bed half an hour earlier that night. The next morning, get up half an hour earlier, and so on. How long you will have to do this depends on how late you're used to getting up.

Step 8: Get Your Act Together

Time to complete: 10 minutes to read; time to complete will vary
Activity: Complete Final Preparations worksheet
You're in control of your mind and body; you're in charge of test anxiety, your preparation, and your test-taking strategies. Now it's time to take charge of external factors, like the testing site and the materials you need to take the exam.

Find Out Where the Test Is and Make a Trial Run

You'll know ahead of time when and where your exam is being held. But do you know how to get to the testing site? Do you know how long it will take to get there? If not, make a trial run, preferably on the same day of the week at the same time of day. Make note, on the Final Preparations worksheet, of the amount of time it will take you to get to the exam site. Plan on arriving 10–15 minutes early so you can get the lay of the land, use the bathroom, and calm down. Then figure out how early you will have to get up that morning, and make sure you get up that early every day for a week before the exam.

Gather Your Materials

The night before the exam, lay out the clothes you will wear and the materials you have to bring with you to the exam. Plan on dressing in layers; you won't have any control over the temperature of the examination room. Have a sweater or jacket you can take off if it's warm. Use the checklist on the Final Preparations worksheet to help you pull together what you'll need.

Don't Skip Breakfast

Even if you don't usually eat breakfast, do so on exam morning. A cup of coffee doesn't count. It's not a good idea to eat doughnuts or other sweet foods, either. A sugar high will leave you with a sugar low in the middle of the exam. A mix of protein and carbohydrates is best: cereal with milk and just a little sugar, or eggs with toast, will do your body a world of good.

Step 9: DO IT!

Time to complete: 5 minutes, plus test-taking time
Activity: Ace the CBEST!
Fast forward to exam day. You're ready. You made a study plan and followed through. You've practiced your test-taking strategies while working through this book. You're in control of your physical, mental, and emotional state. You know when and where to show up

22

LEARNINGEXPRESS TEST PREPARATION SYSTEM

and what to bring with you. In other words, you're better prepared than most of the other people taking the CBEST with you. You're psyched!

Just one more thing. When you're done with the CBEST, you will have earned a reward. Plan a celebration for exam night. Call up your friends and plan a party, or have a nice dinner for two—whatever your heart desires. Give yourself something to look forward to.

And then do it. Go into the exam full of confidence, armed with test-taking strategies you've practiced till they're second nature. You're in control of yourself, your environment, and your performance on the exam. You're ready to succeed. So do it! Go in there and ace the exam! And look forward to your future career in education!

Final Preparations

Getting to the Exam Site

Location of exam: _____

Date: _____

Time of exam: _____

Do I know how to get to the exam site?   Yes____   No____

(If no, make a trial run.)

Time it will take to get to exam site: _____

Things to Lay Out the Night Before

Clothes I will wear   ____

Sweater/jacket   ____

Watch   ____

Admission card   ____

Photo ID   ____

4 #2 pencils   ____

CHAPTER 3 ▶ Diagnostic CBEST Exam

CHAPTER SUMMARY
This is the first of the three practice tests in this book based on the California Basic Educational Skills Test (CBEST). Use this test to see how you would do if you were to take the exam today.

This diagnostic practice exam is of the same type as the real California Basic Educational Skills Test you will be taking. Like the real exam, it is divided into three sections. The Reading Comprehension section consists of 50 multiple-choice questions on reading passages that vary from a few sentences to between 100 and 200 words. The Mathematics section consists of 50 multiple-choice questions. The Essay Writing section consists of two topics on which you are asked to write essays; one essay is based on a situation or statement, the other on a personal experience.

The answer sheet you should use for the multiple-choice questions is on the following page. (Write your essay on a separate piece of paper.) Then comes the exam itself, and after that is the answer key. Each answer on the test is explained in the answer key to help you to find out why the correct answers are right and the incorrect answers wrong. You'll also find scoring criteria for the essay section and sample essays based on the topics in the exam. The answer key is followed by a section on how to score your exam.

LEARNINGEXPRESS CALIFORNIA BASIC EDUCATIONAL SKILLS TEST ANSWER SHEET

Section 1: Reading Comprehension

1. ⓐ ⓑ ⓒ ⓓ ⓔ	21. ⓐ ⓑ ⓒ ⓓ ⓔ	41. ⓐ ⓑ ⓒ ⓓ ⓔ	
2. ⓐ ⓑ ⓒ ⓓ ⓔ	22. ⓐ ⓑ ⓒ ⓓ ⓔ	42. ⓐ ⓑ ⓒ ⓓ ⓔ	
3. ⓐ ⓑ ⓒ ⓓ ⓔ	23. ⓐ ⓑ ⓒ ⓓ ⓔ	43. ⓐ ⓑ ⓒ ⓓ ⓔ	
4. ⓐ ⓑ ⓒ ⓓ ⓔ	24. ⓐ ⓑ ⓒ ⓓ ⓔ	44. ⓐ ⓑ ⓒ ⓓ ⓔ	
5. ⓐ ⓑ ⓒ ⓓ ⓔ	25. ⓐ ⓑ ⓒ ⓓ ⓔ	45. ⓐ ⓑ ⓒ ⓓ ⓔ	
6. ⓐ ⓑ ⓒ ⓓ ⓔ	26. ⓐ ⓑ ⓒ ⓓ ⓔ	46. ⓐ ⓑ ⓒ ⓓ ⓔ	
7. ⓐ ⓑ ⓒ ⓓ ⓔ	27. ⓐ ⓑ ⓒ ⓓ ⓔ	47. ⓐ ⓑ ⓒ ⓓ ⓔ	
8. ⓐ ⓑ ⓒ ⓓ ⓔ	28. ⓐ ⓑ ⓒ ⓓ ⓔ	48. ⓐ ⓑ ⓒ ⓓ ⓔ	
9. ⓐ ⓑ ⓒ ⓓ ⓔ	29. ⓐ ⓑ ⓒ ⓓ ⓔ	49. ⓐ ⓑ ⓒ ⓓ ⓔ	
10. ⓐ ⓑ ⓒ ⓓ ⓔ	30. ⓐ ⓑ ⓒ ⓓ ⓔ	50. ⓐ ⓑ ⓒ ⓓ ⓔ	
11. ⓐ ⓑ ⓒ ⓓ ⓔ	31. ⓐ ⓑ ⓒ ⓓ ⓔ		
12. ⓐ ⓑ ⓒ ⓓ ⓔ	32. ⓐ ⓑ ⓒ ⓓ ⓔ		
13. ⓐ ⓑ ⓒ ⓓ ⓔ	33. ⓐ ⓑ ⓒ ⓓ ⓔ		
14. ⓐ ⓑ ⓒ ⓓ ⓔ	34. ⓐ ⓑ ⓒ ⓓ ⓔ		
15. ⓐ ⓑ ⓒ ⓓ ⓔ	35. ⓐ ⓑ ⓒ ⓓ ⓔ		
16. ⓐ ⓑ ⓒ ⓓ ⓔ	36. ⓐ ⓑ ⓒ ⓓ ⓔ		
17. ⓐ ⓑ ⓒ ⓓ ⓔ	37. ⓐ ⓑ ⓒ ⓓ ⓔ		
18. ⓐ ⓑ ⓒ ⓓ ⓔ	38. ⓐ ⓑ ⓒ ⓓ ⓔ		
19. ⓐ ⓑ ⓒ ⓓ ⓔ	39. ⓐ ⓑ ⓒ ⓓ ⓔ		
20. ⓐ ⓑ ⓒ ⓓ ⓔ	40. ⓐ ⓑ ⓒ ⓓ ⓔ		

Section 2: Mathematics

1. ⓐ ⓑ ⓒ ⓓ ⓔ	21. ⓐ ⓑ ⓒ ⓓ ⓔ	41. ⓐ ⓑ ⓒ ⓓ ⓔ	
2. ⓐ ⓑ ⓒ ⓓ ⓔ	22. ⓐ ⓑ ⓒ ⓓ ⓔ	42. ⓐ ⓑ ⓒ ⓓ ⓔ	
3. ⓐ ⓑ ⓒ ⓓ ⓔ	23. ⓐ ⓑ ⓒ ⓓ ⓔ	43. ⓐ ⓑ ⓒ ⓓ ⓔ	
4. ⓐ ⓑ ⓒ ⓓ ⓔ	24. ⓐ ⓑ ⓒ ⓓ ⓔ	44. ⓐ ⓑ ⓒ ⓓ ⓔ	
5. ⓐ ⓑ ⓒ ⓓ ⓔ	25. ⓐ ⓑ ⓒ ⓓ ⓔ	45. ⓐ ⓑ ⓒ ⓓ ⓔ	
6. ⓐ ⓑ ⓒ ⓓ ⓔ	26. ⓐ ⓑ ⓒ ⓓ ⓔ	46. ⓐ ⓑ ⓒ ⓓ ⓔ	
7. ⓐ ⓑ ⓒ ⓓ ⓔ	27. ⓐ ⓑ ⓒ ⓓ ⓔ	47. ⓐ ⓑ ⓒ ⓓ ⓔ	
8. ⓐ ⓑ ⓒ ⓓ ⓔ	28. ⓐ ⓑ ⓒ ⓓ ⓔ	48. ⓐ ⓑ ⓒ ⓓ ⓔ	
9. ⓐ ⓑ ⓒ ⓓ ⓔ	29. ⓐ ⓑ ⓒ ⓓ ⓔ	49. ⓐ ⓑ ⓒ ⓓ ⓔ	
10. ⓐ ⓑ ⓒ ⓓ ⓔ	30. ⓐ ⓑ ⓒ ⓓ ⓔ	50. ⓐ ⓑ ⓒ ⓓ ⓔ	
11. ⓐ ⓑ ⓒ ⓓ ⓔ	31. ⓐ ⓑ ⓒ ⓓ ⓔ		
12. ⓐ ⓑ ⓒ ⓓ ⓔ	32. ⓐ ⓑ ⓒ ⓓ ⓔ		
13. ⓐ ⓑ ⓒ ⓓ ⓔ	33. ⓐ ⓑ ⓒ ⓓ ⓔ		
14. ⓐ ⓑ ⓒ ⓓ ⓔ	34. ⓐ ⓑ ⓒ ⓓ ⓔ		
15. ⓐ ⓑ ⓒ ⓓ ⓔ	35. ⓐ ⓑ ⓒ ⓓ ⓔ		
16. ⓐ ⓑ ⓒ ⓓ ⓔ	36. ⓐ ⓑ ⓒ ⓓ ⓔ		
17. ⓐ ⓑ ⓒ ⓓ ⓔ	37. ⓐ ⓑ ⓒ ⓓ ⓔ		
18. ⓐ ⓑ ⓒ ⓓ ⓔ	38. ⓐ ⓑ ⓒ ⓓ ⓔ		
19. ⓐ ⓑ ⓒ ⓓ ⓔ	39. ⓐ ⓑ ⓒ ⓓ ⓔ		
20. ⓐ ⓑ ⓒ ⓓ ⓔ	40. ⓐ ⓑ ⓒ ⓓ ⓔ		

▶ Section 1: Reading Comprehension

Answer questions 1–8 on the basis of the following passage.

(1) The coast of the State of Maine is one of the most irregular in the world. A straight line running from the southernmost city in Maine, which is Kittery, to the northernmost coastal city, Eastport, would measure about 225 miles. If you followed the coastline between the same two cities, you would travel more than ten times as far. This irregularity is the result of what is called a *drowned coastline*. The term refers to the results of the glacial activity of the Ice Age. At that time, the whole area that is now Maine was part of a mountain range that towered above the sea. As the glacier descended, however, it expended enormous force on those mountains and they sank into the ocean.

(2) As the mountains sank, ocean water charged over the lowest parts of the remaining land, forming a series of twisting inlets and lagoons, of contorted grottos and nooks. Once the glacier receded, the highest parts of the former mountain range that were nearest the shore remained as islands. Although the mountain ranges were never to return, the land rose somewhat over the centuries. On one of the islands that the glacier left behind, marine fossils have been found at 225 feet above today's sea level, indicating that the island was once part of the shoreline.

(3) The 2,500-mile-long rocky and jagged coastline of Maine keeps watch over nearly two thousand islands. Many of these islands are tiny and uninhabited, but many are home to thriving communities. Mt. Desert Island is one of the largest—sixteen miles long and nearly twelve miles wide—and one of the most beautiful of Maine's coastal islands. Mt. Desert Island very nearly formed as two distinct islands. It is split almost in half by Somes Sound, a very deep and very narrow stretch of water seven miles long. On the east side of the island, Cadillac Mountain rises 1,532 feet, making it the highest mountain on the Atlantic seaboard.

(4) For years, Mt. Desert Island, particularly its major settlement, Bar Harbor, afforded summer homes for the wealthy. Recently, Bar Harbor has made a name for itself as a burgeoning arts community as well. But there is much more to Mt. Desert Island than a sophisticated and wealthy playground. A majority of the island is unspoiled forestland, which makes up the greatest part of Acadia National Park. Mt. Desert Island sits on the boundary line between the temperate and sub-Arctic zones. The island, therefore, supports the flora and fauna of both zones, as well as beach, inland, and alpine plants. In addition to its geological treasures, Mt. Desert Island lies in a major bird-migration lane; all kinds of migratory birds pass over the island.

(5) The establishment of Acadia National Park in 1916 means that this diversity of nature will be preserved and that it will be available to all people, not just the wealthy who once had exclusive access to the island's natural beauty. Today, visitors to Acadia may receive nature instruction from the park naturalists, in addition to enjoying the beauty of the island by camping, hiking, cycling, or boating. Or, visitors may choose to spend time at the archeological museum, learning about the Stone Age inhabitants of the island. The best view on Mt. Desert Island, though, is from the top of Cadillac Mountain. From the summit, you can gaze back toward the mainland or out over the Atlantic Ocean and contemplate the beauty created by a retreating glacier.

DIAGNOSTIC CBEST EXAM

1. Which of the following statements best expresses the main idea of paragraph 4?
   a. The wealthy residents of Mt. Desert Island selfishly kept it to themselves.
   b. Acadia National Park is one of the smallest of the national parks.
   c. On Mt. Desert Island, there is great tension between the year-round residents and the summer tourists.
   d. Due to its location and environment, Mt. Desert Island supports an incredibly diverse animal and plant life.
   e. A variety of activities are available to tourists who visit Mt. Desert Island.

2. According to the selection, the large number of small islands along the coast of Maine is the result of
   a. glaciers.
   b. a temperate climate.
   c. volcanic mountains.
   d. floods.
   e. the irregular coastline.

3. According to paragraph 2, one way to tell whether the top of a mountain was once at sea level is to look for
   a. inlets and lagoons.
   b. grottos and nooks.
   c. marine fossils.
   d. islands.
   e. mountains.

4. In the context of paragraph 4, which of the following words or phrases would most logically be substituted for the underlined word *afforded*?
   a. remembered
   b. discouraged
   c. bought for a higher price
   d. caused to exist
   e. endured

5. Paragraph 5 suggests that the writer believes that
   a. the continued existence of national parks is threatened by budget cuts.
   b. the best way to preserve the environment on Mt. Desert Island is to limit the number of visitors.
   c. national parks allow large numbers of people to visit and learn about interesting wilderness areas.
   d. Mt. Desert Island is the most interesting tourist attraction in Maine.
   e. Acadia National Park should be made into a sanctuary for endangered birds.

6. In the first paragraph, the author compares the straight-line distance (225 miles) from Kittery to Eastport with the driving distance (2,250 miles) to illustrate
   a. just how jagged the Maine coastline is.
   b. that Maine's coastline is very mountainous.
   c. that driving the coast of Maine can be dangerous.
   d. difference in appearance between the two cities.
   e. that air travel is the best way to reach Maine's coastal cities.

7. This passage could best be described as
   a. a persuasive essay.
   b. a tourist brochure.
   c. an informative essay.
   d. a description of a fictional setting.
   e. a personal narrative.

8. Paragraph 5 celebrates which of the following aspects of Maine?
   a. its historical interest as a playground of the wealthy
   b. the diversity of its plants and wildlife
   c. its geological origins
   d. its system of national parks
   e. its beautiful shoreline

30

Answer question 9 on the basis of the following passage.

One of the missions of the Peace Corps is to help the people of interested countries meet their need for trained men and women. People who work for the Peace Corps do so because they want to. But to keep the Peace Corps dynamic with fresh ideas, no staff member can work for the agency for more than five years.

9. The paragraph best supports the statement that Peace Corps employees
    a. are highly intelligent people.
    b. must train for about five years.
    c. speak several different languages.
    d. are hired for a limited term of employment.
    e. have both academic and work experience.

Answer questions 10–13 on the basis of the following passage.

Theodore Roosevelt was a city boy with asthma and poor eyesight. Yet this sickly child later won fame as a political leader, Rough Rider, and hero of the common people. To conquer his handicaps, Teddy trained in a gym and became a lightweight boxer at Harvard. Out west, he hunted buffalo and ran a cattle ranch. Back east, he became a civil service reformer and police commissioner. He became President McKinley's Assistant Navy Secretary during the Spanish-American War. Also, he led a charge of cavalry Rough Riders up San Juan Hill in Cuba. After achieving fame, he became Governor of New York and went on to become the Vice-President.

When McKinley was assassinated, Theodore Roosevelt became the youngest U.S. President at forty-two. He is famous for his motto, "Speak softly and carry a big stick." Roosevelt battled for meat inspection and pure food laws. Also, he wanted to save the forests and break up the grip that big business had on steel and oil. Roosevelt persuaded the diplomats of warring Russia and Japan to make peace.

10. Which of the following states the main idea of the passage?
    a. Theodore Roosevelt was a man of many accomplishments.
    b. Presidents should speak softly and carry big sticks.
    c. Presidents can help countries make peace.
    d. A governor can become a president.
    e. Theodore Roosevelt was the youngest U.S. president.

11. What achievement illustrates Roosevelt's ability to overcome personal obstacles?
    a. He led a charge of cavalry Rough Riders in Cuba.
    b. He is famous for his motto, "Speak softly and carry a big stick."
    c. He overcame his asthma by training in gym and became a boxer.
    d. He became Governor of New York.
    e. He was committed to saving the forests.

12. According to the passage, how did Roosevelt first become President?
    a. He won the support of his party in a political campaign.
    b. As Vice-President, he took over the Presidency when McKinley was assassinated.
    c. He won the nation's popular vote.
    d. He won the necessary Electoral College votes.
    e. He was appointed after serving as Governor of New York.

13. He first worked under President McKinley in what capacity?
   a. Assistant Navy Secretary during the Spanish-American War
   b. Back east, he served as a Police Commissioner
   c. Governor of New York
   d. Civil Service reformer
   e. Rough Rider

Answer question 14 on the basis of the following passage

One New York publisher has estimated that 50,000 to 60,000 people in the United States want an anthology that includes the complete works of William Shakespeare. And what accounts for this renewed interest in Shakespeare? As scholars point out, his psychological insights into both male and female characters are amazing even today.

14. The paragraph best supports the statement that
   a. Shakespeare's characters are more interesting than fictional characters today.
   b. people today are interested in Shakespeare's work because of the characters.
   c. academic scholars are putting together an anthology of Shakespeare's work.
   d. New Yorkers have a renewed interest in the work of Shakespeare.
   e. Shakespeare was a psychiatrist as well as a playwright.

Answer question 15 on the basis of the following passage.

Due to downsizing and new technologies, the role of the traditional secretary is declining. At the same time secretaries and administrative assistants are becoming much more important to businesses of all sizes. Although traditional jobs such as typist, stenographer, and data entry specialist have declined by about 33 percent, there has been a sharp increase in jobs such as clerical supervisor and medical and legal secretary.

15. The paragraph best supports the statement that
   a. secretaries are less important now than they once were.
   b. many traditional secretaries have been promoted to clerical supervisors.
   c. due to downsizing, about 33 percent of all typists have recently become unemployed.
   d. advances in technology have contributed to the changing role of the secretary.
   e. downsizing and the new technologies have made the traditional secretary obsolete.

Answer questions 16–19 on the basis of the following passage.

The English language premiere of Samuel Beckett's play, *Waiting for Godot*, took place in London in August 1955. *Godot* is an avant-garde play with only five characters (not including Mr. Godot, who never arrives) and a minimal setting: one rock and one bare tree. The play has two acts; the second act repeats what little action occurs in the first with few changes: the tree, for instance, acquires one leaf. In a statement that was to become famous, the critic Vivian Mercer has described *Godot* as "a play in which nothing happens twice." Opening night, critics and playgoers greeted the play with bafflement and derision. The line, "Nothing happens, nobody comes, nobody goes. It's awful," was met by a loud rejoinder of "Hear! Hear!" from an audience member. _____.
However, Harold Hobson's review in *The Sunday Times* managed to recognize the play for what history has proven it to be, a revolutionary moment in theater.

16. Which sentence, if inserted in the blank space in the passage, would make the best sense in the context of the passage?
    a. The director, Peter Hall, had to beg the theater management not to close the play immediately but to wait for the Sunday reviews.
    b. Despite the audience reaction, the cast and director believed in the play.
    c. It looked as if *Waiting for Godot* was beginning a long run as the most controversial play of London's 1955 season.
    d. *Waiting for Godot* was in danger of closing the first week of its run and of becoming nothing more than a footnote in the annals of the English stage.
    e. The audience and critics all completely misunderstood Beckett's play.

17. Judging from the information provided in the paragraph, which of the following statements is accurate?
    a. The 1955 production of *Waiting for Godot* was the play's first performance.
    b. *Waiting for Godot* was written by Peter Hall.
    c. The sets and characters in *Waiting for Godot* were typical of London stage productions in the 1950s.
    d. *Waiting for Godot* was not first performed in English.
    e. *Waiting for Godot* has a complicated plot.

18. Which of the following provides the best definition of the term "avant-garde" as the author intends it in the passage?
    a. innovative
    b. unintelligible
    c. foreign
    d. highbrow
    e. eccentric

19. Which of the following best describes the attitude of the author of the passage toward the play *Waiting for Godot*?
    a. It was a curiosity in theater history.
    b. It is the most important play of the 20th century.
    c. It had no effect on theater.
    d. It is too repetitious.
    e. It represents a turning point in stage history.

Answer questions 20 and 21 on the basis of the following passage.

May is National Reading Month. In conjunction with the public library, the city is offering half-fare rides to anyone carrying a library card. In order to receive the half-price fare, each passenger must show the driver his or her current library card and deposit one-half the fare in the collection box. Drivers will record these fares in the "special fares" section on the trip sheets for each route.

20. John and Mary Burton get on the bus driven by Operator Hudson at the corner of Sherman Avenue and West 123rd Street. John shows Hudson his library card and deposits half-fare in the collection box. Mary deposits half-fare in the collection box. The couple move toward their seats. What should Operator Hudson do first?
    a. Proceed to the next stop without saying anything
    b. Inform Mary that she must exit the bus
    c. Assume Mary has a library card, too
    d. Inform Mary that she may acquire a library card at any branch of the library
    e. Tell Mary that if she does not have a library card, she will have to pay full fare

33

21. The passage implies that
   a. many bus passengers like to read.
   b. many transit employees have library cards.
   c. bus drivers regularly deal with special fares.
   d. several bus routes service the public library.
   e. literacy rates increase due to government intervention.

Answer question 22 on the basis of the following passage.

In space flight there are the obvious hazards of meteors, debris, and radiation; however, astronauts must also deal with two vexing physiological foes—muscle atrophy and bone loss. Space shuttle astronauts, because they spend only about a week in space, undergo minimal wasting of bone and muscle. But when longer stays in microgravity or zero gravity are contemplated, as in the proposed space station or a two-year round-trip voyage to Mars, these problems are of particular concern because they could become acute.

22. The most appropriate audience for the passage would be students in
   a. a physiology class.
   b. an engineering class.
   c. a physics class.
   d. an astronomy class.
   e. a history of science class.

Answer question 23 on the basis of the following passage.

Light pollution is a growing problem worldwide. Like other forms of pollution, light pollution degrades the quality of the environment. Where once it was possible to look up at the night sky and see thousands of twinkling stars in the inky blackness, one now sees little more than the yellow glare of urban sky glow. When we lose the ability to connect visually with the vastness of the universe by looking up at the night sky, we lose our connection with something profoundly important to the human spirit, our sense of wonder.

23. The passage implies that the most serious damage done by light pollution is to our
   a. artistic appreciation.
   b. sense of physical well-being.
   c. cultural advancement.
   d. spiritual selves.
   e. intellectual curiosity.

Answer questions 24–27 on the basis of the following poem by Emily Dickinson.

   Apparently with no surprise
   To any happy flower,
   The frost beheads it at its play
   In accidental power.

   The blond assassin passes on,
   The sun proceeds unmoved
   To measure off another day
   For an approving God.

24. Which of the following most nearly describes the author's attitude toward nature as expressed in this poem?
   a. delight
   b. dismay
   c. indifference
   d. reverence
   e. deference

25. What is "the blond assassin" referred to in the poem?
    a. the flowers
    b. the frost
    c. the sun
    d. God
    e. nature

26. The poem implies that the attitude of the flowers toward the frost is one of
    a. fear.
    b. horror.
    c. acceptance.
    d. reverence.
    e. awe.

27. The tone of the poem implies that the speaker probably regards God as
    a. benevolent. — kind
    b. just.
    c. cruel.
    d. angry.
    e. non-existent.

Answer questions 28–29 on the basis of the following table.

THE FUJITA–PEARSON TORNADO INTENSITY SCALE

CLASSIFICATION	WIND SPEED	DAMAGE
F0	72 MPH	Mild
F1	73–112 MPH	Moderate
F2	113–157 MPH	Significant
F3	158–206 MPH	Severe
F4	207–260 MPH	Devastating
F5	260–319 MPH	Cataclysmic
F6	319–379 MPH	Overwhelming

28. A tornado with a wind speed of 173 mph would be assigned which classification?
    a. F0
    b. F1
    c. F2
    d. F3
    e. F4

29. The names of the categories in the third column, labeled "Damage," could best be described as
    a. scientific.
    b. descriptive.
    c. objective.
    d. persuasive.
    e. whimsical. — unusual; odd; fantastic

Answer question 30 on the basis of the following passage.

James Carruthers' recent essays attempt to redefine arts criticism as a play of critical intelligence that can take place free from the bonds of political partisanship. In Carruthers' view, this play of the mind, working itself free from constraints, is the only ethical approach to the arts.

30. What is the best definition of the word "play" as it is used in the above passage?
    a. to act or conduct oneself in a specified way
    b. to move or operate freely within a confined space
    c. to pretend to be; mimic the activities of
    d. to behave carelessly or indifferently
    e. to stake or wager in a game

Answer questions 31–36 on the basis of the following passage.

In his famous study of myth, *The Hero With a Thousand Faces*, Joseph Campbell writes about the archetypal hero who has ventured outside the boundaries of the village and, after many trials and adventures, has returned with the boon that will save or enlighten his fellows. Like Carl Jung, Campbell believes that the story of the hero is part of the collective unconscious of all humankind. He likens the returning hero to the sacred or tabooed personage described by James Frazier in *The Golden Bough*. Such an individual must, in many instances of myth, be insulated from the rest of society, "not merely for his own sake but for the sake of others; for since the virtue of holiness is, so to say, a powerful explosive which the smallest touch can detonate, it is necessary in the interest of the general safety to keep it within narrow bounds."

There is _____ between the archetypal hero who has journeyed into the wilderness and the poet who has journeyed into the realm of imagination. Both places are dangerous and full of wonders, and both, at their deepest levels, are journeys that take place into the kingdom of the unconscious mind, a place that, in Campbell's words, "goes down into unsuspected Aladdin caves. There not only jewels but dangerous jinn abide. . . ."

31. Based on the passage, which of the following would best describe the hero's journey?
    a. wonderful
    b. terrifying
    c. awesome
    d. whimsical
    e. mundane

32. The title of Campbell's book, *The Hero With a Thousand Faces*, is meant to convey
    a. the many villagers whose lives are changed by the story the hero has to tell.
    b. the fact that the hero journeys into many different imaginary countries.
    c. the many languages into which the myth of the hero has been translated.
    d. the many adventures the archetypal hero has during the journey into the wilderness.
    e. the universality of the myth of the hero who journeys into the wilderness.

33. Based on the passage, which of the following best describes the story that will likely be told by Campbell's returning hero and Frazier's sacred or tabooed personage?
    a. a radically mind-altering story
    b. a story that will terrify people to no good end
    c. a warning of catastrophe to come
    d. a story based on a dangerous lie
    e. a parable aimed at establishing a religious movement

34. Which of the following is the most accurate definition of "boon" as the word is used in the passage?
    a. gift
    b. blessing
    c. charm
    d. prize
    e. prayer

35. The phrase that would most accurately fit into the blank in the first sentence of the second paragraph is
    a. much similarity.
    b. a wide gulf.
    c. long-standing conflict.
    d. an abiding devotion.
    e. great diversity.

36. As depicted in the last sentence of the passage, "Aladdin's caves" are most likely to be found in
 a. holy books.
 b. fairy tales.
 c. the fantasies of the hero.
 d. the hero's preparation for the journey.
 e. the unconscious mind.

Answer questions 37–40 on the basis of the following passage.

Typically people think of genius, whether it manifests in Mozart's composing symphonies at age five or Einstein's discovery of relativity, as having a quality not just of the supernatural, but also of the eccentric. People see genius as a "good" abnormality; moreover, they think of genius as a completely unpredictable abnormality. Until recently, psychologists regarded the quirks of genius as too erratic to describe intelligibly; however, Anna Findley's ground-breaking study uncovers predictable patterns in the biographies of geniuses. These patterns do not dispel the common belief that there is a kind of supernatural intervention in the lives of unusually talented men and women, however, even though they occur with regularity. _____, Findley shows that all geniuses experience three intensely productive periods in their lives, one of which always occurs shortly before their deaths; this is true whether the genius lives to nineteen or ninety.

37. Which word or phrase, if inserted into the blank space above, best defines the relationship of the last sentence in the passage to the one preceding it?
 a. For example
 b. Despite this
 c. However
 d. In other words
 e. Nevertheless

38. According to the information presented in the passage, what is the general populace's opinion of genius?
 a. It is mystical and magical.
 b. It is predictable and uncommon.
 c. It is supercilious and abnormal.
 d. It is unpredictable and erratic.
 e. It is extraordinary and erratic.

39. Which of the following would be the best title for the passage?
 a. Understanding Mozarts and Einsteins
 b. Predicting the Life of a Genius
 c. The Uncanny Patterns in the Lives of Geniuses
 d. Pattern and Disorder in the Lives of Geniuses
 e. Supernatural Intervention in the Life of the Genius

40. Given the information in the passage, which of the following statements is true?
 a. Anna Findley is a biographer.
 b. All geniuses are eccentric and unpredictable.
 c. A genius has three prolific times in his or her life.
 d. Mozart discovered relativity.
 e. Geniuses experience three fallow periods in their lives.

Answer questions 41 and 42 on the basis of the following passage.

Scientists have developed an innovative magnetic resonance imaging (MRI) procedure that reveals details of tissues and organs which are difficult to see by conventional MRI. By using this new procedure, which detects inert gases, scientists have taken the first clear MRI pictures of human lungs and airways. Conventional MRI, because it images water protons, provides poor images of the lungs, which are filled, not with water, but with air. Chest X rays can detect tumors or inflamed regions in the lungs but provide poor soft-tissue contrast and no clear view of air passages. Computed tomography can provide high resolution images of the walls of the lungs and its airways but gives no measure of function.

41. According to information in the passage, the MRI innovation is different from standard imaging procedures in that it
  a. distinguishes gases rather than simply distinguishing fluids.
  b. can detect tumors or inflamed regions in the lungs.
  c. provides high resolution images of the walls of the lungs.
  d. provides better images of water-filled tissues.
  e. uses computed tomography.

42. According to information in the passage, the inability to generate satisfactory images of air routes is a deficiency of
  a. computed tomography.
  b. hyperpolarization.
  c. high resolution images.
  d. X rays.
  e. MRI operators.

Answer question 43 on the basis of the following passage.

Over the last twenty years, worldwide illiteracy rates have consistently declined. The main reason for this decline is the sharp increase of literacy rates among young women, which is the result of campaigns to increase educational opportunities for girls. For example, between 1970 and 1990, the literacy rate among women in the United Arab Emirates increased from seven percent to 76 percent.

43. Based on the passage, the author would tend to agree with which of the following statements?
  a. Men and women should have equal access to education.
  b. It has been shown that women with increased education have fewer children.
  c. Males traditionally have a greater need for higher education.
  d. Countries should be required to demonstrate increased literacy rates in order to qualify for U.S. foreign aid.
  e. Throughout the world, women need medical care more than the ability to read.

Answer question 44 on the basis of the following passage.

Jessie Street is sometimes called the Australian Eleanor Roosevelt. Like Roosevelt, Street lived a life of privilege, while at the same time devoting her efforts to working for the rights of the disenfranchised, including workers, women, refugees, and Aborigines. In addition, she gained international fame when she was the only woman on the Australian delegation to the conference that founded the United Nations—just as Eleanor Roosevelt was for the United States.

44. Which of the following inferences may be drawn from the information presented in the passage?
   a. Eleanor Roosevelt and Jessie Street worked together to include women in the United Nations Charter.
   b. Usually, people who live lives of privilege do not spend much time participating in political activities.
   c. Discrimination in Australia is much worse than it ever was in the United States.
   d. At the time of the formation of the United Nations, few women were involved in international affairs.
   e. The United Nations has been ineffective in helping the disenfranchised all over the world.

Answer questions 45 and 46 on the basis of the following passage.

One out of five Americans suffers from an allergic disease, which results from the immune system reacting to a normally innocuous substance such as pollen or dust. An allergic response begins with a process called sensitization. When a foreign substance—an allergen such as pollen, for example—first enters the body of an allergic person, cells called macrophages engulf the invader, chop it into pieces and display the pieces on their surfaces. T-helper cells recognize certain allergen fragments and bind to the macrophages. This process causes the T-helper cells to secrete signaling molecules, including interleukin-4 (IL-4). IL-4, in turn, spurs nearby B cells to mature into plasma cells. Plasma cells produce Y-shaped antibody proteins.

45. An allergic disease occurs when the body's immune system reacts to a substance that is usually
   a. common.
   b. toxic.
   c. irritating.
   d. airborne.
   e. harmless.

46. Cells that surround allergens within the body are known as
   a. T-helper cells.
   b. macrophage cells.
   c. B cells.
   d. plasma cells.
   e. IL-4.

Answer questions 47–50 on the basis of the following passage.

Mental and physical health professionals may consider referring clients and patients to a music therapist for a number of reasons. It seems a particularly good choice for the social worker who is coordinating a client's case. Music therapists use music to establish a relationship with the patient and to improve the patient's health, using highly structured musical interactions. Patients and therapists may sing, play instruments, compose music, dance, or simply listen to music.

The course of training for music therapists is comprehensive. In addition to their formal musical and therapy training, music therapists are taught to discern what kinds of interventions will be most beneficial for each individual patient. Since each patient is different and has different goals, the music therapist must be able to understand the patient's situation and choose the music and activities that will do the most toward helping the patient achieve his or her goals. The referring social worker can help this process by clearly articulating each client's history.

Although patients may develop their musical skills, that is not the main goal of music therapy. Any client who needs particular work on communication or on academic, emotional, and social skills, and who is not responding to traditional therapy, is an excellent candidate for music therapy.

47. Which of the following would be the most appropriate title for this passage?
 a. The Use of Music in the Treatment of Autism
 b. How to Use Music Combat Depression
 c. Music Therapy: A Role in Social Work?
 d. Training for a Career in Music Therapy
 e. The Social Worker as Music Therapist

48. According to information presented in the passage, music therapy can be prescribed for social work clients who
 a. need to develop coping skills.
 b. were orphaned as children.
 c. need to resolve family issues.
 d. are under the age of 18.
 e. need to improve social skills.

49. Which of the following inferences can be drawn from the passage?
 a. Music therapy can succeed where traditional therapies have failed.
 b. Music therapy is a relatively new field.
 c. Music therapy is particularly beneficial for young children.
 d. Music therapy probably will not work well for psychotic people.
 e. Music therapy is only appropriate in a limited number of circumstances.

50. Which of the following best organizes the main topics addressed in this passage?
 a. I. The role of music therapy in social work
    II. Locating a music therapist
    III. How to complete a music therapist referral
 b. I. Using music in therapy
    II. A typical music therapy intervention
    III. When to prescribe music therapy for sociopaths
 c. I. Music therapy and social work
    II. Training for music therapists
    III. Skills addressed by music therapy
 d. I. How to choose a music therapist
    II. When to refer to a music therapist
    III. Who benefits the most from music therapy
 e. I. Music therapy as a cost-effective treatment
    II. Curriculum of a music therapy program
    III. Music therapy and physical illness

► Section 2: Mathematics

1. Which of the following numbers is NOT between −0.02 and 1.02?
   a. −0.15
   b. −0.015
   c. 0
   d. 0.02
   e. 1.015

Use the graph below to answer question 2.

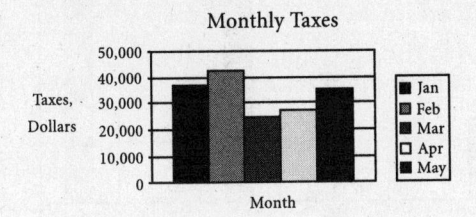

Monthly Taxes

2. What were the total taxes collected for January, February, and April?
   a. $78,000
   b. $98,000
   c. $105,000
   d. $115,000
   e. $132,000

Use the table below to answer question 3.

BLUE ROUTE BUS SCHEDULE		
	Depot	Washington St.
Bus 1	6:00	6:53
Bus 2	6:30	7:23
Bus 3	7:00	7:53
Bus 4	7:20	
Bus 5	7:40	8:33

3. What time is Bus 4 scheduled to arrive at Washington St.?
   a. 8:03
   b. 8:10
   c. 8:13
   d. 8:18
   e. 8:23

4. Membership dues at Arnold's Gym are $53 per month this year, but were $50 per month last year. What was the percentage increase in the gym's prices?
   a. 5.5%
   b. 6.0%
   c. 6.5%
   d. 7.0%
   e. 7.5%

5. In the figure below, angle POS measures 90 degrees. What is the measure of angle ROQ?

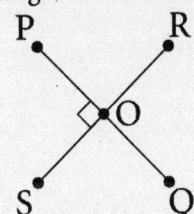

   a. 30 degrees
   b. 45 degrees
   c. 90 degrees
   d. 180 degrees
   e. 270 degrees

DIAGNOSTIC CBEST EXAM

6. What is the value of X in the figure below?

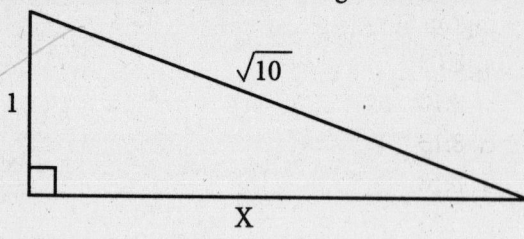

a. 3
b. 4
c. 5
d. 9
e. 10

7. If the figure below is a regular decagon with a center at Q, what is the measure of the indicated angle?

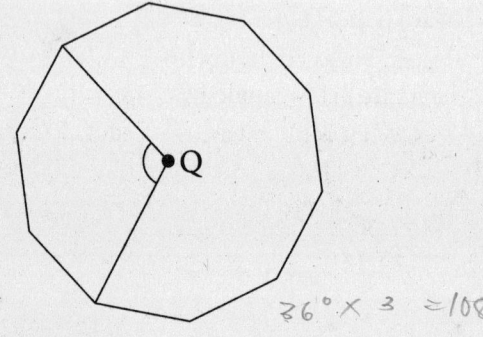

a. 36 degrees
b. 45 degrees
c. 80 degrees
d. 90 degrees
e. 108 degrees

Answer questions 8–10 by referring to the following graph, which shows wildfire trends in a particular region.

WILDFIRE TRENDS (WESTERN U.S., INTERMOUNTAIN REGION)

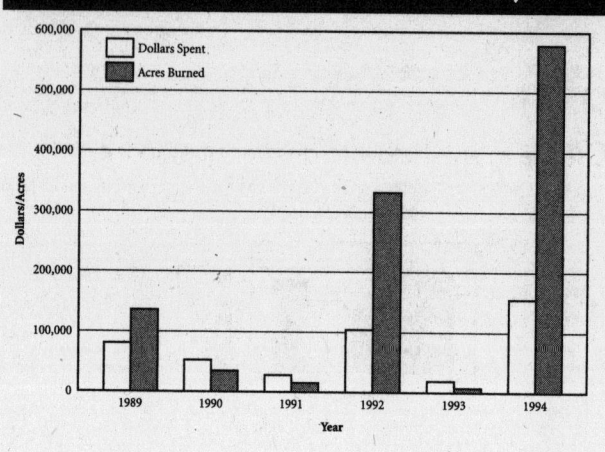

8. In which of the following years were the fewest acres burned?

a. 1989
b. 1990
c. 1991
d. 1992
e. 1993

9. About how much money was spent fighting wildfires in the Intermountain Region during 1992?

a. $90,000
b. $100,000
c. $110,000
d. $300,000
e. $320,000

10. In which of the following years was the cost per acre of fighting wildfires the lowest?
   a. 1989
   b. 1990
   c. 1991
   d. 1993
   e. 1994

Answer questions 11–13 by referring to the following graph, which compares the average annual rainfall with the actual rainfall for one year in a particular city.

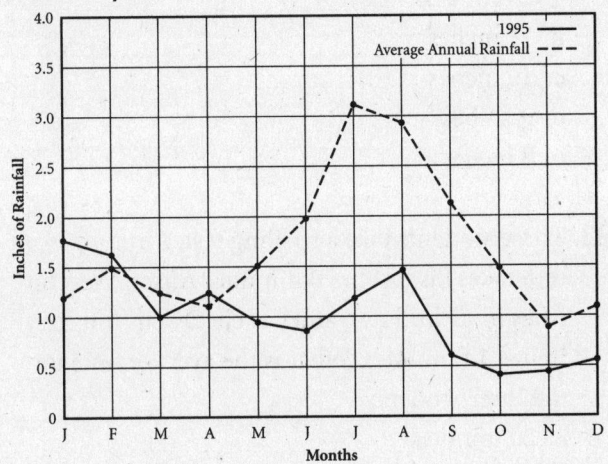

11. In which of the following months during 1995 was the rainfall nearest normal?
   a. April
   b. May
   c. June
   d. July
   e. August

12. What is the average rainfall amount for the month of September?
   a. 0.5 inches
   b. 0.7 inches
   c. 2.0 inches
   d. 2.1 inches
   e. 2.5 inches

13. During 1995, how many months had above-average rainfall amounts?
   a. 2
   b. 3
   c. 6
   d. 9
   e. 10

14. Which of these numbers has a 9 in the thousandths place?
   a. 3.00950
   b. 3.09050
   c. 3.90050
   d. 3.00590
   e. 3.00509

15. Benito earns $12.50 for each hour that he works. If Benito works 8.5 hours per day, five days a week, how much does he earn in a week?
   a. $100.00
   b. $106.25
   c. $406.00
   d. $531.25
   e. $743.75

16. Melissa can grade five of her students' papers in an hour. Joe can grade four of the same papers in an hour. If Melissa works for three hours grading, and Joe works for two hours, what percentage of the 50 students' papers will be graded?
   a. 44%
   b. 46%
   c. 52%
   d. 54%
   e. 56%

17. James has a length of rope that he measures with a yardstick to be 28 inches long. By laying the yardstick end-to-end with the rope, what is the longest distance that he can measure accurately?
  a. 28 inches
  b. 36 inches
  c. 40 inches
  d. 54 inches
  e. 64 inches

18. A rectangular area has one side that measures 15 inches and another side one-third as long. What is the area of the rectangle?
  a. 37.5 square inches
  b. 40 square inches
  c. 55 square inches
  d. 75 square inches
  e. 85 square inches

19. Des Moines recently received a snowstorm that left a total of eight inches of snow. If it snowed at a consistent rate of three inches every two hours, how much snow had fallen in the first five hours of the storm?
  a. 3 inches
  b. 3.3 inches
  c. 5 inches
  d. 7.5 inches
  e. 8 inches

20. The number of red blood corpuscles in one cubic millimeter is about 5,000,000 and the number of white blood corpuscles in one cubic millimeter is about 8,000. What, then, is the ratio of white blood corpuscles to red blood corpuscles?
  a. 1:400
  b. 1:625
  c. 1:40
  d. 4:10
  e. 5:1,250

21. The perimeter of a rectangle is 148 feet. Its two longest sides add up to 86 feet. What is the length of each of its two shortest sides?
  a. 31 feet
  b. 42 feet
  c. 62 feet
  d. 72 feet
  e. 74 feet

22. A piece of ribbon 3 feet 4 inches long was divided into 5 equal parts. How long was each part?
  a. 1 foot 2 inches
  b. 11 inches
  c. 10 inches
  d. 9 inches
  e. 8 inches

23. Three students take a spelling test. Anthony Herrera takes his test in 20 minutes. Alison West finishes in 17 minutes, and Gracie Owens finishes in just 14 minutes. What is the average time for the three students?
  a. 20 minutes
  b. 19 minutes
  c. 17 minutes
  d. 14 minutes
  e. 12 minutes

24. A steel box has a base length of 12 inches and a width of 5 inches. If the box is 10 inches tall, what is the total volume of the box?
  a. 480 cubic inches
  b. 540 cubic inches
  c. 600 cubic inches
  d. 720 cubic inches
  e. 1200 cubic inches

DIAGNOSTIC CBEST EXAM

25. A builder uses 27 cubic feet of concrete to pave a sidewalk whose length is 6 times its width. The concrete is poured 6 inches deep. How long is the sidewalk?
a. 9 feet
b. 12 feet
c. 15 feet
d. 18 feet
e. 20 feet

26. After three days, a group of hikers discovers that they have used $\frac{2}{5}$ of their supplies. At this rate, how many more days can they go forward before they have to turn around?
a. 0.75 days
b. 1.5 days
c. 3.75 days
d. 4.5 days
e. 7.5 days

27. A supply truck can carry 3 tons. A breakfast ration weighs 12 ounces, and the other two daily meals weigh 18 ounces each. On a ten-day trip, how many troops can be supplied by one truck?
a. 100
b. 150
c. 200
d. 320
e. 600

28. A clerk can process 26 forms per hour. If 5,600 forms must be processed in an 8-hour day, how many clerks must you hire for that day?
a. 24 clerks
b. 25 clerks
c. 26 clerks
d. 27 clerks
e. 28 clerks

29. On the same latitude, Janice travels east at 35 miles per hour and Harriet travels west at 15 miles per hour. If the two women start out 2,100 miles apart, how long will it take them to meet?
a. 30 hours
b. 42 hours
c. 60 hours
d. 105 hours
e. 140 hours

30. During the last week of training on an obstacle course, a runner achieves the following times in seconds: 66, 57, 54, 54, 64, 59, and 59. The runner's three best times this week are averaged for her final score on the course. What is her final score?
a. 57 seconds
b. 55 seconds
c. 59 seconds
d. 61 seconds
e. 56 seconds

31. Twelve less than 4 times a number is 20. What is the number?
a. 2
b. 4
c. 5
d. 6
e. 8

45

DIAGNOSTIC CBEST EXAM

Use the information below to answer question 32.

A family eats at Joe's Grill and orders the following items from the menu:

Hamburger	$2.95
Cheeseburger	$3.35
Chicken Sandwich	$3.95
Grilled Cheese	$1.95

32. If the family orders 2 hamburgers, 1 cheeseburger, 2 chicken sandwiches, and 1 grilled cheese, what is the total cost of their order?
    a. $12.20
    b. $15.15
    c. $17.10
    d. $18.05
    e. $19.10

33. If Rachel has worked a total of $26\frac{1}{4}$ hours so far this week, and has to work a total of $37\frac{1}{2}$ hours, how much longer does she have to work?
    a. $10\frac{1}{4}$ hours
    b. $11\frac{1}{4}$ hours
    c. $11\frac{3}{4}$ hours
    d. $13\frac{1}{2}$ hours
    e. $13\frac{3}{4}$ hours

34. If candy bars cost $0.40 and soft drinks cost $0.50, what is the cost of four candy bars and three soft drinks?
    a. $2.10
    b. $2.30
    c. $2.60
    d. $3.10
    e. $4.00

35. On Roy's daily jog, he travels a distance of $\frac{1}{2}$ mile to get to the track and $\frac{1}{2}$ mile to get home from the track. One lap around the track is $\frac{1}{4}$ mile. If Roy jogs 5 laps around the track, what is the total distance that he travels?
    a. $2\frac{1}{4}$ miles
    b. $2\frac{1}{2}$ miles
    c. 3 miles
    d. $3\frac{1}{4}$ miles
    e. 4 miles

36. A teacher spacing desks in a classroom determines that she can have 4 rows of desks if she spaces them 4 feet apart. Each desk is 3 feet wide. If there is 4 feet from the wall to the rows of desks on the edges, how wide is the classroom?
    a. 20 feet
    b. 28 feet
    c. 32 feet
    d. 36 feet
    e. 40 feet

37. Kathy was half the age of her mother 20 years ago. Kathy is 40 now. How old is Kathy's mother?
    a. 50
    b. 60
    c. 70
    d. 80
    e. 100

Use the information below to answer question 38.

A used car dealer has 40 cars on his lot. Fifteen of them are Fords, 9 are Chevrolets, 10 are Dodges, and 6 are foreign models. The dealer sells 2 cars after a day.

38. Which of the following statements can be determined from the information above?
    a. the number of cars remaining on the lot after the day ends
    b. the number of Toyotas on the lot
    c. the cost of a Dodge
    d. the amount the dealer earned in sales
    e. the number of Fords sold

Use the information below to answer question 39.

Ms. Margaret Richbody wishes to insure items of jewelry valued as follows:

- 1 gold watch, valued at $240
- 2 rings, each valued at $150
- 1 ring, valued at $70

39. Ms. Richbody's insurance agent, Bill Ratchet, is preparing a report on the jewelry. Which one of the following represents the total value?
   a. $460
   b. $545
   c. $610
   d. $705
   e. $785

Use the information below to answer question 40.

A man turns in a woman's handbag to the Lost and Found Department of a large downtown store. The man informs the clerk in charge that he found the handbag on the floor beside an entranceway. The clerk estimates that the handbag is worth approximately $150. Inside, the clerk finds the following items:

- 1 leather makeup case valued at $65
- 1 vial of perfume, unopened, valued at $75
- 1 pair of earrings valued at $150
- Cash $178

40. The clerk is writing a report to be submitted along with the found property. What should he write as the total value of the found cash and property?
   a. $468
   b. $608
   c. $618
   d. $638
   e. $718

Use the information below to answer questions 41–43.

The cost of movie theater tickets is $7.50 for adults and $5 for children ages 12 and under. On Saturday and Sunday afternoons until 4:00 P.M., there is a matinee price: $5.50 for adults and $3 for children ages 12 and under. Special group discounts are available for groups of 30 or more people.

41. Which of these can be determined from the information given in the above passage?
   a. how much it will cost a family of 4 to buy movie theater tickets on Saturday afternoon
   b. the difference between the cost of two movie theater tickets on Tuesday night and the cost of one ticket on Sunday at 3:00 P.M.
   c. how much movie theater tickets will cost each person if he or she is part of a group of 40 people
   d. the difference between the cost of a movie theater ticket for an adult on Friday night and a movie theater ticket for a 13 year old on Saturday afternoon at 1:00 P.M.
   e. the total money saved by a group of 35

42. Based on the passage, how much will movie theater tickets cost for two adults, one 15-year-old child and one 10-year-old child at 7:00 P.M. on a Sunday night?
   a. $17.00
   b. $19.50
   c. $25.00
   d. $26.50
   e. $27.50

43. Using the passage, how can you find the difference in price between a movie theater ticket for an adult and a movie theater ticket for a child under the age of 12 if the tickets are for a show at 3:00 P.M. on a Saturday afternoon?
   a. subtract $3.00 from $7.50
   b. subtract $5.00 from $7.50
   c. subtract $7.50 from $5.50
   d. add $5.50 and $3.00 and divide by 2
   e. subtract $3.00 from $5.50

44. It takes a typing student 0.75 seconds to type one word. At this rate, how many words can the student type in 60 seconds?
   a. 4.5 words
   b. 8.0 words
   c. 45.0 words
   d. 75.0 words
   e. 80.0 words

45. If a physical education student burns 8.2 calories per minute while riding a bicycle, how many calories will the same student burn if she rides for 35 minutes?
   a. 246 calories
   b. 286 calories
   c. 287 calories
   d. 387 calories
   e. 980 calories

46. Pediatric specialist Dr. Drake charges $36.00 for an office visit, which is $\frac{3}{4}$ of what general practitioner Dr. Jarmuth charges. How much does Dr. Jarmuth charge?
   a. $48.00
   b. $27.00
   c. $38.00
   d. $57.00
   e. $28.80

Use the information below to answer question 47.

A bicycle shop has a total of 55 bicycles in stock. Twelve are red, 5 are green, and 15 are blue. The bicycles are made by three different manufacturers: Trek, Schwinn, and GT.

47. Which of the following facts can be determined from the information given above?
   a. the number of Trek bicycles
   b. the number of yellow bicycles
   c. the cost of a red Schwinn
   d. the ratio of road bicycles to mountain bicycles
   e. the ratio of red bicycles to green bicycles

Use the information below to answer questions 48 and 49.

Basic cable television service, which includes 16 channels, costs $15 a month. The initial labor fee to install the service is $25. A $65 deposit is required but will be refunded within two years if the customer's bills are paid in full. Other cable services may be added to the basic service: the movie channel service is $9.40 a month; the news channels are $7.50 a month; the arts channels are $5.00 a month; the sports channels are $4.80 a month.

48. A customer's cable television bill totaled $20 a month. Using the passage above, what percentage of the bill was for basic cable service?
   a. 25 percent
   b. 33 percent
   c. 50 percent
   d. 75 percent
   e. 85 percent

49. A customer's first bill after having cable television installed totaled $112.50. This customer chose basic cable and one additional cable service. Which additional service was chosen?
   a. the news channels
   b. the movie channels
   c. the arts channels
   d. the sports channels
   e. no additional services were chosen

50. Out of 100 students polled, 80 said they would favor being offered a course in parenting skills at their high school. How many students out of 30,000 could be expected to favor being offered such a course?
   a. 2,400
   b. 6,000
   c. 16,000
   d. 22,000
   e. 24,000

▶ **Section 3:** Essay Writing

Carefully read the two essay-writing topics that follow. Plan and write two essays, one on each topic. Be sure to address all points in the topic. Allow about 30 minutes for each essay.

Topic 1
Should public school students be required to wear uniforms? Supporters argue that, among other things, uniforms would improve discipline and build a strong sense of community and identity. On the other hand, opponents believe that uniforms limit students' freedom of expression and their development as individuals.

Write an essay in which you take a position on whether or not public school students should be required to wear uniforms to school. Be sure to support your position with logical arguments and specific examples.

Topic 2
Bob Maynard has said that "Problems are opportunities in disguise."

Write an essay describing a time in your life when a problem became an opportunity. How did you transform the situation? Explain what you did to turn the problem into an opportunity and how others can benefit from your experience.

Answers and Explanations

Section 1: Reading Comprehension

1. **d.** See the second to last sentence, which speaks of Mt. Desert Island as supporting *the flora and fauna of both zones, as well as beach, inland, and alpine plants*. The other choices are not mentioned in paragraph 4.
2. **a.** See the final sentence of paragraph 1 and the second sentence of paragraph 2. There is no support for the other choices.
3. **c.** Although all the choices are related to the glacial disturbance of the Maine shoreline, only marine fossils are spoken of as evidence that a mountain was once at shoreline level.
4. **d.** This is the choice that makes the most sense. Since the summer homes of the wealthy existed for years and apparently still exist at the time of the writing of the passage, it is illogical to say that they were either *remembered* (choice a) or *discouraged* from existing there (choice b), or that the town *endured* them (choice e). It is unreasonable to suppose that a town would pay for summer homes for wealthy people (choice c).
5. **c.** Paragraph 5 (see the second sentence) discusses the visitors to Acadia National Park, and what they can learn from their visits. Choices a, b, d, and e are not mentioned in the passage.
6. **a.** This answer is implied by the first three sentences of paragraph 1. Even though Maine was part of a mountain range, there is no evidence that it could now be described as *very mountainous* (choice b) because the original mountains sank into the sea. There is no support for choice c. Choices d and e are not mentioned in the passage.
7. **c.** This passage is factual and informative. Although it may persuade some people to visit Maine, it is not written primarily as a *persuasive* piece (choice a). A *tourist brochure* would try to sell the reader, which rules out choice b. Choice d is a poor choice because this passage is nonfiction. There is no mention of the writer's experience or opinion, so choice e is also incorrect.
8. **b.** See the first sentence of paragraph 5. The general thrust of the paragraph suggests that the author would not care to celebrate the exclusive presence of the wealthy, even in former times (choice a). Earlier parts of the passage described the geological origins of the Maine coastline, but this is not the focus of the final paragraph (choices c and e). The paragraph does celebrate one single national park, Acadia, but does not speak of a *system of national parks* (choice d).
9. **d.** This is the best answer because the final sentence states that staff members in the Peace Corps cannot work more than five years. The other choices are not mentioned in the passage.
10. **a.** The examples in this passage are mainly about Roosevelt's accomplishments.
11. **c.** The third sentence of the first paragraph supports this choice.
12. **b.** In the second paragraph, the first sentence supports this answer.
13. **a.** This is the only choice stated in paragraph 1.
14. **b.** The last sentence in the paragraph clearly gives support for the idea that the interest in Shakespeare is due to the development of his characters. Choice a is incorrect because the writer never makes this type of comparison. Choice c is wrong because even though scholars are mentioned in the paragraph, there is no indication that the scholars are compiling the anthology. Choice d is wrong because there is no support to show that most New Yorkers are interested in this work. There is no support for choice e either.

15. d. The first sentence and the third sentence point to the relationship between technology and the changing role of the secretary. Choice **a** is incorrect because the second sentence indicates that the opposite is true. Choice **b** is not mentioned. Choice **c** is incorrect because there is no indication that typists have not found other jobs. Choice **e** goes far beyond what the passage suggests.

16. d. It is logical that a play would close after such a bad first night reception, and the sentence in choice **d** also uses a metaphor about stage history that is extended in the next sentence. Choices **a**, **b**, and **c** do not fit the sense or syntax of the paragraph, since the *however* in the next sentence contradicts them. Choice **e** claims that all critics misunderstood the play; whereas, the last sentence states that the critic Harold Hobson did see the importance of the play.

17. d. The first line of the passage describes the *English language premiere* of the play, indicating it had previous performances in a different language.

18. a. While the other choices are sometimes connotations of the term *avant-garde*, the author's meaning of *innovative* is supported by the final judgment of the passage on the play as *revolutionary*.

19. e. Although the writer seems amused by the negative criticisms of the play, she does give the opinion that it was *revolutionary* (a word which literally means *a turning point*) the authoritative backing of history. Choice **a** underplays and choice **b** overestimates the importance of the work to the author of the passage. Choice **c** is contradicted by the last sentence of the passage, and choice **d** mistakes Vivian Mercer's opinion for the author's.

20. e. According to the third sentence of the passage, each passenger must show the driver a library card in order to receive half-fare, so choices **a** and **c** would not be appropriate. Choice **d** might be appropriate after the driver has collected the full fare, assuming Mary does not have a library card. Choice **b** is incorrect, because the passage does not say that a person without a card cannot ride the bus, only that he or she cannot ride for half fare.

21. c. According to the last sentence of the passage, the trip sheet has a *special fare* section, implying that drivers regularly deal with special fares. The other choices may be true but are not reflected in the passage.

22. a. Although students in the other classes might find the passage's subject matter somewhat appropriate, the passage talks mainly about physiological changes to astronauts in space.

23. d. The passage says that in the face of light pollution *we lose our connection with something profoundly important to the human spirit, our sense of wonder*. The other choices are not mentioned in the passage.

24. b. The narrator describes nature in terms of the murder of a happy flower; therefore, the most logical description of her attitude would not be *delight*, *indifference*, *reverence*, or *deference*, but rather *dismay*.

25. b. The frost *beheads* the flower and therefore can be thought of as an *assassin*. None of the other choices in the poem directly commits murder.

26. c. The flower in the poem is *happy* and feels *no surprise* at its death, which implies *acceptance*. If there is any hint of *fear* or *horror* in the poem (choices **a** and **b**) it is on the part of the poet. Nothing in the poem is described as feeling either *reverence* or *awe* (choices **d** and **e**).

27. c. A God who would *approve* of a *happy flower*'s being beheaded, while apparently the rest of His creation (as exemplified by the sun) remains *unmoved* is probably not to be regarded as *benev-*

olent or *just* (choices **a** and **b**). Approval does not connote *anger* (choice **d**). The narrator speaks of God as if she is a believer, so God is not *nonexistent* in the poem (choice **e**).

28. **d.** A wind speed of 173 miles per hour falls between 158 and 206, which is the range for an F3 tornado.

29. **b.** Applying words such as *mild, moderate, significant, severe, devastating, cataclysmic,* and *overwhelming* to the kinds of damage done by a tornado is a means of describing the damage. A word like *devastating,* for example, is not what we think of as *scientific* or *objective* (choices **a** and **c**), and most of the words have negative connotations and therefore are not *whimsical* (choice **e**). Neither the table nor the language is trying to *persuade* (choice **d**), except perhaps secondarily.

30. **b.** The connotations of words like *bonds* and *constraints* in the passage suggest a *confined space* of criticism where the mind must be allowed to find some movement or *play*. None of the other choices make sense in the context of the passage.

31. **c.** The word *awe* implies mingled reverence, dread, and wonder, so the adjective *awesome* is the best of all the choices to describe a place that is *dangerous and full of wonders* (second sentence of the second paragraph). Choices **a** and **b** both describe a part of the hero's journey but neither describes the whole of it. Choice **d** is incorrect because the hero's journey is described in the passage in very serious terms, not in *whimsical* (playful or fanciful) terms at all. The words *trials* and *adventures* do not suggest anything mundane.

32. **e.** The first sentence of the passage describes Campbell's hero as *archetypal*. An archetype is a personage or pattern that occurs in literature and human thought often enough to be considered universal. Also, in the second sentence, the author of the passage mentions *the collective unconscious of all humankind*. The *faces* in the title belong to the *hero*, not to villagers, countries, languages, or adventures (choices **a, b, c,** and **d**).

33. **a.** The passage states that the hero's tale will *enlighten* his fellows, but that it will also be *dangerous*. Such a story would surely be radically mind-altering. Choice **b** is directly contradicted in the passage. If the hero's tale would terrify people *to no good end*, it could not possibly be enlightening. There is nothing in the passage to imply that the tale is *a warning of catastrophe, a dangerous lie,* or *a parable* (choices **c, d,** and **e**).

34. **b.** The definition of the word *boon* is *blessing*. What the hero brings back may be a kind of gift, charm, or prize (choices **a, c,** and **d**), but those words do not necessarily connote blessing or enlightenment.

35. **a.** The paragraph describes only the similarity between the hero's journey and the poet's. The other choices are not reflected in the passage.

36. **e.** The last sentence in the passage says that *the kingdom of the unconscious mind* goes down into *unsuspected Aladdin caves*. The story of *Aladdin* is a fairy tale (choice **b**), but neither this nor the other choices are in the passage.

37. **a.** The final sentence is an instance of a regular pattern that still has an uncanny quality. Choices **b, c,** and **e** all would introduce a sentence with an idea contradicting the preceding. Choice **d** would indicate that the final sentence is a restatement of the preceding, which it is not.

38. **e.** The passage says that people in general consider genius *supernatural, but also . . . eccentric;* the pairing of *extraordinary* and *erratic* in choice **e** includes both meanings given in the passage. Choices **a** and **d** cover only one side of the passage's meaning. Choice **b** and **c** contain definitions that the passage does not ascribe to the common view of genius.

39. c. This title covers the main point of the passage that, while there are predictable patterns in the life of a genius, the pattern increases the sense of something supernatural touching his or her life. Choices **a** and **b** are too general. Choice **d** is inaccurate because the passage does not talk about disorder in the life of a genius. Choice **e** covers only one of the two main ideas in the passage.

40. c. All the other statements are inaccurate.

41. a. According to the second sentence of the passage, the new MRI *detects not water but inert gases.* Choices **b**, **c**, and **d** are contradicted in the passage, and choice **e** is not reflected in the passage.

42. d. See the next-to-last sentence of the passage, which states specifically that chest X rays cannot provide a clear view of air passages.

43. a. Choices **b**, **d**, and **e** may be opinions held by the author, but they are far beyond the content of the passage and a reader could not tell if the author believed them. Choice **c** reflects a traditional view that the author probably does not hold; the passage indicates that the author approves of a change in this attitude. Choice **a** is therefore the best choice.

44. d. Because the author mentions two women who attended an international conference as an accomplishment for which at least one of them *gained international fame*, the reader can surmise that it was a rare occurrence and choice **d** is the best answer. Choices **b**, **c**, and **e** are far beyond the scope of the passage; choice **a** might be true but would require information not contained in the passage.

45. e. The first paragraph notes that an allergic disease results from *the immune system reacting to a normally innocuous substance . . .* Choices **b** and **c** are contradicted in the passage by this statement. Choices **a** and **d** are not reflected in the passage.

46. b. See the third sentence, which says, in part, that *cells called macrophages engulf the invader* (that is, the allergen).

47. c. This passage provides information to social workers about music therapy, as the title in choice **c** indicates. Choice **e** is incorrect because the first sentence speaks of mental and physical health professionals *referring* their clients and patients to music therapists; the second sentence indicates that *It* (meaning a *referral*) *seems a particularly good choice for the social worker.* Choice **d** is possible, but does not summarize the passage as well as choice **c**. Choices **a** and **b** refer to topics not covered in the passage.

48. e. Although the other choices may be correct, they require knowledge beyond the passage. Based on the information in the passage, **e** is the best choice.

49. a. Based particularly on the last sentence of the passage, **a** is the best choice. The other choices are beyond the scope of the passage.

50. c. Choice **c** provides the best outline of the passage. The other choices all contain points that are not covered by the passage.

Section 2: Mathematics

1. a. −0.15 is less than −0.02, the smallest number in the range.

2. c. January is approximately 38,000; February is approximately 41,000, and April is approximately 26,000. These added together give a total of 105,000.

3. c. The buses arrive 53 minutes after they leave. Therefore, the bus will arrive at 8:13.

4. b. $3 divided by $50 is .06. This is an increase of 0.06, or 6%.

5. c. PQ and RS are intersecting lines. The fact that angle POR is a 90-degree angle means that PQ and RS are perpendicular, indicating that all the angles formed by their intersection, including ROQ, measure 90 degrees.

6. **a.** The Pythagorean theorem states that the square of the length of the hypotenuse of a right triangle is equal to the sum of the squares of the other two sides, so we know that the following equation applies: $1^2 + X^2 = (\sqrt{10})^2$, so $1 + X^2 = 10$, so $X^2 = 10 - 1 = 9$, so $X = 3$.

7. **e.** If the figure is a regular decagon, it can be divided into ten equal sections by lines passing through the center. Two such lines form the indicated angle, which includes three of the ten sections. $\frac{3}{10}$ of 360 degrees is equal to 108 degrees.

8. **e.** According to the graph, of the choices given, the fewest acres burned in 1993.

9. **c.** The bar on the graph is over the 100,000 mark.

10. **e.** To answer this question, both *Acres Burned* and *Dollars Spent* must be considered. The ratio between the two is greater in 1994 than in the other years.

11. **a.** In April, the dotted line (representing the average) is closest to the solid line (representing 1995 rainfall).

12. **d.** Read the dotted line for September.

13. **b.** The graph shows that during January, February, and April, rainfall amounts were above average.

14. **a.** In choice **b**, the 9 is in the hundredths place; in **c** it is in the tenths place, in **d** in the ten-thousandths place, and in **e** in the hundred-thousandths place.

15. **d.** $12.50 per hour × 8.5 hours per day × 5 days per week is $531.25. This can be estimated by multiplying $12 × 8 × 5 = $500. Because he earns $0.50 more an hour and works a half-hour more per day, you know that his actual earnings are just a little more than 500, and so the only reasonable answer is **d**.

16. **b.** The number of papers graded is arrived at by multiplying the rate for each grader by the time spent by each grader. Melissa grades 5 papers an hour for 3 hours, or 15 papers; Joe grades 4 papers an hour for 2 hours, or 8 papers, so together they grade 23 papers. Because there are 50 papers, the percentage graded is $\frac{23}{50}$ which is equal to 46%.

17. **e.** A yardstick is 36 inches long; add that to the 28 inches of rope, and you will get 64 inches as the longest distance James can measure.

18. **d.** Obviously, since the two sides have different measurements, one is the length and one the width. The area of a rectangle is found by multiplying length times width: Length = 15 inches. Width = 15 divided by 3, or 5 inches. 5 inches × 15 inches = 75 square inches.

19. **d.** 3 inches every 2 hours = 1.5 inches per hour × 5 hours = 7.5 inches.

20. **b.** The unreduced ratio is 8,000:5,000,000 or 8:5,000. 5,000 divided by 8 equals 625, for a ratio of 1:625.

21. **a.** The first step in solving the problem is to subtract 86 from 148. The remainder, 62, is then divided by 2 to get 31 feet.

22. **e.** Three feet equals 36 inches; add 4 inches to get 40 inches total; 40 divided by 5 is 8.

23. **c.** To find the average time, you add the times for all the students and divide by the number of students. 20 plus 17 plus 14 is 51. 51 divided by 3 equals 17.

24. **c.** The volume will equal the length times the width times the depth or height of a container: (12 inches) (5 inches) (10 inches) = 600 cubic inches.

25. **d.** The volume of concrete is 27 cubic feet. As noted in the previous answer explanation, the volume is length times width times depth or height,

or (L)(W)(D), so (L)(W)(D) equals 27. We're told that the length L is 6 times the width W, so L equals 6W. We're also told that the depth is 6 inches, or 0.5 feet. Substituting what we know about the length and depth into the original equation and solving for W, we get (L)(W)(D) = (6W)(W)(0.5) = 27. $3W^2$ equals 27. W^2 equals 9, so W equals 3. To get the length, we remember that L equals 6W, so L equals (6)(3), or 18 feet.

26. a. First, you find out how long the entire hike can be, based on the rate at which the hikers are using their supplies. $\frac{\frac{2}{5}}{3} = \frac{1}{x}$, where 1 is the total amount of supplies and x is the number of days for the whole hike. Cross-multiplying, you get $\frac{2}{5}x = 3$, so that $x = \frac{(3)(5)}{2}$, or $7\frac{1}{2}$ days for the length of the entire hike. This means that the hikers could go forward for 3.75 days altogether before they would have to turn around. They have already hiked for 3 days. 3.75 minus 3 equals 0.75 for the amount of time they can now go forward before having to turn around.

27. c. Three tons is 6,000 pounds. 6,000 pounds times 16 ounces per pound is 96,000 ounces. The total weight of each daily ration is 12 ounces plus 18 ounces plus 18 ounces, or 48 ounces. 96,000 divided by 48 equals 2,000 troops supplied. 2,000 divided by 10 days equals 200 troops supplied.

28. d. 26 forms times 8 hours is 208 forms per day per clerk. 5,600 divided by 208 is approximately 26.9. Since you can't hire 0.9 of a clerk, you have to hire 27 clerks for the day.

29. b. The women's combined rate of travel is 35 miles per hour plus 15 miles per hour, which is equal to 50 miles per hour. 2,100 miles divided by 50 miles per hour equals 42 hours.

30. b. The runner's three best times are 54, 54, and 57, or 165. The average of these is 165 divided by 3, or 55.

31. e. Solve this problem with the following equation: $4x - 12 = 20$; $4x = 32$; $x = 8$.

32. e. This can be most quickly and easily solved by rounding the numbers to the nearest ten cents. Therefore, $2 \times \$3 + \$3.40 + 2 \times \$4 + \$2 = \$19.40$. The nearest and most reasonable answer would be e or $19.10.

33. b. Solve this problem with the following equation: $37\frac{1}{2}$ hours $- 26\frac{1}{4}$ hours $= 11\frac{1}{4}$ hours.

34. d. Solve this problem with the following equation: 4 candy bars $\times \$0.40 +$ 3 soft drinks $\times \$0.50 = \$3.10$.

35. a. Solve this problem with the following equations: $\frac{1}{2} + \frac{1}{2} = 1$. $5 \times \frac{1}{4} = 1\frac{1}{4}$. $1 + 1\frac{1}{4} = 2\frac{1}{4}$.

36. c. There are 5 spaces of 4 feet and 4 desks of 3 feet; this adds to 32 feet.

37. b. An algebraic equation should be used: $K - 20 = \frac{1}{2}(M - 20)$; $K = 40$. Therefore, $M = 60$.

38. a. The number of cars originally is known, and the number sold is known, so the number remaining can be calculated.

39. c. The two rings valued at $150 have a total value of $300, but remember that there is another ring valued at only $70, so the correct answer is $610.

40. c. The value of the handbag ($150) must be included in the total of $618.

41. d. Choices a, b, and e can be ruled out because there is no way to determine how many tickets are for adults or for children. Choice c can be ruled out because the price of group tickets is not given.

42. e. Because the 15-year-old requires an adult ticket, there are 3 adult tickets at $7.50 each and one child's ticket at $5 for a total of $27.50.

43. e. The adult price on Saturday afternoon is $5.50; the child's price is $3.00. By subtracting

$3.00 from $5.50, you can find the difference in price.

44. e. This problem is solved by dividing 60 (the words) by 0.75 (the time), which gives 80 words.

45. c. This is a simple multiplication problem, which is solved by multiplying 35 times 8.2 for a total of 287.

46. a. You know the ratio of Dr. Drake's charge to Dr. Jarmuth's charge is 3:4, or $\frac{3}{4}$. To find what Dr. Jarmuth charges, you use the equation $\frac{3}{4} = \frac{36}{x}$, or $3x = (4)(36)$. 4 times 36 equals 144, which is then divided by 3 to arrive at $x = 48$.

47. e. Because the only categories quantified are colors of bikes, only the ratio of red bikes to green bikes can be found.

48. d. The basic cable service fee of $15 and the bill is $20: $15 divided by $20 will give you 0.75, or 75 percent.

49. a. The labor fee ($25) plus the deposit ($65) plus the basic service ($15) equals $105. The difference between the total bill, $112.50, and $105 is $7.50, the cost of the news channels.

50. e. Eighty out of 100 is 80 percent. Eighty percent of 30,000 is 24,000.

Section 3: Essay Writing

Following are the criteria for scoring CBEST essays.

A "4" essay is a coherent writing sample that addresses the assigned topic and is aimed at a specific audience. Additionally, it has the following characteristics:

- A main idea and/or a central point of view that is focused; its reasoning is sound
- Points of discussion that are clear and arranged logically
- Assertions that are supported with specific, relevant detail
- Word choice and usage that is accurate and precise
- Sentences that have complexity and variety, with clear syntax; paragraphs that are coherent (minor mechanical flaws are acceptable)
- Style and language that are appropriate to the assigned audience and purpose

A "3" essay is an adequate writing sample that generally addresses the assigned topic, but may neglect or only vaguely address one of the assigned tasks; it is aimed at a specific audience. Generally, it has the following additional characteristics:

- A main idea and/or a central point of view and adequate reasoning
- Organization of ideas that is effective; the meaning of the ideas is clear
- Generalizations that are adequately, though unevenly, supported
- Word choice and language usage that are adequate; mistakes exist, but these do not interfere with meaning
- Some errors in sentence and paragraph structure, but not so many as to be confusing
- Word choice and style is appropriate to a given audience

A "2" essay is an incompletely formed writing sample that attempts to address the topic and to communicate a message to the assigned audience but is generally incomplete or inappropriate. It has the following additional characteristics:

- A main point, but one which loses focus; reasoning that is simplistic
- Ineffective organization that causes the response to lack clarity
- Generalizations that are only partially supported; supporting details that are irrelevant or unclear

- Imprecise language usage; word choice that distracts the reader
- Mechanical errors; errors in syntax; errors in paragraphing
- Style that is monotonous or choppy

A "1" essay is an inadequately formed writing sample that only marginally addresses the topic and fails to communicate its message to, or is inappropriate to, a specific audience. Additionally, it has the following characteristics:

- General incoherence and inadequate focus, lack of a main idea or consistent point of view; illogical reasoning
- Ineffective organization and unclear meaning throughout
- Unsupported generalizations and assertions; details that are irrelevant and presented in a confusing manner
- Language use that is imprecise, with serious and distracting errors
- Many serious errors in mechanics, sentence syntax, and paragraphing

Following are examples of scored essays for Topics 1 and 2.

TOPIC 1

Pass—Score = 4

Though it may seem to contradict the ideal of democracy upon which our public school system is based, requiring public school students to wear uniforms is a good idea. In fact, uniforms would help schools provide a better education to all students by evening out socio-economic differences and improving discipline among students.

Style is important, especially to children and teenagers who are busy trying to figure out who they are and what they believe in. But in many schools today, kids are so concerned about what they wear that clothing becomes a major distraction—even an obsession. Many students today are too busy to study because they're working after school so they can afford the latest fashions. If students were required to wear uniforms, they would have less pressure to be "best dressed" and more time to devote to their studies.

More importantly, the competition over who has the hottest clothes can be devastating to the self-esteem of students from lower income families. Because uniforms would require everyone to wear the same outfits, students from poorer families would not have to attend school in beat-up hand-me-downs and wouldn't have to face the kind of teasing they often get from students who can afford Tommy Hilfiger and $150 Reeboks. True, students from wealthier families will be able to wear nicer shoes and accessories, but in general the uniforms will create an evening-out that will enable poorer students to stop being ashamed of their poverty and develop a stronger sense of self.

Contrary to what opponents argue, uniforms will not create uniformity. Just because students are dressed the same does not mean they won't be able to develop as individuals. In fact, because uniforms enable students to stop worrying so much about their appearance, students can focus more on who they are on the inside and on what they're supposed to be learning in the classroom.

Furthermore, uniforms will improve discipline in the schools. Whenever a group of people dresses alike, they automatically have a sense of community, a sense of common purpose. Uniforms *mean* something. School uniforms will constantly remind students that they *are* indeed in school—and they're in school to learn. Getting dressed for school itself will be a form of discipline that students will carry into the classroom.

Though many students will complain, requiring public school students to wear uniforms makes sense. Students will learn more—both about themselves and about the world around them.

Marginal Pass—Score = 3

I don't think that requiring public school students to wear uniforms is a good idea. The way the student dresses makes a powerful statement about who he or she is, and the school years are an important time for them to explore their identities. Uniforms would undermine that. They would also have little, if any, positive affect on students with disipline problems.

Each student has their own personality, and one way he expresses who he is is through his clothing. Clothes are an important way for young people to show others how they feel about themselves and what is important to them. If public school students are forced to wear uniforms, this important form of self-expression will be taken away.

I remember back when I was in junior high school. My parents had given me complete freedom to buy my back to school wardrobe. They took me to the mall and let me choose everything, from sweaters and shirts to socks and shoes. I'll never forget how independent that made me feel. I could choose clothing that *I* liked. I did make a few bad choices, but at least those were *my* choices. Students today, I am sure, would feel the same way.

Besides, America values individuality. What happens to that value in an environment where everybody looks the same?

Though disipline in schools is a serious concern, uniforms are not the answer. Disipline problems usually come from a lack of disipline at home, and that's a problem that uniforms can't begin to address. A student who is rowdy in the classroom isn't going to change their behavior because they are wearing a white shirt and tie. In fact, disipline problems might *increase* if students are required to wear uniforms. Students often make trouble because they want attention. Well-behaved students who used to get attention from how they dressed might now become trouble-makers so they can continue to get attention.

Uniforms are not the answer to the problems public school students face. In fact, because they'll restrict individuality and may even increase disiplinary problems, they'll only add to the problem.

Marginal Fail—Score = 2

I don't think that requiring public school students to wear uniforms is a good idea. Each student has their own identity and express who he is through clothing. The school years are an important in finding one's personality. Uniforms would also have little, if any, positive affect on students with disipline problems.

In junior high school I let my children buy their back-to-school wardrobe, anything they wanted. I let them choose everything. I'll never forget how that made them feel. As they would say, awesome! They could choose clothing that they liked.

We are told to be yourself. But how can a young person be in a country where everybody is the same.

Disipline in schools is of a serious concern, uniforms are not the answer. It is the home life of many students that make bad behavior. If the parents use drugs or dont disipline children at home, thats a problem that the school and uniforms can't do anything about. A student who is causing trouble at school isn't going to change their behavior because they are wearing a white blouse or pleated skirt. In fact, disipline problems might even get worse if students are required to wear uniforms because of not getting enough attention about the way he or she is dressed.

Uniforms are not the answer to the problems public school students face. In fact, because they will keep them from being who they are they will make it worse.

Fail—Score = 1

Public school students should wear uniforms to. Not just private school students. I do not want to teach in a private school; but I like them wearing a uniform every day. The look neat and well-groom no matter if they are low income or high income. Social level doesnt matter.

Wearing uniforms is good because they build a sense of community. Everyone from the same school wear the same clothes. The students know if someone is from there school right away. It makes it easier for students, rich or poor, to make friends with people. They don't have to worry about what to wear in the morning because they always know.

Also they don't have to spend as much money on cloths.

Many students think it is unfair that public school students could wear whatever they wanted. Maybe private school students shouldn't wear uniforms either. Then everyone would be able to dress the way they want to and be individulistic.

Some people say uniforms would make bad students behave better. Because they wouldn't always be talking about who has a better sneakers or better jeans. They might have paid more attention in school like they should of, and then everyone could learn more.

TOPIC 2

Pass—Score = 4

Life is full of problems, but how we approach those problems often determines whether we're happy or miserable. Bob Maynard says that "Problems are opportunities in disguise." If we approach problems with Maynard's attitude, we can see that problems are really opportunities to learn about ourselves and others. They enable us to live happier and more fulfilling lives.

Maynard's quote applies to all kinds of problems. I faced a problem just last week when our family's kitchen sink developed a serious leak. There was water all over our kitchen floor and piles of dishes to be washed. But our landlord was out of town for the week. I come from a big family—I have six brothers and sisters—so we couldn't afford to wait until he got back, and my mom couldn't afford a couple hundred dollars to pay for a plummer on her own. So I took the opportunity to learn how to fix it myself. I went to the library and found a great fix-it-yourself book. In just a few hours, I figured out what was causing the leak and how to stop it. If it weren't for that problem, I probably would have relied on plummers and landlords all my life. Now I know I can handle leaky pipes by myself.

I think it's important to remember that no matter how big a problem is, it's still an opportunity. Whatever kind of situation we face, problems give us the chance to learn and grow, both physically and mentally. For example, when I had a problem with my car and couldn't afford the repairs right away, my problem became an opportunity to get some exercise—something I'd been wanting to do anyway. I had to walk a mile each day to get to the bus stop and back. But in the meantime, I got the chance to start getting back in shape, and I saved a lot on gas.

I've come to realize that problems are really part of what makes life worth living. Problems challenge us and give us the opportunity to do things we've never done before, to learn things we never knew before. They teach us what we're capable of doing. They give us the chance to surprise ourselves.

Marginal Pass—Score = 3

Just the word "problem" can send some of us into a panic. But problems can be good things, too. Problems are situations that make us think and force us to be creative and resourceful. They can also teach us things we didn't know before.

For example, I had a problem in school a few years ago when I couldn't understand my math class. I started failing my quizzes and homework assignments. I wasn't sure what to do, so finally I went to the teacher and asked for help. She said she would arrange for me to be tutored by another student who was her best student. In return, though, I'd have to help that student around school. I wasn't sure what she meant by that until I met my tutor. She was handicapped.

My job was to help her carry her books from class to class. I'd never even spoken to someone in a wheelchair before and I was a little scared. But she turned out to be the nicest person I've ever spent time with. She helped me understand everything I need to know for math class and she taught me a lot about what it's like to be handicapped. I learned to appreciate everything that I have, and I also know that people with disabilities are special not because of what they can't do, but because of who they are.

So you see that wonderful things can come out of problems. You just have to remember to look for the positive things and not focus on the negative.

Marginal Fail—Score = 2
The word "problem" is a negative word but its just an opportunity as Mr. Bob Maynard has said. It can be teaching tool besides.

For example, I had a problem with my son last year when he wanted a bigger allowance. I said no and he had to earn it. He mowed the lawn and in the fall he raked leaves. In the winter he shovelled the walk. After that he apreciated it more.

Its not the problem but the sollution that matters. My son learning the value of work and earning money. (It taught me the value of money to when I had to give him a bigger allowance!) After that he could get what he wanted at Toys Are Us and not have to beg. Which was better for me too. Sometimes we forget that both children and there parents can learn a lot from problems and we can teach our children the value of over-coming trouble. Which is as important as keeping them out of trouble. As well we can teach them the value of money. That is one aspect of a problem that we manytimes forget.

So problems are a good teaching tool as well as a good way to let you're children learn, to look at the silver lining behind every cloud.

Fail—Score = 1
I agree with the quote that problems are opportunities in disguise. Sometimes problems are opportunities, too.

I have a lot of problems like anyone else does. Sometimes there very difficult and I don't no how to handle them. When I have a really big problem, I sometimes ask my parents or freinds for advise. Sometimes they help, sometimes they don't, then I have to figure out how to handle it myself.

One time I had a big problem. Where someone stole my wallet and I had to get to a job interview. But I had no money and no ID. This happened in school. So I went to the principles office and reported it. He called the man I was supposed to interview with. Who rescheduled the intervew for me. So I still had the opportunity to interview and I'm proud to say I got the job. In fact I'm still working there!

Problems can be opportunities if you just look at them that way. Instead of the other way around.

▶ Scoring

Because it is necessary for you to do well on all three sections of the CBEST—Reading Comprehension, Mathematics, and Essay Writing—you must figure your score on each section separately. Reading Comprehension and Mathematics are scored the same way: First find the number of questions you got right in each section. Questions you skipped or got wrong don't count; just add up how many questions you got right out of the 50 questions in each section. If you get approximately 70% of the answers right on each section, you will pass the test. The table below will help you check your math by giving you percentage equivalents for some possible scores.

Number of questions right	Approximate percentage
50	100%
46	92%
43	86%
39	78%
35	70%
32	64%
28	56%
25	50%

You should get a score of at least 70% on both the Reading Comprehension section and the Mathematics section to be absolutely certain to pass those portions of the CBEST. (The actual number you receive on the real CBEST will *not* be "70," however, as the scores are converted from raw scores to scaled scores. But for the purpose of finding out if you passed the practice exams in this book, a percentage is just fine.)

In addition to achieving a score of 70% on the Reading Comprehension and Mathematics sections, you must receive a passing score on the Essay Writing section of the CBEST. On this portion, each essay you write will be scored by two readers who have been especially trained for this task. The criteria are outlined in detail in Section 3 on pages 56–57, but generally the essays are scored as follows:

4 = Pass (an excellent and well-formed essay)
3 = Marginal Pass (an average and adequately-formed essay)
2 = Marginal Fail (a partially-formed but substandard essay)
1 = Fail (an inadequately-formed essay)

Your score will be a combination of the two readers' judgments, somewhere between a possible high of 8 to a low of 2. The best way to see how you did on your essays for this diagnostic exam is to give your essays and the scoring criteria to a teacher and ask him or her to score your essays for you.

What's much more important than your scores, for now, is how you did on each of the basic skills tested by the exam. You need to diagnose your strengths and weaknesses so that you can concentrate your efforts as you prepare for the exam.

Use your percentage scores in conjunction with the LearningExpress Test Preparation system in Chapter 2 of this book to help you devise a study plan. Then turn to the CBEST Mini-Course in Chapter 4, which covers each of the basic skills tested on the CBEST in 24 half-hour lessons. You should plan to spend more time on the lessons that correspond to the questions you found hardest and less time on the lessons that correspond to areas in which you did well.

CHAPTER

4 ▶ CBEST Mini-Course

CHAPTER SUMMARY
The CBEST Mini-Course gives you the essentials you need to pass the CBEST in just 24 lessons. By spending just half an hour on each lesson—more on the areas that give you trouble, less on the areas you feel confident about—you can increase your CBEST score and earn your California or Oregon teaching credentials.

Each of the 24 lessons in this chapter reviews one important CBEST skill. You can either move through the Mini-Course sequentially or choose the areas you need to study most. If you find you need more help after completing the lessons in one area, be sure to consult the More Help section at the end of this chapter.

Here's an outline of what you'll find in this Mini-Course:

Reading 1: General Strategies (page 64)
Reading 2: Organization Questions (page 66)
Reading 3: Unmasking the Main Idea (page 70)
Reading 4: About the Author (page 73)
Reading 5: Definite Details and Tables of Contents (page 76)
Reading 6: Impressive Implications (page 79)
Reading 7: Wizard Words, Departed Parts, and Other Oddities (page 81)
Reading 8: Graphs (also applies to Math) (page 87)

Math 1:   Words, Words, Words (page 90)
Math 2:   Numbers Working Together (page 93)
Math 3:   Rounding, Estimation, and Decimal Equivalents (page 97)
Math 4:   Fractions (page 101)
Math 5:   Measurement, Perimeter, and Area (page 104)
Math 6:   Ratios, Proportions, and Percents (page 109)
Math 7:   Algebra (page 114)
Math 8:   Averages, Probability, and Combinations (page 118)
Math 9:   The Word Problem Game (page 123)
Math 10:   The CIA Approach to Word Problems (page 127)
Math 11:   Logic and Venn Diagrams (page 130)
Writing 1: Outlining the Essay (page 133)
Writing 2: Writing the Introduction (page 136)
Writing 3: The Sandwich Paragraphs and the Last Slice (page 140)
Writing 4: Sentence Doctor (page 143)
Writing 5: Finishing Touches (page 147)

More Help with Reading, Math, and Writing (page 151)

Most types of questions discussed in each lesson are accompanied by a gray box that gives success steps for solving that type of question. Look for the gray box on each page and read it before you try the sample questions.

▶ Reading 1: General Strategies

The reading comprehension section is composed of 50 questions on a variety of passages. The passages are created to simulate high school and college-level materials, student textbooks, teacher's guides and enrichment material, and books on student behavior or psychology. The questions are a variety of types. This section explores some general strategies for all kinds of passages and questions. The sections that follow look in detail at each kind of question you might be asked.

Seven Approaches

How do you approach reading comprehension questions? Below are some suggestions from former CBEST takers.

- **The Concentrator:** "I read the passage thoroughly before I look at the questions. After concentrating on the passage, I can find the answers to the questions if I don't already know the answer from my careful reading."
- **The Skimmer:** "I skim the passage before looking at the questions. I can always go back and find the answers once I know how the passage is arranged."
- **The Cautious Reader:** "I read the questions first with all their answer choices. I want to know what they will ask me before I read the passage so I can be on the lookout. Then I read the passage two or three times until I am sure I understand it completely."
- **The Game Player:** "I read the questions first and try to answer them from what I already know or can guess. Then I read the passage to see whether I am right. After guessing the answers, I am familiar with the questions enough to recognize the answers when I find them."
- **The Educated Guesser:** "I read the questions first, but not the answers. When I find the answer in the passage, I look for it among the answer choices."
- **The Psychic:** "I believe the test makers would put the questions for the first part of the passage first. So I read the first question and go back to the passage for the answer, and then I do the second."
- **The Efficiency Expert:** "First I look at the questions and do the questions that have line numbers that indicate where the answer is to be found.

Then I skim the passage for the key words I read in the other questions. This way I sometimes do not even have to read the whole passage."

If you don't already have a preferred method, try some of these approaches as you work through the practice exercises in this book. See which method fits your own mix of talents.

Hints for Reading the Passages

Try Short Cuts
The purpose of a reading comprehension problem is to be as accurate as possible in the given amount of time. Practice will help you determine whether you need to read the questions first, the answers first, or some combination thereof. Try some of the shortcuts listed above to find out which works for you.

Associate with the Passage
Every passage has something to do with real-life situations. Your mission is to discover the answers to such questions as:

- What is the author trying to express?
- Who might the author be?
- Does the author tell readers in the beginning what to expect later in the passage?
- How does the author structure the work to convey meaning?
- Does the author make any statements that might surprise or interest you?
- To what conclusions is the author leading readers? What conclusions are stated?

If the passage seems boring or on a topic that is foreign to you, try imagining that your best friend is talking to you on the same subject, and it totally interests him or her. It might not be your thing, but it's your friend's, so listen to every detail and nuance of what your friend has to say and try to associate with it.

To Mark or Not to Mark
Some test takers find it helpful to underline text or make notes in the margins to designate the stated subject, supporting facts, conclusions, etc. For others, marking a passage seems a waste of time. You are free to make as many marks as you want on the test booklet, so if marking helps, go for it. If you are not sure, now is the time to try out this method. If you decide to mark a passage, don't mark so much that the meat of the passage is obscured. Marking a few key words and ideas is more helpful than underlining the majority of the passage.

Notice Transitions
Pay special attention to words that give you an insight into the author's purpose or that change the context of the passage, such as *however, nevertheless,* etc. In at least one passage, these words will be left for you to fill in. This topic will be discussed in more detail in Reading Lesson 7.

Hints for Reading the Questions
Reading the questions carefully is just as important as reading the answers.

Read the Questions as Carefully as the Passage
It is crucial that you read the questions and answers as carefully as you read the passage. Should you read all the answer choices or stop when you have found one that seems right? Test takers differ on this. Some who read all the answers become confused or worry about wasting time. Others feel more secure when they can eliminate every answer but the right one. It's up to you to find the best method.

Know Question Types

If, for example, you answer an implication question as a detail question, you will get the answer wrong, even though the answer you chose is in the passage. The lessons after this one will show you how to recognize the different question types and how to quickly choose the best answer.

Avoid Controversial Answers

There will probably be some type of ethnic or environmental passage on your CBEST. Stay away from answers that seem negative toward any ethnic or gender group or any environmental issues. Test makers usually steer clear of right answers that say something negative or controversial.

Answer Only from the Passage

Everything you need to know has to be somewhere in the passage. While it is helpful to have some knowledge of the subject in order to better understand the author, don't rely on your experience to answer the question. An answer can be true and still not be the correct answer.

Not or *Except*

Look for words in the question such as NOT or EXCEPT, especially if you cannot find your answer or there seem to be more than one answer. For example, a question might read: "Which of the following facts is NOT stated in the passage?"

Eliminate

Eliminate all the answers that are obviously off the subject or otherwise wrong. Physically cross off the obviously wrong answers in your test booklet so you won't waste time reading them again. Test takers say that they are often left with two close answers. There has to be one answer that is better than the other. Check the passage for clue words that might point to one choice over the other. If, after trying out all the strategies you learn in this book, you are still left with two answers, go ahead and guess, and get on with the test.

None Left?

If you eliminate all of the answers, go back over the eliminated answers to determine whether there might be another meaning for any of them. Try to find a reason that would make each answer correct. If there is no possible way an answer could be right—for example, it is completely off the subject—then eliminate that answer. Choose the answer that is the least wrong.

Marking the Unknown Question

Should you mark questions to come back to later? If you do, you will probably have to read the passage again, which can waste valuable time. If an answer jumps out at you after reading the passage once or twice, choose it. Many teachers and test takers recommend going with your first answer, your "gut" instinct. To save time and avoid dealing with passages more than once, answer all the questions about one passage before continuing on to the next passage.

Using the Steps

The lessons that follow discuss types of reading questions you may encounter. They offer sample question beginnings, as well as steps for solving each type of problem. There is no need to memorize all the steps. They are tips that clue you into what the test makers expect. You may be able to find the answer by your own methods without looking at the steps. So much the better. The steps are not there to bog you down, but if any of them can help you, use them.

CBEST MINI-COURSE

▶ Reading 2: Organization Questions

Passages on the CBEST are always organized logically. Learning to recognize that organization may also give you some ideas on organizing your essays in the Writing section. In this lesson, you'll learn about two types of organization questions: structure and misplaced sentences.

Structure Questions

Structure questions have stems (the question part) that start out like these:

- Which of the following best represents the arrangement of the passage?
- Which of the following best describes the organization of the passage?
- The sequence of the passage is best represented by which of the following?

Where to Find Structure Answers in the Passage

To answer structure questions, you will need to skim the passage carefully enough to discover the gist of each sentence; that is, whether it is a statistic, an example, a quote, an opinion, and so on.

Practice Passage and Questions

Try the six Success Steps on the structure questions that follow this passage.

Many extended-time programs use heterogeneous grouping of multi-age and/or multi-ability students. Mixed-ability grouping is based on the theory that lower-ability students benefit from working in small groups with their higher-achieving peers, and high-ability students reinforce their knowledge by sharing with their lower-achieving peers. Researchers also have found that multi-age grouping benefits students' mental health as well as academic achievement and contributes to positive attitudes toward school.

Because the voluntary nature of participation in an extended-time program results in a range of student ages and skills, heterogeneous groups may result naturally. Often, however, extended-time program planners arrange groups so that high- and low-ability students work together—with the expectation of cooperative rather than competitive learning. In Chicago's ASPIRA program, students are selected for participation with a goal of mixing high achievers and at-risk participants—and these groups work together closely in all activities.

Six Success Steps for Structure Passages

1. Skim the passage or read the topic sentences to understand the general topic and the purpose of the passage.
2. Notice the logical sequence of ideas that the author uses.
3. The description of sentences in the answers goes in the same order as the sentences in the passage. So notice the first sentences. Do they state a theory, introduce a topic, quote a famous person, or . . . ?
4. Look at the answer choices. If the first few sentences state a theory, then the first part of the correct answer should say that the author stated a theory, gives a hypothesis, or other words to that effect. Eliminate any answers that do not match.
5. Go back to 3 and 4 above; look at the next few sentences.
6. You should have eliminated at least one or two answers. When only two or three are left, read them to see what possibilities they reveal for the rest of the passage. Read the next sentences of the passage and find the answer that matches the rest of the structure.

Two Success Steps for Misplaced Sentences

1. Read the passage to determine the main idea.
2. Be suspicious of any sentence that has nothing to do with the main idea.

---

1. Which of the following best describes the structure of the passage?
   a. The passage begins with a hypothesis, and then gives an explanation and support for this theory.
   b. The passage starts with a main idea, gives an example, and then draws a conclusion.
   c. The passage opens with an introduction to the topic, then gives a more detailed account of the topic.
   d. The passage begins with a statement, supports that statement with research, and gives real life examples.
   e. The passage begins with an event and then continues the narrative.

2. Which of the following would be the best outline for the passage?
   a. I. Statement
      II. Facts
      III. Quotations
   b. I. Theory
      II. Practices
   c. I. Research
      II. Discussion
      III. Example
   d. I. Question
      II. Answer
      III. Support
   e. I. Quote
      II. Thesis
      III. Examples

Answers

Here's how you could use the six Success Steps to answer question 1.

1. It seems as though the passage is about students of different ages and abilities learning together.
2. The first paragraph tells why and the second tells how students come to be in groups of mixed age and ability.
3. The first sentence states a fact. The other sentences in the paragraph seem to cite research. It doesn't say so at first, but later it says, "Researchers also found . . ." which implies that research was involved in the theories before that sentence.
4. Answers c and e are out. The passage does not give much introduction to the topic, and does not start with an event.
5. The next sentences support the topic sentence with research. The answer must be d.
6. For this question, you don't need to use this hint.

If you use the same method to answer question 2, you will quickly eliminate answers d and e on the basis of the first few sentences. You eliminate a because there are no quotations. You are left with b and c, which are very close. Answer c contains a vague word, *discussion*, which could be almost any kind of structure. Answer b is more precise. The first paragraph in the passage gives the theory, and the second gives the application of the theory. The better answer is b.

Misplaced Sentences

You may be asked to find the sentence that does not logically flow, or that is not necessary to the purpose of the passage. Such questions often start out like this:

- Which sentence, if omitted from the passage, would be least likely to interrupt the sequence of ideas?

68

Seven Success Steps for Simple Main Idea Questions

1. While reading or skimming the passage, notice the general topic.
2. Go through the answer choices. Cross out any that are completely off the topic.
3. Cross out any answer choices that are too broad for a short passage. ("The constellations" might be the subject of a book, but not the main idea for a paragraph or two.)
4. Eliminate any answer that is on the general topic, but not the specific topic of the passage.
5. Cross out any that only deal with one sentence of a paragraph, or one paragraph of a longer passage.
6. If you are still left with two answers that seem to fit most of the sentences in the passage, then choose the one that is most precise or specific.
7. If you have crossed them all out, check the choices again. Carefully try to decide whether there is another meaning to any of the answer choices. If you're still stumped, go back to the answer that was the most specific and seemed to cover more of the passage than the others.

- Which of the following is least relevant to the main idea of the passage?

Where to Find Misplaced Sentences
You will usually be directed to a particular paragraph. If the first sentence states the main idea of the paragraph, it is unlikely to be the misplaced sentence. Check all others.

Sample Passage and Question
The goal is to discover the sequence of bases in the DNA. If this is a mitochondrial DNA fragment, the sequence will be like the person's mother and maternal relatives. The DNA is divided down the center like unzipping a zipper. Heat is used to cause the division. Only one half (side of the zipper) is used. The sequence of bases will be discovered by recreating the other half.

(This passage will be continued in the next section, Reading 3.)

3. Which of the sentences in the first paragraph is least relevant to the main idea of the paragraph?
   a. Heat is used to cause the division.
   b. The DNA is divided down the center like unzipping a zipper.
   c. The goal is to discover the sequence of bases in the DNA.
   d. If this is a mitochondrial DNA fragment, the sequence will be like the person's mother and maternal relatives.
   e. Only one half (side of the zipper) is used.

Answer
The passage describes the process of reading DNA. The second sentence has nothing to do with the process. It should have been placed in a paragraph that discussed vocabulary. The answer is d.

Preparing for Organization Questions
To further prepare for the test, as you read any book, magazine, or paper, you might want to take note of different ways paragraphs are structured and how sentences follow in a logical sequence.

Reading 3: Unmasking the Main Idea

Main idea questions can be put in three categories. The first asks for a simple sentence or title that includes the main topic of the passage. The second asks questions about the author and what the author had in mind. Then there are those that ask for a paraphrase of all the main ideas in the passage.

Pure and Simple

Simple main idea questions take a variety of forms:

- What is the main idea of the passage?
- The best title for this passage would be . . .
- What is the theme of the passage?
- The central thought of the passage is . . .

How to Find Main Idea Answers in the Passage

To answer main idea questions, you sometimes do not have to read the whole passage. Often the main idea is stated at the beginning or end of the passage. Sometimes you can glean the main idea by paying attention to the topic sentences of each paragraph of the passage.

Sample Passage and Question

This passage continues the passage on DNA that you began in the previous section.

> The goal is to discover the sequence of bases in the DNA. If this is a mitochondrial DNA fragment, the sequence will be like the person's mother and maternal relatives. The DNA is divided down the center like unzipping a zipper. Heat is used to cause the division. Only one half (side of the zipper) is used. The sequence of bases will be discovered by recreating the other half.
>
> The next goal is to use the half of the DNA which was saved to reconstruct the other half. This process will show the sequence of bases. Bases A and T always bind to each other. Bases C and G always bind to each other. The idea is to put one-half of a DNA strand in a test tube with some free bases and an enzyme that causes the free bases to attach to the half strand—rezipping the zipper. Modified bases are also added so that the location of that base on the "zipper" can be marked. In this way, the sequence of bases can be discovered. Each test tube contains thousands of copies of the saved half of the DNA strand, and a radioactive primer which will attach at the start location of every strand so that all operations start at the same place on every strand. Also included are DNA polymerase, which is an enzyme that acts as a "glue" to attach the free bases to the half DNA strand, and all four bases, which are free and unattached. There is also a modified base— each test tube has a different base which has been modified to act as a marker during reconstruction.
>
> At the end of the process, thousands of reconstructed strands will be in each test tube. Some of these strands will be complete, but some of them will have been terminated by a modified base so they will be shorter. All of them will have the same sequence of bases but will terminate at different positions where A is found. The reason that some of the strands did not terminate at base A is that a normal instead of a modified base A attached at some of the base A locations. There is a test tube for each base. Therefore, there are reconstructed strands which terminate with C in the test tube with modified C bases, strands which terminate with G in the test tube with modified G bases, and strands which terminate with T in the test tube with modified T bases. The four test tubes are used in order to tell the difference between bases since the strands and bases all look alike. However, the same test can be done in one test tube if fluorescent dyes are used to tag the modified bases.

1. Which of the following best describes the main topic of the passage?
   a. DNA can be linked to clues in a criminal investigation.
   b. Learning about the genetic code is important.
   c. The role of modified bases is part of reading DNA.
   d. Dyes are used to tell the difference between bases.
   e. Reading base A strands is done at the end of the process.

Answer
Use the Success Steps to help you answer the question.

1. The general topic seems to have to do with the DNA strands in the test tube and some marked ends that help people read them.
2. It looks as though a is off the topic because the passage does not mention criminal investigations.
3. Answer b seems too broad.
4. There don't seem to be any answer choices that are on the general topic but not the specific topic.
5. Answers d and e have to do with only one part of the passage.

You don't have to use steps 6 and 7, because you have one answer left: choice c seems to fit.

Sample Passage and Question
Try your hand at another passage and main idea question.

Successful programs make the extended-time curriculum challenging but not overwhelming. Research indicates that a challenging curriculum should accommodate individual student needs, coordinate with other instruction, and focus on more than remedial work. For example, the TAP Summer Youth Employment Program, which serves a large number of students living in housing projects, teaches basic skills that students need for communicating with employers and co-workers, and it also provides students with the challenge of putting these skills to use while working in their communities.

2. Which of the following would be the best title for the passage?
   a. Appropriately Challenging Curriculum
   b. Successful Programs
   c. Individualized Learning
   d. Curriculum Innovation
   e. The TAP Summer Youth Employment Program

Answer
Again, apply the seven Success Steps.

1. The passage seems to be about the curriculum for a program outside of school.
2. It looks as if all the choices are on the general topic.
3. Answers b and d are too broad.
4. Answer c is on the general topic, but not on the subject of the paragraph.
5. Answer e has to do with only a part of the passage. The paragraph is mostly about appropriately challenging curriculum. Therefore, answer a would make the best title. Once again, you did not have to use steps 6 and 7.

Perfect Paraphrases
There will probably be at least one question that asks you to paraphrase the entire passage. Paraphrase questions are the most troublesome of all the main idea questions because the choices are so long. Realize, however, that the test makers had to make four of the choices wrong in some way. Your task is to discover the errors.

Seven Success Steps for Paraphrase Questions

1. Read or skim the passage, noting or underlining main ideas as they flow from one to the other.
2. Look for phrases that restate the main ideas you underlined.
3. Eliminate answers that contain phrases that contradict ideas in the passage.
4. Eliminate answers that are off the topic or only deal with part of the passage.
5. Eliminate answers that state one or more ideas that the author has not mentioned.
6. If left with two choices, choose the most complete one.
7. If you have eliminated them all, take the paraphrase that contains the most main ideas without adding new ideas.

Paraphrase questions tend to start out like this:

- Which of the following best paraphrases the ideas in the passage?
- The best summary of the passage is ...
- Which of the following is the best summation of the ideas in the passage?
- Which of the following best restates the main ideas of the passage?

How to Find Paraphrase Answers in the Passage

The main ideas of the passage can be found in each of the paragraphs, or in sections of the paragraphs. If you can follow the way the author has logically arranged the passage, you are more likely to find the correct answer to a paraphrase question.

Sample Passage and Question

Extended-time programs often feature innovative scheduling, as program staff work to maintain participation and respond to students' and parents' varied schedules and family or employment commitments. Offering students flexibility and some choice regarding when they participate in extended learning may be as simple as offering homework sessions when children need them most—after school and before dinner—as do Kids Crew and the Omaha After-School Study Centers. Or it may mean keeping early and late hours to meet the child care needs of parents who work more than one job or support extended families, as does Yuk Yau Child Development Center. Similarly, the Florida Summer Institute for At-Risk Migrant Students is a residential program so that students' participation does not disrupt their migrant families' travels.

3. Which of the following paraphrases best summarizes the passage above?
   a. After-school programs should help children finish their homework after school.
   b. Kids Crew and other programs meet the needs of children.
   c. There are several ways to schedule programs outside school time to meet the needs of students and families.
   d. Extended-time programs can be innovative, and Yuk Yau Child Development Center is an example of this.
   e. Extended hours may need to be late or early to accommodate needs.

Answer

Walk through the steps:

1. The flow goes like this: innovative scheduling—family needs—examples: after school, early and late care, residential.
2. Answers a, c, d, and e have words and ideas noted in step 1.
3. None of the answers are contrary to the passage. That tactic is usually used with persuasive passages.

Seven Success Steps for Author Questions

1. For author-purpose questions, eliminate answers that do not match the general topic. If it is a scientific passage, the author is probably objectively trying to disseminate information, so you should eliminate answers that suggest the author is trying to change the reader's behavior in any way. If it is a persuasive paragraph, however, the author is not just simply conveying information. For questions on the author's intended audience, eliminate audiences that are significantly less or more technical than the author's style.
2. Eliminate answers that say the opposite of what the author is trying to say.
3. Look for a climax in the passage, a sentence or two that describes the author's purpose or audience. Then look for an answer that says the same thing in different words. Also, be on the lookout for clue words that could hint at the audience.
4. Look for words that indicate a change or shift in the author's meaning. Sometimes the author's purpose will follow words such as "however," or be found somewhere in sentences beginning with words like "although" or "instead of."
5. If you are looking for an author's tone, put the answer choices in order from very negative to very positive. Look for adjectives that describe the way the author feels about a topic; then look for synonyms or the same tone in the answer choices.
6. If you are left with two choices, look at the topic of the passage and decide what might be an appropriate response to the topic. If the topic discusses a dangerous future situation, an appropriate response of the author might be a warning.
7. Avoid controversy. Test makers will probably not create a correct answer that displays intolerance or promotes illegal activities.

---

4. The answers are all on the topic, but a, b, and e only deal with part of the paragraph.
5. All the ideas are in the passage.
6. You are left with answers c and d. Answer d only mentions one example and the passage gives three. Answer c does not mention any examples specifically, but includes all the examples as well as the idea of the paragraph. You can conclude that the answer is c, and you don't have to use step 7.

Preparing for Main Idea Questions

For extra practice, check out all the test books you can from the library that have a reading comprehension section and answer as many main idea questions as you can until you feel very confident.

▶ Reading 4: About the Author

Most passages were not written to torture test takers. Authors write to communicate; that is, they *want* you to understand their ideas and arguments. To that end, they usually will try to write as clearly and logically as possible. To read these passages efficiently, therefore, you need to get involved with the author in the subject. Give this author your undivided attention and try to understand what the author took the time and trouble to write. As you read, ask yourself these questions:

- Who is this person?
- Can I detect anything about the author?
- From what perspective does the author write?
- How does the author think?

- What was the author trying to accomplish?
- For whom was the author writing?

Sample question stems for author questions might include the following:

- The author's primary purpose is to...
- The author is primarily concerned with...
- The main focus of the author is...
- In what publication might this passage be found?
- The author is writing primarily for what kind of audience?
- Which best describes the author's relationship with...
- Which best describes the feeling of the author toward his subject?
- The attitude of the author toward...

How to Find Author Answers in the Passage

You may discover the purpose of the author, like the main idea, in the first or last sentence of the passage, or by looking at the topic sentences of the paragraphs. You can also skim the passage for descriptive words that reveal the bias of the author. The subject of the passage and the absence or presence of technical language are two of the main clues toward discovering the author's intended audience.

Sample Passage and Questions

Lincoln's 1863 Thanksgiving Proclamation

It is the duty of nations as well as of men to own their dependence upon the overruling power of God; to confess their sins and transgressions in humble sorrow, yet with assured hope that genuine repentance will lead to mercy and pardon; and to recognize the sublime truth, announced in the Holy Scriptures and proven by all history, that those nations are blessed whose God is the Lord.

We know that by His divine law, nations, like individuals, are subjected to punishments and chastisements in this world. May we not justly fear that the awful calamity of civil war which now desolates the land may be a punishment inflicted upon us for our presumptuous sins, to the needful end of our national reformation as a whole people?

We have been the recipients of the choicest bounties of heaven; we have been preserved these many years in peace and prosperity; we have grown in numbers, wealth and power as no other nation has ever grown.

But we have forgotten God. We have forgotten the gracious hand which preserved us in peace and multiplied and enriched and strengthened us, and we have vainly imagined, in the deceitfulness of our hearts, that all these blessings were produced by some superior wisdom and virtue of our own. Intoxicated with unbroken success, we have become too self-sufficient to feel the necessity of redeeming and preserving grace, too proud to pray to the God that made us.

It has seemed to me fit and proper that God should be solemnly, reverently and gratefully acknowledged, as with one heart and one voice, by the whole American people. I do therefore invite my fellow citizens in every part of the United States, and also those who are at sea and those who are sojourning in foreign lands, to set apart and observe the last Thursday of November as a day of Thanksgiving and praise to our beneficent Father who dwelleth in the heavens.

1. Lincoln's purpose in proclaiming a holiday was to
   a. make peace with Native Americans.
   b. celebrate cultural awareness.
   c. thank God for blessings and favor.
   d. bring complaints as well as thankfulness before God.
   e. promote separation of church and state.

Answers

Use the seven Success Steps to answer the question.

1. Answers **a** and **b** do not match the general topic.
2. Answer **e** says the opposite of what Lincoln meant; he was proposing that all Americans thank God.
3. The last sentence seems to be a climax. Both **c** and **d** contain the idea of thankfulness.
4. The word *but* at the beginning of the fourth paragraph seems to indicate a shift, but that shift is really part of Lincoln's meaning; he is contrasting the blessings America has experienced with Americans' having forgotten God.
5. This isn't a tone question, so you don't need this step.
6. You're left with answers **c** and **d**. The holiday was about thanking God, not bringing complaints. Look again for a mention of complaints in the passage. There isn't one, so the closest answer is **c**.
7. Controversy isn't likely to arise in a passage like this one.

Sample Passage and Questions

Now try the steps on the questions that follow this passage.

> The most significant research results produced are as follows: In the area of micro-ecological adaptation and evolutionary process, our research has shown that regardless of the complexity of the selection force and the biological traits, the rate of evolutionary change of the plant populations has been rapid and the results are even better than we expected. Further study of the interactions between plants and their soil environments found that a successful colonization of plant species in soils with elevated toxic levels of soil chemical compounds such as selenium may be achieved in the presence of other chemical compounds (such as sulfate) that could alleviate the toxic effects and improve the conditions for colonization. The knowledge generated by these ecological studies has made it possible to apply the research with more confidence.

2. In what publication might this passage be published?
   a. a college *Introduction to Biology* textbook
   b. a general encyclopedia
   c. a bulletin to parents
   d. a science teacher's manual
   e. a book of dissertation abstracts

3. Which of the following can best describe the author's attitude toward the results of the research?
   a. pompous
   b. satisfied
   c. apologetic
   d. elated
   e. unbiased

Answers

Here's how you could use the steps on question 2.

1. This is a rather technical passage. Eliminate **c** and maybe even **a**.
2. Although no choice disagrees with the author, a science teacher's manual would have hints in it for teaching children. There are no clues that this is a teacher's manual; **d** is gone.
3. There is no climax.
4. There are clue words, though they're not easy to find. The author mentions *research* that is being done. Encyclopedias don't include current research, so **b** is eliminated. That leaves you with **e**. This makes sense because a dissertation is someone's research. (You don't need to use steps 5–7.)

Six Success Steps for Detail Questions

1. When reading the passage, notice the way the passage is arranged. For example, if the passage is on the intelligence of bees, the bees' sense of direction might be in the first paragraph. The bees' communication system might be discussed in the second paragraph.
2. Check the question for the detail you are looking for and search in the proper section of the paragraph. For example, if you were asked about the bees' inner compass, you would look in the first paragraph of the two mentioned above.
3. Skim for key words. Look for the words that are in the question. Once you find the words, find the answer in that sentence.
4. Eliminate answers that contain facts not found in the paragraph. If an answer choice is not in the paragraph, it is not the right answer, even if it is true. Also eliminate choices that are found in the passage, but that do not answer the question.
5. If the paragraph is complex, and you are having trouble trying to find the answer, you may need to start up to five lines above the key word. For example, suppose the paragraph is comparing two kinds of fish, and the question asks for the head size of one kind. You find the word *head* in a context like this: "Although their tails are the same, the 4-inch head size of the latter is about twice the head size of the former, which makes them easier to prey upon." You may need to go back a sentence or two to discover which fish has the bigger head and is easier to prey upon.
6. Do not let technical words stop you from answering the question. You are not being tested on technical language alone. There is always enough information in the paragraph to answer a detail question without previous knowledge of the topic.

For question 3, you have an attitude question.

1. This is a scientific paper so it has to be fairly objective.
2–4. You don't need these steps for an attitude question.
5. From negative to positive you might rank the answer choices like this: *apologetic, pompous, unbiased, satisfied, elated.* The first two are hard to rank; they seem to have about the same degree of negativity. There are some clue words; "even better than we expected" and "more confidence" sound as though you should look on the positive side of the list, which includes choices b and d.
6. This is a research report. Probably *elated* would not be appropriate. The author might be elated, but there are no clues in the passage that the author is that happy. *Satisfied,* answer **b,** seems the closest choice.
7. There's no controversy in the passage or question.

▶ Reading 5: Definite Details and Tables of Contents

Most people find both detail questions and questions on tables of contents fairly easy to answer, because the answers are right there in the passage or table of contents. You have probably been answering detail questions most of your life. In every subject, most of the questions at the end of the chapters in your textbook have been detail questions—and you used the table of contents to find the chapter you wanted quickly and easily. These questions mean (relatively) easy points for you. All you need are some strategies that may help enhance your speed and accuracy.

Detail questions ask about one specific fact in the passage. They are signaled by question words such as *what, when,* or *where.* You'll often find the phrase "according to the passage" in a detail question.

How to Find Detail Answers in the Passage

Detail answers are usually in the body of the paragraphs. Usually they are not in the main idea sentences.

Sample Passage and Questions

Normal aging is associated with the oxidation of a wide range of cellular proteins, and it has been proposed that reactive oxygen species (ROS) selectively modify some proteins, ultimately resulting in a loss of calcium homeostasis. We propose that two of these proteins are CaM and the Ca-ATPase. Calmodulin (CaM) is a ubiquitous eukaryotic calcium binding protein that serves as an intermediary in the amplification of transient increases in intracellular calcium, and plays a central role in the regulation of numerous cellular processes, including neurotransmission, neuronal plasticity, muscle contraction, cytoskeletal assembly, and a host of reactions involved in the energy and biosynthetic metabolism of the cell. The plasma membrane (PM) Ca-ATPase is the major high affinity, high capacity calcium transport protein that ultimately maintains normal (low) intracellular calcium concentrations through its activation by calcium-bound CaM. Our long-term goal is to identify mechanistic relationships between oxidative damage and these key calcium regulatory proteins and function.

As a first step, we propose to identify both the sensitivity of CaM and the PM-Ca-ATPase to physiologically relevant ROS, and the structural and functional consequences relating to oxidative dam-

age. The second theme, and ultimate goal of the project, is to apply these methods to identify the specific ROS and the functional consequences associated with the age-related (post-translational) modification of these calcium regulatory proteins and the associated lipids. An identification of the ROS involved in the modification of CaM and the PM-Ca-ATPase will ultimately suggest possible therapies that could alleviate the decline in cellular functions associated with aging.

1. Which fact CANNOT be found in the passage?
   a. Both (PM) Ca-ATPase and calmodulin (CaM) are calcium regulators.
   b. Reactive oxygen causes a lack of calcium balance in the body.
   c. (PM) Ca-ATPase is a protein.
   d. Calmodulin (CaM) is a kind of calcium.
   e. Calmodulin (CaM) is necessary for the energy and biosynthetic metabolism of the cell.

2. According to the passage, which substance is responsible for beginning the process of aging?
   a. PM-Ca-ATPase
   b. calmodulin
   c. ROS
   d. eukaryotic calcium
   e. cytoskeletal assembly

3. With which of the following would the author be most likely to agree?
   a. Ca-ATPase causes aging.
   b. Research on ROS can lead to a reversal of the aging process.
   c. The aging process is not connected with the plasma membrane.
   d. Calmodulin causes oxidative damage.
   e. Calcium assimilation is regulated by bone marrow.

Four Success Steps for Table of Contents Questions

1. Read the questions and answers first. Then skim down the list marking all possible sections that might contain the information you are seeking.
2. Look at the answer choices and eliminate any that clearly don't make sense.
3. If you are left with two choices, choose the one that best fits the subject.
4. If you are asked for the organization of an outline, look through the answers. One has to describe the table. Choose the one that offers the best description.

Answers

For detail questions, you don't necessarily have to work through all the steps. Here are some tips on how you might have answered the questions.

1. Because you are being asked to look up each answer in the passage to see whether it is there, this is really five questions in one. If you decide to take the time to answer this question at all, you should leave it until you have answered the other questions about this passage. By then, you will have discovered how the passage is arranged, and you may have even noticed some of the facts in the passage. Answer **a** is found at the end of the first paragraph: "these key calcium regulatory proteins and function." "These" refers to the two proteins mentioned in the question. The first sentence tells us that ROS results in "a loss of calcium homeostasis." Even if you do not know what homeostasis is, you know that something is wrong or out of balance, so **b** can be verified. You can find all the answers but **d** in a similar fashion. The passage states that calmodulin (CaM) is a protein, not a calcium. The answer is **d**.
2. The first sentence tells you that ROS is up to no good. The answer is **c**.
3. The last sentence points directly to answer **b**.

Table of Contents Questions

Questions on tables of contents are among the easiest in the Reading section. Watch for traps, but view these as free points. You'll know a table of contents question immediately by the passage. Questions may ask something like the following:

- On which pages could one find . . . ?
- In what general category is . . . ?
- How is the table of contents organized?

How to Find Answers to Table of Contents Questions

The answers to these questions have to be in the table of contents. There are usually fewer words in the tables than in passages, making them easier to skim, and usually the contents are logically arranged.

Sample Table of Contents and Questions

Preparing Your Family for an Earthquake
The Plan 2
General Tips 4
Essentials 5
Sanitation 6
Safety 6
Cooking 7
Tools 9

4. On what page would you look to find a recommendation for stocking paper plates and cups?
   a. 2
   b. 4
   c. 6
   d. 7
   e. 9

5. In what way is this table of contents arranged?
   a. alphabetical
   b. by category
   c. chronological — *arranged in order of occurrence*
   d. by age
   e. by task

Answers

Here's how you would use the steps on question 4:

1. Looking down the table of contents, mark *Essentials*, *Sanitation*, and *Cooking*.
2. Eliminate **a, b,** and **e**.
3. The *Essentials* page is not listed in the answers, so that leaves you with *Sanitation* and *Cooking*. The choice that best fits the subject is *Cooking*, answer **d**.
4. This step doesn't apply.

Question 5 deals with organization, so go straight to step 4. Looking at the answer choices, it is fairly obvious that the list is not alphabetical, so eliminate answer **a**. Answers **c** and **d** are not relevant to the subject. Choice **b** is better than **e** because the table is not talking necessarily about things to do, but categories of survival aids. Choice **b** is the correct answer.

▶ Reading 6: Impressive Implications

Implication questions can be easily confused with detail questions. The same answer that might be correct for a detail question, however, will be wrong for an implication question. Of all the question types, some find detail questions to be the easiest and implication questions to be the most difficult. Knowing how implication questions are likely to be phrased will help you distinguish between the two question types. Implication question stems usually include words like the ones that are highlighted below:

- The author **implies** that . . .
- The author **suggests** that . . .
- It can be **concluded** from this passage that . . .
- The passage **implies** that . . .
- The narrator **hints** that . . .
- It can be **inferred** from the passage that . . .
- Which of the following is **closest** to the author's **outlook** on . . . ?
- The feature that ____ and ____ have in common is . . .

How to Find Implication Answers

Implications are not directly stated in the passage. If you find an answer choice in the passage, it is not the right answer. Look, however, for items, people, events, or ideas in the passage that might relate to other items, people, events, or ideas in the passage.

Sample Passage and Question

Many educational reformers have focused their efforts over the last decade on instructional practices such as cooperative learning that emphasize problem solving and decision making over solitary reliance on memorization of facts and theories. Further, programs that emphasize problem solving and decision making directly address the national education goal of helping prepare students "for responsible citizenship, further learning, and productive employment in our modern economy." Several programs described here offer strategies for addressing problem solving and decision making, ranging from in-class discussions and the use of board games to designing and conducting community service activities. For example, tutors at Raising Academic Achievement focus on problem-solving skills and are trained to help students "think, explore, solve, and look back" when working on mathematics problems.

Nine Success Steps for Implication Questions

1. Skim the passage to discover how the passage is organized and find the sentences that deal with the topic.
2. Eliminate any answers that are off the topic.
3. Eliminate any answers that parrot sentences in the passage, using the same or similar words.
4. Look for an answer choice that says the same thing in an opposite way. For example, if the passage says that all unripe fruit is green, look for an answer choice that states that no unripe fruit is orange or red. If you find one like that, great! Some implication answers are not that easy.
5. Eliminate any answers that are unreasonable, that cannot be drawn from facts in the passage.
6. Eliminate any answers that can be concluded from the statements in the passage, but do not answer the question.
7. Ask yourself these questions:
   - If the author were to write another paragraph following this one, what might it be about?
   - If the author were to explain the ideas in the paragraph in more detail or more explicitly, what more would be written?
   - If the author could draw a conclusion from what has been written so far, what facts could be put together to form that conclusion and what would that conclusion be?
8. If you are still left with two answers, choose the answer that is only one step removed from the statements in the passage. Choose the one that can be the most clearly concluded from the statements in the passage.
9. If you have no answers left, look in another part of the passage for additional clue facts. Any choice using the same words as the passage is definitely not the correct answer. Check for answer choices that may mean something different from what you read. Check for choices that may contain answers to the questions you asked yourself in step 7 above. If all the other choices are bizarre, look for a choice saying the same thing with different wording, using synonyms. This is weak as an implication answer, but could be the best answer of the lot.

---

1. Which of the following can be inferred from the information in the passage?
   a. Tutors at Raising Academic Achievement help ensure that students will be productively employed when they become adults.
   b. Cooperative learning emphasizes problem-solving techniques.
   c. Playing board games increases problem-solving skills.
   d. Responsible citizenship should be taught in school.
   e. Tutors at Raising Academic Achievement help students solve math problems.

Answer

Walk through the steps.

1. The passage is short and the question offers no topic or location clues.
2. It looks as though d is off the topic since the paragraph is not about teaching responsible citizenship; it is only mentioned in passing.
3. Answer b is mentioned in the first sentence. Choices c and e are also mentioned. That gives us our answer already. Is a the answer? The passage does not explicitly state that the tutors will help future employment, but it does say tutors help

80

with problem-solving skills and that problem-solving skills will help with future employment. Statement **a** is one step removed from the facts of the passage, so it is the right answer.

You didn't need to use steps 4–9.

Sample Passage and Questions

Student-teacher interaction increases with instruction provided in one-on-one or small-group situations, where teachers give substantive feedback to students. This individualized attention is especially beneficial to low achievers. Effective extended-time programs establish individual goals for each student and work closely with the student to reach these goals. For example, in the Educational Program for Homeless Children and Youth in Devil's Lake, North Dakota, teachers evaluate each child before the program begins to identify academic weaknesses; subsequent individual tutoring focuses on the weak areas.

2. The passage implies that
   a. children in the Educational Program for Homeless Children and Youth in Devil's Lake receive personal evaluation.
   b. one-on-one instruction enables children to receive more attention from teachers.
   c. small group situations do not help high achievers.
   d. the larger the group, the less children can learn.
   e. a large group enables teachers to identify and focus on weak areas.

Answer

Here's how you could use the nine Success Steps to answer question 2.

1. There are no topic or location clues in the question.
2. All the answers seem to be on topic.
3. Answers **a** and **b** mimic the language of the passage.
4. The passage says, "This individualized attention is especially beneficial to low achievers." This seems to be the opposite of choice **c**. A more careful look reveals that the passage was in no way implying that high achievers could not be helped at all by a small group; it only stated that low achievers could benefit the most.
5. Because **c** is unreasonable, it should be eliminated. Choice **e** looks very good, but a careful reading shows it says just the opposite of what the passage is saying. It should start, "A SMALL group...." Answer **d** is the only one left, but you should check it. It seems to be a legitimate implication. The passage was talking about small groups providing more feedback, and answer **d** says the same thing in an opposite way. This is a legitimate implication.

▶ Reading 7: Wizard Words, Departed Parts, and Other Oddities

This section will review most of the rest of the kinds of reading questions you will be likely to encounter on the CBEST: words in context, fill-in-the-blanks, extra evidence, order, and opinion vs. fact. Many of these types are an easy way to gain points by using your common sense. Most test takers report that they can read to find the order of facts without much trouble, and they are pretty good at opinion vs. fact. This lesson is a little longer than the rest, but you can easily accomplish it in half an hour by skimming over the passages, working on the sample questions, and then concentrating on any of the question types that give you trouble.

Six Success Steps for Word-in-Context Questions

1. Locate the word and read at least five lines above the word to catch the context. Notice any context clues—words or phrases that explain the meaning of the word.
2. Eliminate all answers that have nothing to do with the passage or the context.
3. If you are lucky, you may encounter an answer choice that is a different part of speech from the word or phrase in the question. Think for a minute to make sure this answer choice doesn't have an alternate meaning that is the same part of speech, and if it doesn't, eliminate it.
4. Place the remaining words in the blank and read to see which one fits best.
5. If you know the word, make sure the passage uses the word in the same way. Many of the answers will be different possible meanings of the word in question.
6. Look for clues in root words, prefixes and suffixes.

WORDS IN CONTEXT

Questions on words in context have stems like these:

- What is the best synonym for _____ as it is used in the passage?
- Which of the following is the best meaning of _____ as it is used in the second sentence?

How to Find Word-in-Context Answers

Answers to word-in-context questions are found in the sentences immediately preceding, including, and following the word. Usually there is some explanation nearby—some synonym for the word or paraphrase of its meaning.

Sample Passage and Question

An upsurge of new research suggests that animals have a much higher level of brainpower than previously thought. If animals do have intelligence, how do scientists measure it? Before defining animals' intelligence, scientists defined what is **not** intelligence. Instinct is not intelligence. It is a skill programmed into an animal's brain by its genetic heritage. Rote conditioning is also not intelligence. Tricks can be learned by repetition, but no real thinking is involved. Cuing, in which animals learn to do or not do certain things by following outside signals, does not demonstrate intelligence. Scien-

— beliefs yet to be proven as facts

tists believe that insight, the ability to use tools, and communication using human language are effective measures of the mental ability of animals.

When judging animal intelligence, scientists look for insight, which they define as a flash of sudden understanding. When a young gorilla could not reach fruit from a tree, she noticed crates scattered about the lawn near the tree. She piled the crates into a pyramid, and then climbed on them to reach her reward. The gorilla's insight allowed her to solve a new problem without trial and error.

The ability to use tools is also an important sign of intelligence. Crows use sticks to pry peanuts out of cracks. The crow exhibits intelligence by showing it has learned what a stick can do. Likewise, otters use rocks to crack open crab shells in order to get at the sweet meat. In a series of complex moves, chimpanzees have been known to use sticks and stalks in order to get at a favorite snack—termites. To make and use a termite tool, a chimp first selects just the right stalk or twig. He trims and shapes the stick, then finds the entrance to a termite mound. While inserting the stick carefully into the entrance, the chimpanzee turns it skillfully to fit the inner tunnels. The chimp attracts the insects by shaking the twig. Then it pulls the tool out without scraping off any termites. Finally, he uses his lips to skim the termites into his mouth.

Three Success Steps for Fact vs. Opinion Questions

1. Read through the sentences looking for opinion words.
2. If a sentence sounds as though could be a news item, found in a textbook, or otherwise verified, it is probably a fact. If it sounds like a judgment that can't be proven, then it is probably an opinion.
3. If you are left with two answers, choose the one that is most strongly a *value judgment*.

Many animals have learned to communicate using human language. Some primates have learned hundreds of words in sign language. One chimp can recognize and correctly use more than 250 abstract symbols on a keyboard. These symbols represent human words. An amazing parrot can distinguish five objects of two different types. He can understand the difference between the number, color and kind of object. The ability to classify is a basic thinking skill.

The research on animal intelligence raises important questions. If animals are smarter than once thought, would that change the way humans interact with them? Would humans stop hunting them for sport or survival? Would animals still be used for food or clothing or medical experimentation? Finding the answer to these tough questions makes a difficult puzzle even for a large-brained, problem-solving species like our own.

1. The word *upsurge*, as it is used in the first paragraph of the passage, most nearly means
   a. an increasingly large amount.
   b. a decreasing amount.
   c. a well-known amount.
   d. an ancient amount.
   e. an unknown amount.

Answer
The overall content of the passage is about the growing interest and research into chimp intelligence. The question in the first paragraph asks how scientists measure intelligence and gives a clue that there has been interest in the field. By definition, the word upsurge means a rising or swelling and is used as an analogy to illustrate the large and increasing amount of research in animal intelligence. Choice **a** is the best answer.

Opinion vs. Fact
A statement is considered a fact if every person shares the experience that the statement is true. An opinion is any statement that might be disputed by others. "The sky is blue" is a fact. Everyone sees it and shares the same experience. "The sky is lovely today" is an opinion. Someone might not like blue or was hoping that some rain might stop the drought. They could not disagree the sky was blue, but they could disagree on what they consider lovely. *Lovely* is a judgment or opinion word. Opinion-vs.-fact questions have stems like these:

- Which of the following is a statement of fact?
- Which of the numbered sentences constitutes an opinion, not a fact?

How to Find Opinion-vs.-Fact Answers
You don't have to read the passage to find the answer if the statements and opinions are listed in the answers. If you are referred to numbered sentences, look there.

Two Success Steps for Order Questions

1. Skim the passage for key words found in the question.
2. Read the section mentioned and then read the sentences immediately after or before the section depending on the question. If the question asks what happened last, look toward the end of the passage and look for key words such as "finally" or "in conclusion."

Sample Question

This question is on the passage about animal intelligence, on page 83.

2. Which of the following sentences is NOT a fact?
   a. Instinct is not intelligence.
   b. Rote conditioning is also not intelligence.
   c. Tricks can be learned by repetition.
   d. Cuing, does not demonstrate intelligence.
   e. The ability to use tools measures the mental ability of animals.

Answer

A look through the first paragraph will verify that choices a, b, c, and d are facts. Choice e is the opinion of the scientists who have set out to find a way to measure animals' intelligence. Many scientific theories begin with beliefs that have to be proven as fact.

Order

Order questions are easy to spot; they ask you what comes before or after some other incident or event. Question stems look like these:

- In the paragraph, what event immediately follows...?
- What incident precedes...?
- In what order should you...?
- According to the passage, what should you do after...?

How to Find Order Answers

Usually a part of the passage is mentioned in order questions. The question will let you know whether to look *after* or *before* the section you found. The question could also point you directly to a part of the passage such as the beginning or the end.

Sample Question

Go back to the passage about animal intelligence to find the answer to this question.

3. According to the passage, a chimp can make and use a termite tool by finding just the right stalk or twig. What does a chimp do after he finds just the right stalk or twig?
   a. The chimp inserts the stick carefully into a termite mound.
   b. The chimp attracts the insects by shaking the twig.
   c. The chimp trims and shapes the stick.
   d. The chimp finds the entrance to a termite mound.
   e. The chimp pulls the stick full of insects from the termite mound.

Answer

The order of complex moves made by a chimp when making a termite tool is detailed in the third paragraph. It is important in this case to refer back to the passage. Choices a, b, d, and e are all steps the chimp takes, however they are out of order.

Fill In the Blanks

Fill-in-the-blank questions come in two types. One asks you to fill in a couple of words. The other asks you to fill in a whole sentence. Turn to **Additional Information** (page 86), for the kind that deals with a whole sentence. Questions that ask you for a few words have stems like these:

Seven Success Steps for Fill-in-the-Blank Questions

1. Read the entire sentence, or pair of sentences, that contains the blanks.
2. The sentences should give you all the clues you need. Each sentence is likely to be made up of two statements that are compatible or contradictory. If they are compatible, words like "also" or "because" should be used. If they are contradictory, you will need words such as "while," "even if," or "although."
3. Decide whether the first or last blank has the most clues and work with that one first.
4. If one sentence gives you all the clues you need, look at the answer choices to see which one contains a word in the right location that will fit. For example, if the first sentence contains two statements that contradict each other, cover the second set of words in each choice and look only at the first words. Eliminate any choices such as "because" or "since" that do not suggest there will be a contradiction or turn in the sentence. Eliminate the whole answer. Do not even consider the second part of the answer.
5. Next turn to the other blank. If it is a structure blank, the word might indicate its placement in the sentence. For example, "finally" or "as a result" would probably be answers for an end of a passage, not a beginning. "However" cannot begin a passage.
6. Note the type of passage. A story might use the word "meanwhile," directions would use "next" or "finally," and "consequently" or "as a result" might be used in a persuasive or scientific passage.
7. Substitute the remaining words in the remaining blank and choose the one that fits the best.

- Which words, if inserted in order, would best complete the second paragraph?
- Which of the following phrases would best fit in the blanks?

How to Find Fill-in-the-Blank Answers

There are two kinds of word blanks. One can be filled by reading the sentence. The other requires an understanding of the structure of the passage.

Sample Passage and Question

Yesterday was the 16-month anniversary of the TWA 800 tragedy. _____ the National Transportation Safety Board (NTSB) was seeking to determine what happened to Flight 800, the FBI and the other members of the law enforcement team were working with them to discover any possible criminal connection to the event. The FBI and the law enforcement team became involved in the investigation because initial reports were that a TWA Flight was "in the water," that there had been a large explosion and fireball, that all communications from the plane were normal and no distress calls were issued, and the reports of numerous eyewitnesses seeing "flarelike objects" and other events in the sky. If there was even a chance, whether it was 10% or 90%, that this catastrophe was criminal, it was critical that the proper investigation take place immediately. The mission of the law enforcement team was to determine whether a criminal act was responsible for this disaster.

The time has arrived to report to the American people the results of our efforts.

Following 16 months of unprecedented investigative effort which extended from the shores of Long Island to several countries abroad—an investigation where hundreds of investigators conducted thousands of interviews—an investigation which was confronted with the obstacle of having the most critical pieces of evidence lying in 130 feet of water at the bottom of the Atlantic Ocean, we must report that . . .

NO EVIDENCE HAS BEEN FOUND WHICH WOULD INDICATE THAT A CRIMINAL ACT

Four Success Steps for Additional Information Questions

1. If there is a blank to fill, read the passage up to the blank line and then the sentence following it. Notice the relationship between the sentence before and after it. If there is no blank, skim the passage for a main idea or hypothesis.
2. Choose the sentence to fit in the blank that best continues the flow of the paragraph. If the sentence after the blank shows there was a turn in thought, choose the answer that turns the thought.
3. If there is no blank, choose the answer that might complete the thought of the author.
4. If the question calls for the least likely statement, use a sentence that breaks the flow or contradicts the author. The same is true for a question that calls for a statement that would weaken the stand of the author.

WAS THE CAUSE OF THE TRAGEDY OF TWA FLIGHT 800.

We do know one thing, _____. The law enforcement team has done everything humanly possible—has pursued every lead—and has left no stone unturned.

4. Which words or phrases, in order, can best be inserted in the blanks of the passage above?
   a. In spite of the fact that, finally
   b. However, because
   c. As a result, meanwhile
   d. While, however
   e. Because, probably

Answer

The first blank is easier to work with. Covering up the second half of the answers, assess the first words and phrases only. The **a** answer is controversial. It implies that the NTSB was interfering with the FBI. The phrase in the sentence "with them" gives us further cause to cross out **a**. Answer **b** makes no sense. Answer **c** seems to make sense for the first part of the sentence, but it doesn't fit with the second part of the sentence. Choices **d** and **e** sound as though they would fit.

Because we have eliminated all but **d** and **e**, we have two choices for our second blank. "Probably" is too weak for the context of the second blank. The answer has to be **d**.

Additional Information

Some questions may ask you to identify additional information that would fit in the passage, either in the form of a blank sentence that has been left in the passage or in the form of a question about what information would help or hurt the author's argument. The questions look like this:

- Which sentence, if inserted in the blank, would best complete the meaning of the paragraph?
- Which statement, if true, would most strengthen the author's argument?
- Which of the following facts would most weaken the author's argument?

How to Find Additional Information Answers

To find the answer to these questions, you need to skim the paragraph or passage for a main idea, purpose, or hypothesis.

Sample Question

Go back to the passage on TWA Flight 800 to answer this question.

5. Which fact, if true, would be LEAST likely to strengthen the argument that the crashing of the TWA flight was a criminal act?
   a. A thorough and reliable check had been made of the plane just before departure.
   b. Other similar older planes had never misfunctioned.
   c. The FBI agent in charge of the investigation had been offered a bribe, which he refused to accept.
   d. Scuba divers had brought up a jet engine from the ocean floor.
   e. There had been an anonymous phone call warning the airlines of a bomb on board the plane, but no bomb had been found.

Answer

You need to find a sentence that the author would *not* put in the passage. The passage indicates that the communications from the plane had been normal. Choices a or b would further strengthen the argument that the plane was normal, so that criminal activity may have been responsible for the crash. Choices c and e also point to criminal activity. That leaves d. Pulling an engine out of the ocean by itself would not be relevant to the case. It could have been any engine in any ocean. Even if the engine could have provided a clue, that fact was not mentioned in the answer choice. So d is the answer.

▶ **Reading 8: Graphs**

Graphs are found in both the reading and the math sections of the test. This section will give examples of the different types of graphs you may encounter on the CBEST. Try your hand at the sample graphs and questions in this section.

Histograms and Bar Graphs

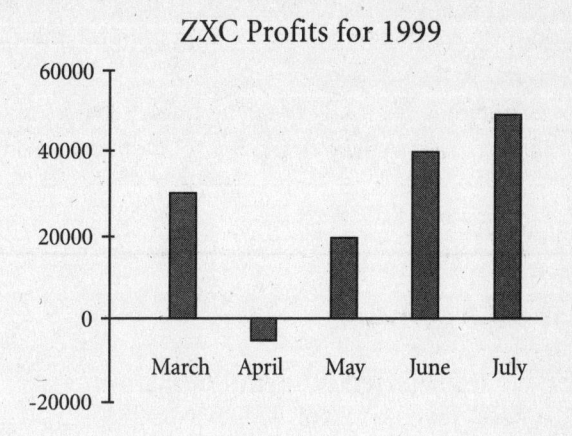

ZXC Profits for 1999

1. Between which two months was the change in profits for ZXC the greatest?
   a. February–March
   b. March–April
   c. April–May
   d. May–June
   e. June–July

2. Between which two months did the profits for ZXC increase the most?
   a. February–March
   b. March–April
   c. April–May
   d. May–June
   e. June–July

Answers

1. b. The change was the greatest between March and April. The a answer is irrelevant. February is not mentioned on the graph.
2. c. April's bar ends on the downward side. Measuring with a piece of paper, you can see that it is farther from April's bottom to May's top than it is from May's top to June's top. You do not need to use the numbers for these questions because the questions did not ask you to read the amounts of the actual profits.

Three Success Steps For Working With Graphs

1. Read the graph carefully. Read all around the graph, including the title and the key.
2. Some questions may try to trick you by leaving out numbers. If all the numbers are not given, it is a very good idea to fill in all the missing numbers on the graph. To do this, you will need to know the value of each increment.
3. Sometimes, instead of reading bars or lines, you can compare differences by using a piece of your test booklet to measure from one point to another or from the end of one bar to the end of another.

Line Graphs

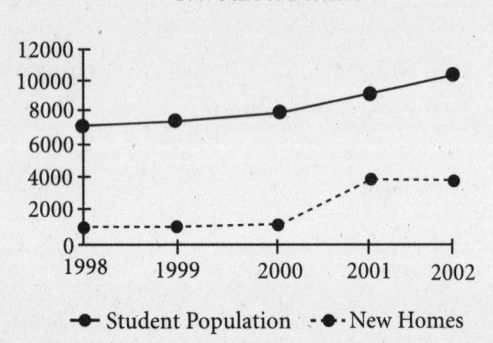

Projected Student Population
P.V. School District

[Line graph showing Student Population and New Homes from 1998 to 2002]

3. In what year is the increase in student population projected to be less than the increase in number of new homes built?
   a. 1998
   b. 1999
   c. 2000
   d. 2001
   e. 2002

Answer
The answer is **c**. A look at the graph shows that during the year 2000 there was a sharper increase in the number of new homes built than in student population. The line slopes up steeper there for houses than it does for student population. Percent of increase is a different question and might yield a different answer. Check Ratios, Proportions, and Percents (p. 109) on percents for details.

Picture Graphs

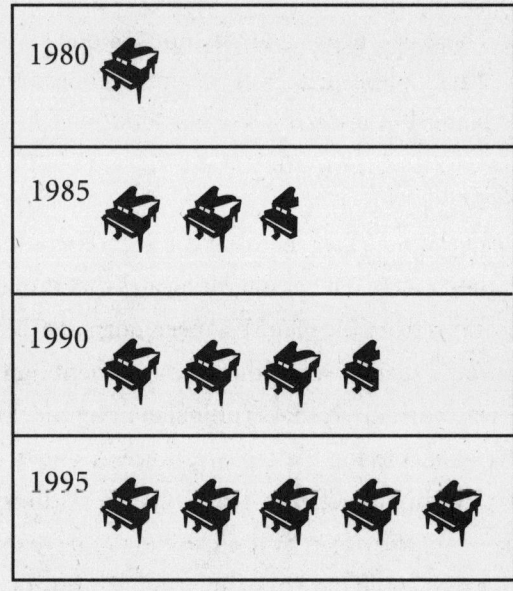

MEMBERSHIP OF THE MTAC

[Picture graph showing pianos for years 1980, 1985, 1990, 1995]

🎹 REPRESENTS 500 MEMBERS

4. How many MTAC members were there in 1990?
   a. $3\frac{1}{2}$
   b. 350
   c. 700
   d. 1,750
   e. 2,250

Answer
It is important to read the key at the bottom of the graph. Each piano represents 500 members. $\frac{1}{2}$ a piano represents 250 members. 1990 has $3\frac{1}{2}$ pianos. This represents 1,750 members. The answer is **d**.

Circle Graphs

Save the Caves Income

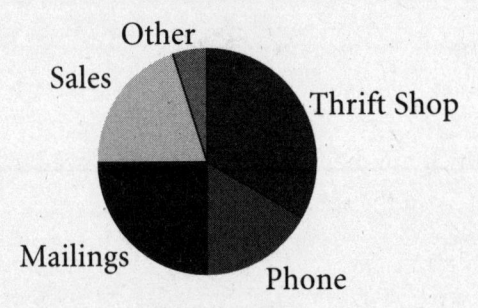

[pie chart with sections: Other, Sales, Thrift Shop, Mailings, Phone]

5. For which category was the income for the Save the Caves Foundation approximately $\frac{1}{4}$?
   a. Mailings
   b. Sales
   c. Thrift Shop
   d. Phone
   e. Other

Answer
Look for the section that takes up approximately $\frac{1}{4}$ of the circle. The answer is **a**.

Here's a different kind of circle graph question.

6. Which of the following could include a representation of expenditures of 25% and 33%?

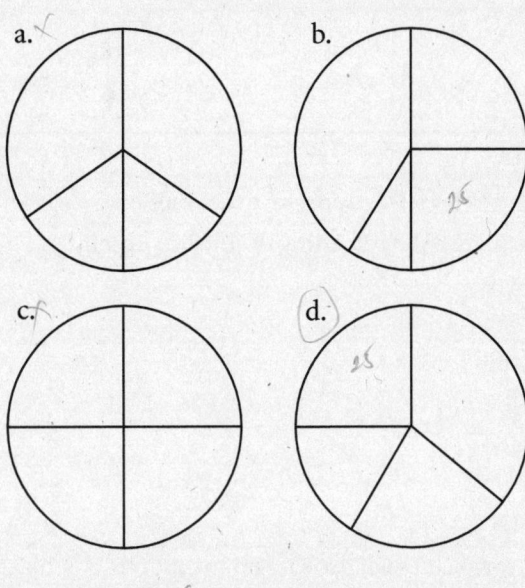

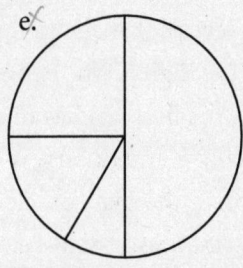

a. [circle divided into 3 sections]
b. [circle divided with 25% section]
c. [circle divided into 4 quarters]
d. [circle with 25% section and other sections]
e. [circle divided into sections]

Answer
25% is the same as $\frac{1}{4}$. 33% is close to $\frac{1}{3}$. The only answer with areas of $\frac{1}{4}$ and $\frac{1}{3}$ of the circle is answer **d**. Choice **b** is close, but the larger area seems a little large for $\frac{1}{3}$.

Oddballs

Some graphs are just plain odd.

7. The circles above represent the dials on an electric meter. What reading do they represent?
   a. 476
   b. 465
   c. 466
   d. 486
   e. 487

Answer

There are no clues whatsoever on the graphs. A look at the answer choices reveals that all are three digits and that all begin with the digit 4. Maybe each circle represents a digit. If so, the first dial has to represent 4. If the first dial represents 4, and the arrow is nearly halfway around (assuming the dials go clockwise), then half is probably 5. In that case, the last circle represents 5, which tells you your answer, choice **b**. It makes sense that the middle digit of 465 is 6, since the middle circle's arrow goes just a bit past the 5 mark. In order to correctly answer this question, it was important that you didn't assume the graphs represent clocks. Questions similar to this have been on the test before.

All right, here's a challenge.

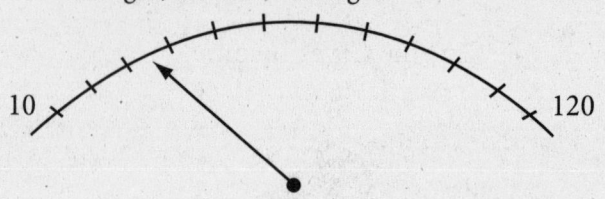

8. Which number best represents the speed indicated on the speedometer above?
   a. $12\frac{1}{2}$
   b. $30\frac{1}{2}$
   c. 35
   d. $40\frac{1}{2}$
   e. 45

Answer

It is very important to label the graph in order to answer this question. If there are 11 segments between 10 and 120, each segment must represent 10 mph. The arrow is pointing halfway between 30 and 40. Halfway between 30 and 40 is 35. The answer is **c**.

▶ Math 1: Words, Words, Words

Many times, an otherwise simple problem may seem difficult merely because the test writers have used terms that you are not familiar with. An understanding of mathematical terms will enable you to understand the language of the problem and give you a better chance of solving that problem. This lesson presents a list of words used when speaking about numbers.

Here is a sample question that will show you why knowing these words is important. Once you've learned the words in this sample question, you should be able to answer it. You can check your answer against the explanation given later in this lesson.

CBEST MINI-COURSE

Sample Definition Question

1. If x is a whole number and y is a positive integer, for what value of x MUST $x < y$ be true?
   a. -3
   b. 0
   c. $\frac{1}{2}$
   d. 3
   e. Any value of x must make the statement true.

Definitions

Below are definitions of words you need to know to answer CBEST math questions. If some of these words are unfamiliar, put them on flash cards: the word on one side, and the definition and some examples on the other side. Flash cards are handy because you can carry them around with you to review at odd moments during the day. If you use this method, it won't take you long to learn these words.

Integer

An integer is simply a number with no fraction or decimal attached $\{\ldots -2, -1, 0, 1, 2 \ldots\}$. Integers include both negative (-5) and positive $(9,687)$ numbers. Zero is also an integer, but is considered neither negative nor positive in most mathematical texts.

Positive Integer

A positive integer is an integer, according to the definition above, that is **greater than zero.** Zero is not included. Positive integers begin with 1 and continue infinitely $\{1, 2, 3 \ldots\}$. Examples of positive integers are 5, 6,000 and 1,000,000.

Negative Integer

A negative integer is an integer that is **less than zero.** Zero is not included. The highest negative integer is negative one (-1). The negative integers go down infinitely $\{\ldots -3, -2, -1\}$. Some examples of negative integers are $-10, -8, -1,476$. The following numbers do not fit the definition of a negative integer: -4.5 (not an integer because of the decimal), 0, and 308.

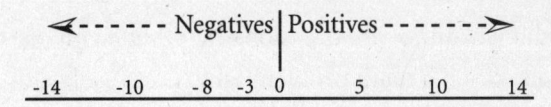

<------ Negatives | Positives ------>
    -14 -10 -8 -3 0   5   10 14

HOT TIP
Negative numbers appear smaller when they are larger. To help you make sense of this concept, think of the degrees below zero on a thermometer. Three degrees below zero is hotter than 40 degrees below, so -3 is greater than -40, even though 40 appears to be a larger number. Test makers like to test your grasp of this principle.

Zero

Zero is an integer that is neither positive nor negative.

Whole Numbers

Whole numbers include all positive integers, as well as zero $\{0, 1, 2, 3 \ldots\}$. Like integers, whole numbers do not include numbers with fractions or decimals.

Digit

A digit is a single number symbol. In the number 1,246, each of the four numerals is a digit. Six is the *ones* digit, 4 is the *tens* digit, 2 is the *hundreds* digit, and 1 is the *thousands* digit. Knowing place names for digits is important when you're asked on a test to round to a certain digit. Rounding will be covered in the third math lesson.

Real Numbers

Real numbers include all numbers: negative, positive, zero, fractions, decimals, most square roots, and so on. Usually, the numbers used on the CBEST will be real numbers, unless otherwise stated.

Variables

Variables are letters, such as *x* and *y*, that are used to replace numbers. The letter is usually a letter of the alphabet, although occasionally, other symbols are used. When a math problem asks you to "solve for *y*," that means figure out what number the letter is replacing. At other times, the problem requires you to work with the letters as if they were numbers. Examples of both of the above will be covered in the lesson on algebra on page 114.

Reciprocal

The reciprocal of a fraction is the fraction turned upside down. For example, the reciprocal of $\frac{3}{8}$ is $\frac{8}{3}$ and vice versa. The reciprocal of an integer is one over the integer. For example, the reciprocal of 2 (or $\frac{2}{1}$) is $\frac{1}{2}$ and vice versa. To get the reciprocal of a mixed number such as $3\frac{1}{2}$, first change the number to an improper fraction ($\frac{7}{2}$) and then turn it over ($\frac{2}{7}$).

Numerator and Denominator

The numerator of a fraction is the number on top, and the denominator is the number on the bottom. The numerator of $\frac{6}{7}$ is 6 and the denominator is 7.

= and ≠

The symbol = is called an *equal sign*. It indicates that the values on both sides of the = are equal to each other. For example, 7 = 2 + 5. A line drawn through an equal sign (≠) indicates that the values on either side are not equal: 8 ≠ 4 + 5.

< and >; ≤ and ≥

The symbol < means *less than* and the symbol > means *greater than*. The number on the closed side of the symbol is smaller, and the number on the open side is larger. Thus, 3 < 5 and 10 > 2. Remember: The alligator eats the bigger number.

The symbol ≤ means *less than or equal to*, and the symbol ≥ means *greater than or equal to*. These two symbols operate the same way as the < and >, but the added line means that it's possible that the two sides are equal. Thus, in the equation $x ≥ 3$, *x* can represent 3 or any number greater than 3.

Answer to Sample Definition Question

Using the definitions above, can you solve sample question 1 from the previous page? The variable *x* can be any **whole number** including zero. The variable *y* can be any **positive integer**, which doesn't include zero. The question reads "... for what value of *x* MUST *x* < *y* be true?" *Must* means that *x* has to be less than *y* under *all circumstances*. You are being asked to replace *x* with a number that will be less than any positive integer that replaces *y*. The only whole number that would make *x* < *y* true, no matter what positive integer is put in place of *y*, is zero. Therefore, **b** is the correct answer.

Try another sample question. Again, the definitions above will be useful in solving this problem.

Sample Digits Question

2. In a certain two-digit number, the tens digit is four more than the ones digit. The sum of the two digits is ten. What is the number?
   a. 26
   b. 82
   c. 40
   d. 37
   e. 73

CBEST MINI-COURSE

Answer

There are two requirements for the unknown number: The tens digit has to be four more than the ones digit, and the two digits have to add up to 10. The best way to solve the problem is to eliminate answers that don't meet these two requirements. Consider the second criterion first. A glance at the answers shows that the digits in the answers **a** and **c** do not add up to 10. They can be eliminated. Next, consider the first requirement. Answer **b** contains a tens digit that is six, not four, more than the ones digit. Answer **d** has the ones digit four more than the tens, reversing the requirement. Therefore, **e** is the only number that correctly meets the requirements.

Practice with Definitions

Match the word on the left with the description or example on the right. You may want to write these definitions on flash cards.

_e_ 3. integer
_c_ 4. whole number
_f_ 5. zero
_a_ 6. negative integer
_b_ 7. positive integer
_g_ 8. digit
_i_ 9. <
_h_ 10. >
_k_ 11. ≤
_j_ 12. ≥
_d_ 13. real number

a. {...−3, −2, −1}
b. {1, 2, 3 ...}
c. {0, 1, 2, 3 ...}
d. number set including fractions
e. {...−3, −2, −1, 0, 1, 2, 3 ...}
f. neither negative nor positive
g. one numeral in a number
h. greater than
i. less than
j. greater than or equal to
k. less than or equal to

Answers

3. e.
4. c.
5. f.
6. a.
7. b.
8. g.
9. i.
10. h.
11. k.
12. j.
13. d.

▶ Math 2: Numbers Working Together

In the last lesson, you learned the definitions of several mathematical terms. This lesson will discuss ways in which numbers work together. You will need this information to solve simple algebra and perform certain arithmetic functions that will be part of some CBEST problems.

Adding and Subtracting Integers

The following sample questions are examples of the types of problems about adding and subtracting you may see on the CBEST. The answers are given later in this lesson.

Sample Integer Questions

1. Every month, Alice's paycheck of $1,500 goes directly into her bank account. Each month, Alice pays $800 on her mortgage payment and $500 for food and all other monthly expenses. She spends $1,650 per year on her car (insurance, gas, repairs, and maintenance), $500 per year for gifts, and $450 per year for property tax. What will be her bank balance at the end of a year?
   a. $500
   b. $300
   c. 0
   d. −$200
   e. −$400

93

2. A submarine is submerged 2,000 feet below the sea. An airplane directly above is flying 32,000 feet above sea level. What is the difference in their altitudes?
   a. 30,000 feet
   b. 31,000 feet
   c. 32,000 feet
   d. 33,000 feet
   e. 34,000 feet

Adding Positive Numbers

You already know that if a positive number, such as 5, is added to another positive number, such as 7, the answer will turn out to be a positive number: 12.

Adding Negative Numbers

Suppose you had two negative numbers to add together, such as −5 and −7. Here are two methods that make working with negative numbers easier:

- **Number line:** If you were to add −5 and −7 on a number line, you would start from 0. You would then proceed back five numbers to −5. From there, you would proceed back seven more (−7), which would leave you at the answer: −12.

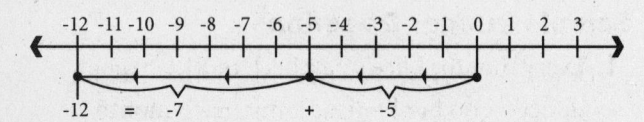

- **Bank account:** Negative numbers put you more in debt. If you started with a balance of zero and withdrew $5, you would have a balance of −5. If you withdrew $7 more, you would be in debt $12, or −12.

> **HOT TIP**
> When adding two negative numbers, just add the two numbers and place a negative sign before the answer. For instance, in the problem (−3) + (−6), first think 3 + 6 = 9, and then add a negative to the answer: −9.

Adding a Negative Number to a Positive Number

When adding a positive number and a negative number, such as 8 + (−15), you can use the number line or the bank account approach.

- **Number line:** Start from 0. Go 8 to the right and then move 15 spaces to the left. This will leave you at the correct answer: −7.

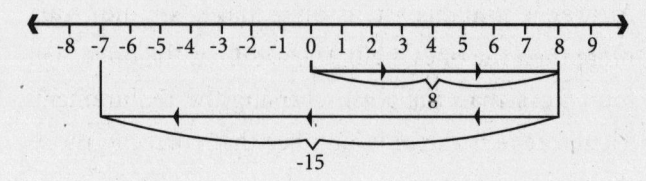

- **Bank account:** You put $8 in your bank account and take out $15. Oops, you've overdrawn, and you're left with a balance of −7.

Now try a problem with the negative number first: −6 + 7.

- **Number line:** Start from 0. Go 6 to the left since 6 is negative, then 7 to the right. You'll end up on the answer: 1.

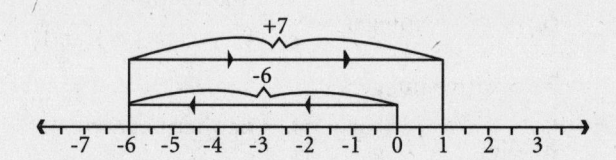

- **Bank account:** You take $6 out of your bank account and put in $7. You have one dollar more than you had before.

> **HOT TIP**
> When adding a positive and negative number, simply subtract the smaller from the larger as usual and give the answer the sign (− or +) of the larger number.

Subtracting Negative Numbers

Two minus signs next to each other may look strange, but they actually indicate one of the simplest operations; two negative signs together can be changed into one plus sign. For instance, the problem 9 – (–) 7 will give you the same answer as 9 + 7.

- **Number line:** From 0, go 9 to the right. The first minus would send the 7 to the left, but another negative sign *negates* that operation, so 7 ends up going to the right as though there had been no negatives at all. The answer is 9 + 7 or 16.

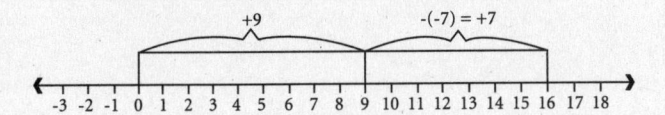

- **Bank account:** You deposit $9 in the bank. A negative would be a withdrawal, but there is another negative, so do a negative withdrawal; that is, deposit another $7. You have deposited a total of $16.

> **HOT TIP**
> When subtracting a negative number, change the two minus signs to an addition sign.

Answers to Sample Integer Questions

1. **d.** One way to find this answer is to first figure out Alice's monthly balance—what's left after she pays her monthly expenses: $1,500 – ($800 + $500), which equals $200. Then multiply this by 12 months to get $2,400, which is her yearly balance. Her yearly spending is $2,600 ($1,650 + $500 + $450). Her yearly balance minus her yearly spending will give you the answer: $2,400 – $2,600 = –$200.

2. **e.** The airplane's altitude is a positive 32,000 feet above sea level, and the submarine is a negative 2,000 below the water. Finding the difference between the two looks like this: 32,000 – (–2,000). Even though the question asked for the *difference*, you need to add the two numbers, giving you a total distance of 34,000 feet.

Multiplying and Dividing Integers

Multiplying and dividing integers is not as complicated as adding and subtracting them.

Two Positives

When a positive number is multiplied or divided by a positive number, the result is positive: 4 × 50 = 200 and 50 ÷ 2 = 25.

> **HOT TIP**
> Multiplication can be written three different ways and division two ways.
> - **Multiplication:** You can write 3 × 4, 3(4), and 3 · 4. When working with a variable, such as z, 3 × z may be written 3z, without parentheses. Additionally, a negative sign directly outside a parentheses means to multiply anything inside the parentheses by negative 1. For example: $-(a) = -a$, and $-(xy) = -xy$.
> - **Division:** You can write 30 ÷ 4, or $\frac{30}{4}$. Variables in division can come in various forms. It's important to know these different forms when taking a multiple choice exam. For example, $\frac{1}{2}y$ is the same as $\frac{y}{2}$, not $\frac{1}{2y}$.

Two Negatives

When two negative numbers are multiplied or divided, the result is positive: –5 × –5 = + 25 and –36 ÷ –6 = + 6. Commit this rule to memory.

Negative and Positive

When a negative number is multiplied by a positive number, the result is negative. Multiplying –3 by 6 means that six –3's are added together, so of course you will get a negative answer, –18. On the number line, you will go back three units six times. In your bank account, you will end up owing $18 after $3 is removed from your bank account six times.

Order of Operations

You may be given a problem with more than one operation, like this:

$$3 + 5 \times 2^2 + \frac{14}{(2+5)}$$

If you simply work from left to right, your answer will be 140, and it will be wrong. But, be assured, 140 will probably be one of the multiple choice answers. The phrase below will help you remember the correct order of operations:

Please Excuse My Dear Aunt Sally

1. P stands for *Parentheses*. In the above example, 2 + 5 is in parentheses. That operation should be done first: $3 + 5 \times 2^2 + \frac{14}{7}$.

2. E stands for *Exponents*. Those are the numbers that are smaller in size and higher on the page than the others and indicate the number of times to multiply the number by itself. Thus, 5^3 means $5 \times 5 \times 5$. In the problem above, 2^2 means that 2 should be multiplied by itself twice: $2 \times 2 = 4$. So now the problem reads $3 + 5 \times 4 + \frac{14}{7}$.

3. M and D stand for *Multiplication* and *Division*. The next step is to do the multiplication and division from left to right: $3 + 20 + 2$.

4. A and S stand for *Addition* and *Subtraction*. The last step is to add and subtract from left to right: 25.

Practice

Match the descriptions in the first column with an appropriate answer from the second column. The answers may be used more than once.

___ 3. negative times or divided by a negative
___ 4. negative times or divided by a positive
___ 5. negative plus a negative
___ 6. positive minus a negative
___ 7. negative minus a negative
___ 8. positive plus a negative
___ 9. $8 + 3(40 - 10) - 9$
___ 10. $2 + 5 + 6 \times \frac{4}{3} + 69$
___ 11. $-97 - (-8)$
___ 12. $100 + -11$
___ 13. $-21(-4)$
___ 14. $21(-4)$
___ 15. $-21(4)$
___ 16. $-14 - 70$

a. 89
b. 84
c. 56
d. −20
e. −84
f. −89
g. positive
h. negative
i. Change the double negative to a positive and follow rule j below.
j. Subtract one from the other and select the sign of the largest number.

Answers

3. g.	**7.** i.	**11.** f.	**15.** e.
4. h.	**8.** j.	**12.** a.	**16.** e.
5. h.	**9.** a.	**13.** b.	
6. g.	**10.** b.	**14.** e.	

▶ Math 3: Rounding, Estimation, and Decimal Equivalents

The questions on the CBEST will include number rounding, estimation, and decimal equivalents. Most teachers studying for the CBEST only need a very basic brush up on these topics in order to master them. If you need a more thorough review, check out some of the books listed in the "More Help" section at the end of this chapter.

Rounding

Numbers are made up of digits that each represent different values according to their position in the number. For instance, in the number 4,312.796, the 2 is in the ones place and equals 2 units. The 1 is in the tens place and equals 1 ten (10). The 3 is in the hundreds place and equals 3 hundreds (300). The 4 in the thousands place equals 4 thousands (4,000). To the right of the decimal, the 7 is in the tenths place and equals seven tenths (0.7 or $\frac{7}{10}$). The 9 is in the hundredths place and equals 9 hundredths (0.09 or $\frac{9}{100}$). The 6 is in the thousandths place and equals 6 thousandths (0.006 or $\frac{6}{1000}$).

4 3 1 2 . 7 9 6
thousands / hundreds / tens / ones / tenths / hundredths / thousandths

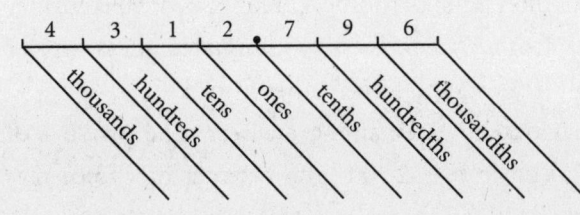

In a rounding question, you will be asked to round to the nearest tenths, hundreds, or other place.

Sample Rounding Question

1. Round 4,312.986 to the nearest tenth.
   a. 4,310
   b. 4,312.8
   c. 4,312.9
   d. 4,313
   e. 4,312.98

Answer
Find the answer by walking through the Success Steps.

1. The digit is 9, so it will either stay 9 or go to 0.
2. 8 is to the right of 9.
3. This step does not apply; 8 is not less than 5.
4. The 9 goes up one because 8 is more than 5.
5. Change 9 to 0 and change 2 to 3. The answer is **d**, 4,313.

(Steps 6 and 7 don't apply.)

Practice
Now try a few more rounding questions.

2. Round 45.789 to the nearest hundredth. *45.79*

3. Round 296.45 to the nearest ten. *300*

4. Round 345,687 to two significant digits. *350,000*

Answers
2. The digit you need to look at is 8; it will either stay 8 or go up to 9. The number 9 is to the right of 8; 9 is more than 5, so you change 8 to 9. The answer is 45.79.

Seven Success Steps for Rounding Questions

1. Locate the place. If the question calls for rounding to the nearest ten, look at the tens place. Notice the place digit. Realize that the place digit will either stay the same or go up one.
2. Look at the digit to the right of the place digit—the **right-hand** neighbor.
3. If the right-hand neighbor is less than 5, the place digit stays the same.
4. If the right-hand neighbor is 5 or more, the place digit goes up one.
5. If the place digit is 9, and the right-hand neighbor is 5 or more, then turn the place digit to 0 and raise the **left-hand** neighbor up one.
6. If instead of a place, the question calls for rounding to a certain number of significant digits, count that number of digits starting from the left to reach the place digit. Now start with step 1.
7. If the specified place was to the left of the decimal point, change all the digits to 0 that are to the right of the place digit.

---

3. The digit is 9; the 9 will either stay 9 or go to 0. The number 6 is to the right of 9; it is more than 5, so change 9 to 0 and apply step 5, raising the 2 to the left of 9 to 3. Now apply step 7, and change digits to the right of the tens place to 0. The answer is 300.
4. Here you need to apply step 6. Two places from the left is the ten thousands digit, a 4. Now apply step 1 and work through the steps: The digit is 4, so it will either stay 4 or go up to 5. Since the right-hand neighbor is 5, change the 4 to 5. Now apply step 7 and change all digits to the right of your new 5 to zero. The answer is 350,000.

Estimation

Estimation requires rounding numbers before adding, subtracting, multiplying, or dividing. If you are given numerical answers, you might just want to multiply the two numbers without estimation and pick the answer that is the closest. Most likely, however, the problem will be more complicated than that.

Sample Estimation Question

5. 42 × 57 is closest to
   a. 45 × 60.
   b. 40 × 55.
   c. 40 × 50.
   d. 40 × 60.
   e. 45 × 50.

Answer to Sample Estimation Question

Here's how you could use the steps to answer the sample question:

1. You can round 42 down and 57 up, resulting in answer **d**.
2. Rounding the numbers to one significant digit yields **d** also.
3. Eliminate. **a.** Eliminated: 45 is further from 42 than is 40. **b.** Maybe. **c.** Eliminated: 50 is further from 57 than is 60. **e.** Eliminated: 45 is further from 42 and 50 is further from 57.
4. Check the remaining answers. The product of choice **b** is 2,200. The product of choice **d** is 2,400. The actual product is 2,394, which makes **d** the closest, and therefore the correct answer.

Four Success Steps for Estimation Problems

To do a problem like this, you might want to try some of the following strategies:

1. See whether you can round one number up and the other one down. This works if by so doing you are adding nearly the same amount to one number as you are subtracting from the other. Rounding one up and one down makes the product most accurate. For example, if the numbers were 71 and 89, you take one from 71 to get 70 and add one to 89 to get 90. 70 × 90 is very close to 71 × 89.
2. An estimation question may be on the test in order to test your rounding skills. Round the numbers to one significant digit, or to the number of significant digits to which the numbers in the answers have been rounded. Find that answer and consider it as a possible right answer.
3. Eliminate answers that are further away from those you obtained after doing steps 1 and 2. For example, for 71 and 89, if answers given were 70 × 85 and 70 × 90, you can eliminate the former choice because 85 is further from 89 than is 90.
4. After eliminating, you can always multiply (subtract, add, divide) out the remaining answers to make sure your answer is correct.

Decimal Equivalents

You may be asked to compare two numbers in order to tell which one is greater. In many cases, you will need to know some basic decimal and percentage equivalents.

Decimal-Fraction Questions

See how many of these you already know. For questions 6–11, state the decimal equivalent.

6. $\frac{1}{2}$
7. $\frac{3}{4}$
8. $\frac{4}{5}$
9. $\frac{1}{8}$
10. $\frac{1}{3}$
11. $\frac{1}{6}$

For questions 12–14, tell which number is greater.

12. a. 0.93
    b. 0.9039

13. a. 0.339
    b. $\frac{1}{3}$

14. a. $\frac{45}{91}$
    b. 0.52

Answers

6. 0.5
7. 0.75
8. 0.8
9. 0.125
10. $0.33\frac{1}{3}$ or 0.33
11. $0.16\frac{2}{3}$ or 0.166
12. a. To compare these numbers more easily, add zeros after the shorter number to make the numbers both the same length: 0.93 = 0.9300. Compare 0.9300 and 0.9039. Then take out the decimals. You can see that 9,300 is larger than 9,039.
13. a. Since $\frac{1}{3}$ = 0.33, extending the number would yield $0.33\overline{3}$. (A line over a number means the number repeats forever.) 333 is smaller than 339.
14. b. Instead of dividing the denominator (91) into the numerator (45), look to see whether the two choices are close to any common number. You might notice that both numbers almost equal $\frac{1}{2}$.

45 is less than half of 91, so $\frac{45}{91}$ is less than half. Half in decimals is 0.5 or 0.50; 0.52 is greater than 0.50, so it is greater than half. Thus, **b** is larger.

Decimal-Percentage Equivalents

You already know that when you deposit money in an account that earns 5% interest, you multiply the money in the bank by 0.05 to find out your interest for the year. 5% in decimal form is 0.05.

> **HOT TIP**
> To change a percent to a decimal, move the decimal point two places to the left. To change a decimal to a percent, move the decimal point two places to the right. If there is no decimal indicated in the number, it is assumed that the decimal is after the ones place, or to the right of the number.

The percent always looks larger. Here are some examples:

Number	Percent
0.05	5%
0.9	90%
0.002	0.2%
0.0004	0.04%
3	300%

Questions

Change the following numbers to percents.

15. 0.07
16. 0.8
17. 0.45
18. 6.8
19. 97

20. 345
21. 0.125

Change the following percents to decimals.

22. 5%
23. 0.7%
24. 0.09%
25. 49%
26. 764%

Answers

15. 7%
16. 80%
17. 45%
18. 680%
19. 9,700%
20. 34,500%
21. 12.5%
22. 0.05
23. 0.007
24. 0.0009
25. 0.49
26. 7.64

CBEST MINI-COURSE

Common Equivalents

Here are some common decimal, percent, and fraction equivalents you should have at your fingertips. A line over a number indicates that the number is repeated indefinitely.

CONVERSION TABLE

Decimal	%	Fraction
0.25	25%	$\frac{1}{4}$
0.50	50%	$\frac{1}{2}$
0.75	75%	$\frac{3}{4}$
0.10	10%	$\frac{1}{10}$
0.20	20%	$\frac{1}{5}$
0.40	40%	$\frac{2}{5}$
0.60	60%	$\frac{3}{5}$
0.80	80%	$\frac{4}{5}$
$0.33\overline{3}$	$33\frac{1}{3}\%$	$\frac{1}{3}$
$0.66\overline{6}$	$66\frac{2}{3}\%$	$\frac{2}{3}$

For more on fraction and decimal equivalents, see the next lesson.

▶ Math 4: Fractions

Fractions are the nemesis of many a CBEST taker. Consider yourself fortunate if you have had few problems with them. Now that you have had a few more years of education and are a little wiser, fractions may not be as intimidating as they once seemed.

Comparing Fractions
The Laser Beam Method

A CBEST question may ask you to compare two fractions, or a fraction to a decimal. To compare two fractions, use the laser beam method: 1. Two laser beams are racing toward each other. 2. They both hit numbers and bounce off up to the number in the opposite corner multiplying the two numbers as they go. 3. Exam-

ine the numbers they came up with. The largest number is beside the largest fraction. Use the laser beam method to compare $\frac{5}{16}$ and $\frac{2}{5}$.

$(25) \frac{5}{16} \times \frac{2}{5} (32)$

$32 > 25$, so $\frac{2}{5} > \frac{5}{16}$

HOT TIP

To change a fraction into a decimal, you simply divide the denominator of the fraction into the numerator, like this:

$\frac{3}{8} = $ 0.375
8 ⟌ 3.000
   2 4
   60
   56
    40

Practice

Which number is the largest?

1. a) 0.25
   b) $\frac{11}{48}$

2. a) $\frac{4}{5}$
   b) 0.75

3. a) $\frac{3}{7}$
   b) $\frac{4}{9}$

Which number is the smallest?

4. a) $\frac{3}{13}$
   b) $\frac{2}{11}$

5. a) 0.95
   b) $\frac{9}{10}$

6. a) $\frac{1}{3}$
   b) 0.3387

Answers

1. a. $11 \div 48 = 0.23 < 0.25$
2. a. $\frac{4}{5} = 0.8$ $80 > 75$
3. b. Use the laser beam method.
4. b. Use the laser beam method.
5. b. $\frac{9}{10} = 0.9$ $90 < 95$
6. a. $\frac{1}{3} = 0.33$ $3,387 > 3,333$

Reducing and Expanding Fractions

Fractions can be reduced by dividing the same number into both the numerator and the denominator.

- $\frac{2}{4} = \frac{1}{2}$ because both the numerator and denominator can be divided by 2.
- $\frac{24}{36} = \frac{2}{3}$ because both the numerator and denominator can be divided by 12.

Fractions can be expanded by multiplying the numerator and the denominator by the same number.

- $\frac{1}{8} = \frac{2}{16} = \frac{5}{40}$ because the original numerator and the denominator are both multiplied by 2, and then by 5.

Adding and Subtracting Fractions

When adding fractions that have the same denominators, add the numerators, and then reduce if necessary:

$$\frac{1}{4} + \frac{5}{4} = \frac{6}{4} = 1\frac{2}{4} = 1\frac{1}{2}$$

When subtracting fractions that have the same denominators, subtract the numerators. Then reduce if necessary:

$$\frac{5}{7} - \frac{3}{7} = \frac{2}{7}$$

When adding or subtracting fractions with different denominators, find common denominators before performing the operations. For example, in the problem $\frac{3}{8} + \frac{1}{6}$, the lowest common denominator of 6 and 8 is 24.

Convert both fractions to 24ths: $\frac{3}{8} = \frac{9}{24}$
$\frac{1}{6} = \frac{4}{24}$

Add the new fractions: $\frac{9}{24} + \frac{4}{24} = \frac{13}{24}$

To subtract instead of add the fractions above, after finding the common denominator, subtract the resulting numerators: $\frac{9}{24} - \frac{4}{24} = \frac{5}{24}$.

When adding mixed numbers, there is no need to turn the numbers into improper fractions. Simply add the fraction parts. Then add the integers. When finished, add the two parts together. Don't forget to "carry" if the fractions add up to more than one.

$$13\frac{5}{7}$$
$$+ 6\frac{6}{7}$$
$$\overline{19\frac{11}{7}}$$

$$\frac{11}{7} = 1\frac{4}{7}$$
$$1\frac{4}{7} + 19 = 20\frac{4}{7}$$

Subtraction uses the same principle. Subtract the bottom fraction from the top fraction, and the bottom integer from the top integer. If the top fraction is smaller than the bottom one, then take the following steps:

1. Notice the common denominator of the fractions.
2. Add that number to the numerator of the top fraction.
3. Subtract 1 from the top integer.
4. Subtract as usual.

Suppose the problem above were a subtraction problem instead of addition:

$$13\tfrac{5}{7}$$
$$-6\tfrac{6}{7}$$

1. Notice the common denominator
   of the fractions: 7
2. Add that number to the numerator
   of the top fraction: $5 + 7 = 12$
3. Subtract one from the top integer: $13 - 1 = 12$
4. Subtract as usual: $12\tfrac{12}{7}$
   $$-6\tfrac{6}{7}$$
   $$6\tfrac{6}{7}$$

> **HOT TIP**
>
> When adding or subtracting fractions, you can use the laser beam method.
>
> 1. First change to improper fractions, then multiply crosswise:
>
> $$\tfrac{1}{6} + \tfrac{3}{7} = \overset{7}{\tfrac{1}{6}} \diagdown\!\!\!\!\diagup \overset{18}{\tfrac{3}{7}}$$
>
> 2. Next, multiply the denominators: $6 \times 7 = 42$
> 3. Add or subtract the top numbers as appropriate and place them over the multiplied denominator to get your answer: $7 + 18 = 25$
>
> $$\tfrac{25}{42}$$

Multiplying and Dividing Fractions

When multiplying fractions, simply multiply the numerators and then multiply the denominators:

$$\tfrac{5}{6} \times \tfrac{7}{8} = \tfrac{35}{48}$$

When dividing, turn the second fraction upside-down, then multiply across:

$$\tfrac{1}{2} \div \tfrac{2}{3} \text{ is the same as } \tfrac{1}{2} \times \tfrac{3}{2} = \tfrac{3}{4}$$

When working with problems that involve mixed numbers such as $6\tfrac{1}{2} \times 5\tfrac{1}{3}$, change the numbers to improper fractions before multiplying. With $6\tfrac{1}{2}$, multiply the denominator, 2, by the whole number, 6, to get 12, then add the numerator, 1, for a total of 13. Place 13 over the original denominator, 2. The result is $\tfrac{13}{2}$.

> **HOT TIP**
>
> When you're working with two fractions where the numerator of one fraction can be divided by the same number as the denominator of the other fraction, you can reduce even before you multiply:
>
> $$6\tfrac{1}{2} \times 5\tfrac{1}{3} = \tfrac{13}{2} \times \tfrac{16}{3}$$
>
> Divide both the 2 and the 16 by 2:
>
> $$\tfrac{13}{\cancel{2}_1} \times \tfrac{\cancel{16}^8}{3} = \tfrac{104}{3} = 34\tfrac{2}{3}$$

When multiplying or dividing a fraction and an integer, place the integer over 1 and proceed as if it were a fraction.

$$13 \times \tfrac{1}{2} = \tfrac{13}{1} \times \tfrac{1}{2} = \tfrac{13}{2} = 6\tfrac{1}{2}$$

Choosing an Answer

When you come up with an answer where the numerator is more than the denominator, the answer may be given in that form, as an improper fraction. But if the answers are mixed numbers, divide the denominator into the numerator. Any remainder is placed over the original denominator. In the case of $\tfrac{208}{6}$, 208 divided by 6 is 34 with a remainder of 4 yielding $34\tfrac{4}{6}$. This answer probably will not be there, so reduce $\tfrac{4}{6}$ to $\tfrac{2}{3}$. If $\tfrac{208}{6}$ is not an answer choice, $34\tfrac{2}{3}$ probably will be. But don't worry about having to choose between these two answers. Since they signify the same amount, the test would not be valid if both $\tfrac{208}{6}$ and $34\tfrac{2}{3}$ were there unless the question specifically asked for a fully reduced answer.

Practice

Have you improved your skills with fractions? Try these for practice:

1. $5\frac{1}{2} + 4\frac{2}{3} + 6\frac{1}{6} =$

2. $3\frac{6}{11} \times 1\frac{1}{39} =$

3. $5\frac{3}{4} - 2\frac{1}{2} =$

4. $8\frac{1}{8} - 2\frac{5}{8} =$

5. A recipe called for $2\frac{3}{4}$ cups of flour. Jessica wanted to triple the recipe. How much flour would she need?
    a. $7\frac{3}{4}$
    b. $7\frac{7}{8}$
    c. $8\frac{1}{4}$
    d. $8\frac{1}{2}$
    e. $8\frac{3}{4}$

Answers

1. $16\frac{1}{3}$. The common denominator is 6 or 12.
2. $\frac{40}{11}$ or $3\frac{7}{11}$
3. $3\frac{1}{4}$
4. $5\frac{1}{2}$
5. Jessica needs to multiply $2\frac{3}{4}$ cups of flour times 3. $2\frac{3}{4} \times 3 = \frac{11}{4} \times \frac{3}{1} = \frac{33}{4} = 8\frac{1}{4}$

For more practice, look at some of the books in the "More Help" section.

▶ Math 5: Measurement, Perimeter, and Area

There are certain numbers, formulas, and measurements, such as decimal equivalents, area formulas, and weight conversions that you will be expected to have at your fingertips when working some CBEST problems. It's a good idea to put them on flash cards for memorization.

Common Measurements

You will be asked to figure problems using measurements of length, weight, and volume as well as speed, time, and temperature. Here are the common measurements you may be asked to use. Knowledge of the metric system was not on the CBEST when this book went to print.

Weight Measurements

Weight measurements are usually measured on a scale.

    1 pound = 16 ounces
    1 ton = 2,000 pounds

Liquid and Dry Measurements

Liquid and dry measurements are usually made in a measuring spoon, cup, or larger container. Think of the dairy department of your grocery store. Units smaller than a cup probably will not be on the test.

    1 cup = 8 ounces
    1 pint = 2 cups = 16 ounces
    1 quart = 2 pints
    1 quart = 4 cups = 32 ounces
    $\frac{1}{2}$ gallon = 2 quarts
    $\frac{1}{2}$ gallon = 4 pints = 8 cups
    $\frac{1}{2}$ gallon = 64 ounces
    1 gallon = 2 half gallons
    1 gallon = 16 cups = 4 quarts
    1 gallon = 128 ounces

Distance

Distance is measured by rulers or tape measures. Miles are measured by odometers.

    1 foot = 12 inches
    1 yard = 3 feet
    1 yard = 36 inches

1 mile = 5,280 feet
1 mile = 1,760 yards

Square and Cubic Measurements

Here are some conversions you should know. You won't need to know any of the larger numbers on the CBEST. For example, you won't need to memorize 1,728—just be able to figure it out if you need it.

1 square foot = 144 square inches
1 cubic foot = 12 × 12 × 12 inches
    or 1,728 cubic inches
1 yard = 3 feet
1 square yard = 9 square feet
1 cubic yard = 27 cubic feet

Temperature

Temperature is measured by a thermometer in degrees. The only tricky thing here is to know that the difference between 40 below 0 and 65 above 0 is not 25, but 105. If you can't visualize the distance between 40 below and 65 above 0, a rereading of Math Lesson 2 on negative numbers might help.

Speed

Speed is usually measured by speedometers in miles per hour. Time, distance, and rate problems are discussed in Math Lesson 7.

Time

Time is measured by a clock or by a calendar. You can figure out the number of seconds in an hour (3,600) by multiplying 60 seconds by 60 minutes.

1 minute = 60 seconds
1 hour = 60 minutes = 3,600 seconds
1 day = 24 hours = 1,440 minutes
1 week = 7 days = 168 hours
1 year = 12 months = 52 weeks = 365 days

Sample Measurement Question

1. Samuel, a friend of yours, has an uncle in the wholesale fertilizer business. "And I don't even have a garden," he remarked to you one day. The two of you decide to make a garden in a 21 feet by 25 feet patch in his back yard. You suggest he put 4 inches of his uncle's fertilizer on the top and then dig it in. He asks you to help him decide how much to order. Try to solve your friend's problem in *cubic feet* and write down your answer.

    You give Samuel your answer and he calls his uncle. His uncle is most obliging, but insists that since he's a wholesale dealer, he can only accommodate orders in cubic yards. He also warns Samuel that his fertilizer does not smell very good, and needs to be dug in right away. You refigure your calculation in terms up cubic yards. You finally come up with a figure and Samuel calls his uncle. What is the amount he orders?
    a. 9,600 cubic yards
    b. 58.3 cubic yards
    c. 19.4 cubic yards
    d. 6.5 cubic yards
    e. none of these

Answer

Look for your answer below and read to discover the exciting conclusion.

a. 9,600 cubic yards. Suddenly, it grows dark. You try looking out the window, but fertilizer is stacked up against the window as high as you can see. You can't even get out of your house. You changed everything to inches and divided by 36 because there are 36 inches in a yard, so how could you have been wrong?

b. 58.3 cubic yards. Suddenly, it grows dark. Your windows are covered with fertilizer. Fertilizer is piled to the roof and the garden is buried. You changed inches to feet and divided by 3, so where did you go wrong?

c. 19.4 cubic yards. There is a pile of fertilizer about three feet high covering your garden. This is more than you expected so you pile it up and give it to your neighbors. You were clued into the cube idea and divided by 9, so why didn't you get it right?

d. 6.5 cubic yards. You spread exactly 4 inches on top of the garden with a rake. Quickly, you and Samuel dig the fertilizer under. You feel proud that you could get the right answer to a complicated math problem.

e. You couldn't find your answer so you redo your math. You choose the closest answer.

In this volume problem, three dimensions need to be multiplied to get a cubic measurement, but they need to be in the *same* units of measurement. You can't multiply 21 *feet* by 4 *inches*. In this case, it is easiest to change the 4 inches into feet. Four inches is $\frac{1}{3}$ of a foot and $\frac{1}{3}$ of 21 is 7, times 25 is 175, the answer to the first part of the question. Now that you're working in cubic feet, you need to convert to cubic yards.

Suppose you had a square with sides of one yard each. Since there are 3 feet in a yard, a square yard would include 9 square feet.

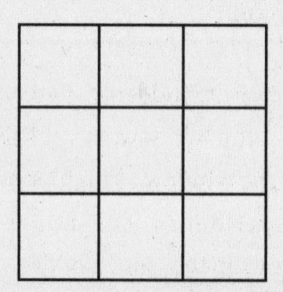

Now suppose you made your square into a cube. You would have 3 layers of 9, or 27 square feet. So since you need 175 cubic feet of fertilizer, you should divide by 27 cubic feet: 175 ÷ 27 ≈ 6.5 cubic yards.

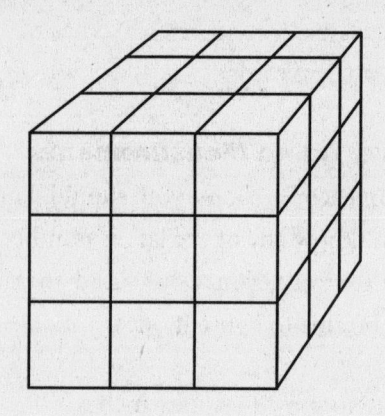

Practice

Try your hand at some additional measurement problems.

2. Casey bought 3 lbs. 5 oz. of boneless chicken at $1.60 per pound. How much did she pay?
   a. $0.50
   b. $4.80
   c. $5.30
   d. $8.80
   e. $12.00

3. Frank cut 2'8" off a 6'3" board. How much was left?
   a. 3'5"
   b. 4'5"
   c. 3'7"
   d. 4'7"
   e. cannot be determined

4. Eight scouts each need two 3' dowels for some banners they are making. Before being cut, the dowels are 10 feet long. How many dowels should the scoutmaster buy?
   a. 2
   b. 3
   c. 4
   d. 5
   e. 6

CBEST MINI-COURSE

5. Three full containers each held one of the following amounts: one ounce, one cup, and one quart. If all three containers were dumped into a gallon jar, how much room would be left?

a. $2\frac{9}{16}$ pints
b. $5\frac{7}{16}$ pints
c. $6\frac{5}{16}$ pints
d. $9\frac{15}{16}$ pints
e. $14\frac{15}{16}$ pints

6. A strip of wallpaper 5 yards long measured 5 inches wide. How many square feet of wallpaper were there?

a. 6.25
b. 8.3
c. 60
d. 12.4
e. 19.7

7. Cooking a turkey takes 20 minutes for every pound in an oven heated to 350 degrees. If a turkey weighing 20 pounds has to be ready by 2:00 P.M., at the latest, when should the turkey be put in the pre-heated oven?

a. 6:20 A.M.
b. 6:40 A.M.
c. 7:00 A.M.
d. 7:20 A.M.
e. 7:40 A.M.

HOT TIP

On the CBEST, there is usually one question that goes something like this:

A school of 240 children want to go on a field trip. A bus can hold 50 children. How many buses are needed? Among the answers are 4, $4\frac{4}{5}$, and 5. Four buses would not be enough. There is no such thing as $\frac{4}{5}$ of a bus. So 5 is the answer.

Answers

2. This problem can be solved at least two ways. You can turn the ounces into $\frac{5}{16}$ of a pound and multiply $1.60 \times 3\frac{5}{16}$. Alternately, you can multiply 1.60 by 3, then multiply 1.60 by $\frac{5}{16}$ and add the two together. Choice **c** is the answer.

3. When subtracting 8 inches from 3 inches, borrow one foot from the 6 feet. Add 12 inches to the 3 inches to get 15″. 15 − 8 = 7 and 5 − 2 is 3. The answer is **c**.

4. The trick here is to realize that the 10' dowels are really only good for 9' since the scouts need 3' pieces. The scouts need a total of 48': 8 × 2 × 3 = 48. Five dowels would only be good for 45', but six dowels would provide more than enough (54'). The answer is **e**.

5. There are 128 ounces in a gallon. 128 − 1 oz. = 127. 127 − 8 oz. (1 cup) = 119 oz. 119 − 32 oz. (1 qt.) = 87 oz. There are 16 ounces in 1 pint, so $\frac{87}{16} = 5\frac{7}{16}$ pt. The correct answer is **b**.

6. The easiest way to do this one is to change everything to feet to begin with. 5 yards is 15 feet × $\frac{5}{12}$ = 6.25. The answer is **a**.

7. Multiply 20 × 20 to get the total time. Convert the answer, 400, from minutes to hours by dividing by 60, to get $6\frac{2}{3}$, or 6 hours, 40 minutes. From noon to 2 p.m. is 2 hours. Subtract the remaining 4 hours and 40 minutes from 12 noon; think of 12 noon as 11 plus 60 minutes. 11:60 − 4:40 = 7:20 A.M.

Perimeter and Area Formulas
Rectangle

Area: length times width $(A = lw)$. One side times the other side tells you how many fit inside.

Perimeter: 2 length + 2 width $(2l + 2w)$. To measure all the way around something rectangular, you need to include 2 lengths and 2 widths—that's all four sides.

CBEST MINI-COURSE

Square
Measuring the area and perimeter of a square is basically the same as a rectangle, only the length and width are the same measurement.

>   Area: side × side
>   Perimeter: side × 4

Triangle
Remember that a triangle is half a rectangle.

>   Area: $\frac{1}{2} b \times h$. Multiply the height and the base. Since the triangle is half, divide by two. Note: The height of a triangle is not always one of the sides. For example, in triangle *ABC* which follows, side *AB* is not the height, *BD* is the height. *AC* is the base. To find the area, ignore all the numbers but the base and the height. The base can be found by adding 4 and 8: 4 + 8 = 12. The height is 5. $\frac{1}{2} \times 5 \times 12 = \frac{60}{2}$ or 30.

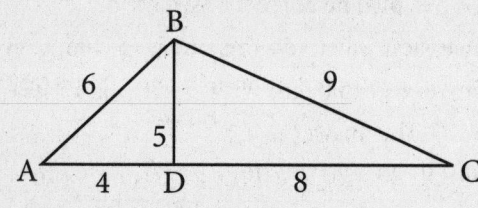

Perimeter: Add the sides all around: 12 + 6 + 9 = 27

Circle

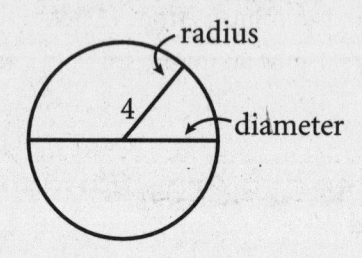

The **diameter** of a circle goes from one point on the circle, through the middle, and all the way across to another point on the circle. The radius *(r)* is half of the diameter. When working with π, consider the following: The symbol π is usually found in the answers so you don't have to worry about converting it to a number. But if π is not found in the answers, and the question calls for an approximate answer, substitute 3 for π. The question may tell you to use $\frac{22}{7}$ or 3.14.

>   Area: πr^2. Square the radius and look at the answers. If π is not found in the answers, multiply by 3. In the example above, $A = \pi 4^2$ or 16π.
>   Circumference: $2\pi r$. Circumference is to a circle what perimeter is to a rectangle. Multiply the radius by 2 and look for the answers. If π is not in the answer choices, multiply by 3. In the example above, the circumference is 2π4, or 8π.

Other Areas
Cut the figure into pieces, find the area of each, and add. If you're asked to find the area of a figure with a piece cut out of it, find the area of the whole figure, find the area of the piece, and subtract.

Other Perimeters
For any perimeter, just add the outside lengths all the way around.

Practice
8. Find the area of a circle with a diameter of 6.
   a. 36π
   b. 24π
   c. 16π
   d. 9π
   e. 6π

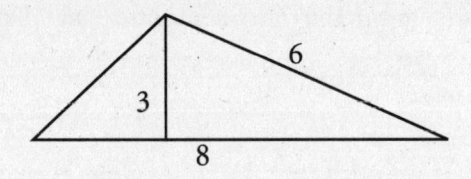

9. What is the area of the triangle above?
a. 48
b. 9
c. 12
d. 18
e. 24

10. A box measured 5" wide, $\frac{1}{2}$' long, and 4" high. How many one-inch cube candies could fit in the box?
a. 10 candies
b. 60 candies
c. 90 candies
d. 120 candies
e. 150 candies

Answers
8. d. If the diameter is 6, the radius is 3. $A = \pi(3)^2 = 9\pi$.
9. c. 8 is the base, b, and 3 is the height, h. $\frac{1}{2} \times 8 \times 3 = 12$.
10. d. The words "one-inch cube" are there to throw you off; volume is always measured in one unit cubic space. Since $\frac{1}{2}$ foot = 6 inches: $6 \times 4 \times 5 = 120$.

▶ Math 6: Ratios, Proportions, and Percents

Ratios and proportions, along with their cousins, percents, are reportedly on every CBEST. A good understanding of these topics can help you pick up valuable points on the math section of the test.

The Three-Step Ratio
The three-step ratio asks for the ratio of one quantity to another.

> **Three Success Steps for Three-Step Ratios**
> 1. Put the quantities in the same units of measurement (inches, yards, seconds, etc.).
> 2. Put the quantities in order and in the form given by the answer choices.
> 3. If the answer you come up with isn't a choice, reduce.

Sample Three-Step Ratio Question
Use the three steps above to help you work out the following problem.

1. Which of the following expresses the ratio of 2 yards to 6 inches?
a. 1:3
b. 3:1
c. 1:12
d. 9:1
e. 12:1

Answer
1. One yard is 36 inches, so 2 yards is 72 inches. Thus, the ratio becomes 72:6. (The quantities can also be put in yards.)
2. This ratio can be expressed as $\frac{72}{6}$ or 72:6. In this problem, 72:6 is the form that is used in the answers.
3. Since the answer is not there, reduce. 72 inches: 6 inches = 12:1. The answer is **e**. Notice that choice **c**, 1:12, is backwards, and therefore incorrect.

Practice

Try the three steps on the following problems.

2. Find the ratio of 3 cups to 16 ounces.
   a. 2:3
   b. 3:16
   c. 16:3
   d. 3:1
   e. 3:2

> **HOT TIP**
> - You can almost do question 2 by the process of elimination. You know that 3:16 or 16:3 can't be right because the units haven't been converted yet. You also know that test makers like to turn the correct ratio around in order to try to catch you, so a or e must be the answer. If you know that 3 cups is more than 16 ounces, you have it made.
> - In question 3, b and c are the same quantity. There can't be two right answers, so they can be eliminated. Why change yards into feet? Six feet is two yards. Reducing 2:20 makes 1:10. Aren't these fun?

3. Find the ratio of 6 feet to 20 yards.
   a. 10:1
   b. 6:20
   c. 3:10
   d. 20:6
   e. 1:10

4. Find the ratio of 2 pounds to 4 ounces.
   a. 2:4
   b. 2:1
   c. 1:8
   d. 8:1
   e. 8:5

5. In a certain class, the ratio of children who preferred magenta to chartreuse was 3:4. What was the ratio of those who preferred magenta to the total students in the class? **Hint:** Add 3 and 4 to get the total.
   a. 7:3
   b. 3:4
   c. 4:3
   d. 3:7
   e. 4:7

6. In a certain factory, employees were either foremen or assembly workers. The ratio of foremen to assembly workers was 1 to 7. What is the ratio of the assembly workers to the total number of employees?
   a. 1:7
   b. 7:1
   c. 7:8
   d. 8:7
   e. 2:14

Answers
2. e.
3. e.
4. d.
5. d.
6. c.

The Four-Step Ratio

The four-step ratio solution is used when there are two groups of numbers: the ratio set, or the small numbers; and the actual, real-life set, or the larger numbers. One of the sets will have both numbers given, and you will be asked to find one of the numbers from the other set.

CBEST MINI-COURSE

> **Four Success Steps for Four-Step Ratios**
>
> 1. Label the categories of quantities in the problem to illustrate exactly what you're working with.
> 2. Set up the complete set in ratio form.
> 3. Set up the incomplete set in ratio form.
> 4. Cross multiply to get the missing figure.

Sample Four-Step Ratio Question

7. The ratio of home games won to total games played was 13 to 20. If home teams won 78 games, how many games were played?

Answer

This problem can be solved in four steps.

1. Notice there are two categories: home team wins and total games played. Place one category over the other in writing.

    $\frac{\text{Home wins}}{\text{Total games}}$ or $\frac{H}{T}$

    Note: This step is frequently omitted by test takers in order to save time, but the omission of this step causes most of the mistakes made on ratio problems. If you reversed the *H* and *T*, putting *T* on top, that is not wrong, as long as you make sure to put the total games on top on both sides of the equation.

2. In the problem above, the small ratio set is complete (13 to 20), and you're being asked to find the larger, real-life set. Work with the complete set first. Decide which numbers from the complete set go with each written category. Be careful; if you set up the ratio wrong, you will most probably get an answer that is one of the answer choices, but it will be the wrong answer.

    Notice which category is mentioned first: "The number of HOME games won to TOTAL games played..." Then check to see what number is first: "...was 13 to 20." Thirteen is first, so 13 goes with home games; 20 goes with the total games.

    $\frac{H}{T} = \frac{13}{20}$

3. Determine whether the remaining number in the problem best fits home wins or total games. "If home teams won 78 games" indicates that the 78 goes in the home-team row. The number of total games played isn't given, so that spot is filled with an *x*.

    $\frac{H}{T} = \frac{13}{20} = \frac{78}{x}$

4. Now cross multiply. Multiply the two numbers on opposite corners: 20 × 78. Then divide by the number that is left (13).

    $\frac{20 \times 78}{13} = \frac{1{,}560}{13} = 120$

> **HOT TIP**
>
> After you cross multiply and wind up with one fraction, you can divide a top number and the denominator by the same factor and thus avoid long computations. In the above example, 13 ÷ 13 = 1 and 78 ÷ 13 = 6.
>
> $\frac{20 \times \cancel{78}^{6}}{\cancel{13}_{1}} = 120$
>
> The problem would then be much simpler: 20 × 6 = 120.

Practice

Try the four steps on the following problems.

8. On a blueprint, $\frac{1}{2}$ inch equals 2 feet. If a hall is supposed to be 56 feet wide, how wide would the hall be on the blueprint?
   a. $1\frac{1}{6}$
   b. $4\frac{2}{3}$
   c. $9\frac{1}{3}$
   d. 14
   e. $18\frac{2}{3}$

9. In a certain recipe, 2 cups of flour are needed to serve five people. If 20 guests were coming, how much flour would be needed?
   a. 50
   b. 30
   c. 12
   d. 10
   e. 8

10. A certain district needs 2 buses for every 75 students who live out of town. If there are 225 students who live out of town, how many buses are needed?
    a. 4
    b. 6
    c. 8
    d. 10
    e. 11

Answers
8. d.
9. e.
10. b.

Percents

There are only five basic types of percent problems on the CBEST. These will be explained below. As is true with most other types of problems on the CBEST, percent problems most often appear in word-problem format. Percents can be done by using ratios or by algebra. Since ratios have just been covered, this section will explain the ratio method.

Eight Success Steps for Solving Percent Problems

Feel free to skip steps whenever you don't need them.

1. Notice the numbers. Usually you are given two numbers and are asked to find a third. Are you given the whole, the part, or both ($\frac{part}{whole}$)? Is the percent given ($\frac{percent}{100}$)? Is the percent large or small? Is it more or less than half? Sometimes you can estimate the answer enough to eliminate some alien answers.
2. If there are pronouns in the problem, write the number to which they refer above the pronoun.
3. Find the question and underline the question word. Question words can include *how much is, what is, find,* etc. In longer word problems, you may have to translate the problem into a simple question you can use to find the answer.
4. Notice the verb in the question. The quantity that is by itself on one side of the verb is considered the *is*. Place this number over the number next to the *of* ($\frac{is}{of}$). If a question word is next to an *is* or *of*, put a variable in place of the number in that spot. If there is no *is* or no *of*, check to see whether one is implied. See whether you can rephrase the question, keeping the same meaning, but putting in the missing two-letter word. If all else fails, check to make sure the part is over the whole.
5. Place the percent over 100. If there is no percent, put a variable over 100 ($\frac{percent}{100}$).
6. Make the two fractions equal to each other.
7. Solve as you would a ratio.
8. Be sure to answer the question that was asked.

Percents can be fairly simple if you memorize these few relationships: $\frac{is}{of}, \frac{part}{whole}, \frac{percent}{100}$.

Sample Question: Finding Part of a Whole

11. There are 500 flights out of Los Angeles every hour. Five percent are international flights. How many international flights leave Los Angeles every hour?

Answer

1. You are being asked to find a part of the 500 flights. The 500 flights is the whole. The percent is 5. You need to find the part. 5% is fairly small, and considering that 20% of 500 is 100, you know your answer will be less than 100.
2. The second sentence has an implied pronoun. The sentence can be rephrased "Five percent *of them* are international flights." "Them" refers to the number 500.
3. The question is "How many. . . ." Use the other sentences to reconstruct the question so it includes all the necessary information. The problem is asking "5% of 500 (them) are how many (international flights)?" The question is now conveniently set up.
4. "Are" is the verb. 500 and 5% are on the left side of the verb and "how many" is on the right side. "How many" is all by itself, so it goes on top of the ratio in the form of a variable. 500 is next to the *of* so it goes on the bottom. At this point, check to see that the part is over the whole.

   $\frac{x}{500} =$

5. The 5 goes over 100.

   $\frac{x}{500} \quad \frac{5}{100}$

6. The two are equal to each other.

   $\frac{x}{500} = \frac{5}{100}$

7. Solve.

   $\frac{500 \times 5}{100} = \frac{\cancel{500} \times 5}{\cancel{100}} = 25$

8. 25 international flights leave every hour.

Sample Question: Finding the Whole

12. In a certain laboratory, 60%, or 12, of the mice worked a maze in less than one minute. How many mice were there in the laboratory?

Answer

Once again, follow the eight Success Steps to solving this problem.

1. 12 is part of the total number of mice in the laboratory. 60 is the percent, which is more than half. 12 must be more than half of the whole.
2. There are no pronouns.
3. The problem is asking, "60% of what number (total mice) is 12?"
4. "Is" is the verb. The 12 is all by itself on the right of the verb. "What number" is next to the *of*. The 12 goes on top, the variable on the bottom.

   $\frac{12}{x}$

5. The 60 goes over 100.

   $\frac{60}{100}$

6. The two fractions are equal to each other.

   $\frac{12}{x} = \frac{60}{100}$

7. Solve.

   $\frac{12 \times 100}{60} = \frac{\cancel{12}^{4} \times \cancel{100}^{5}}{\cancel{60}_{\;1}^{\;3}} = 20$

8. There were 20 mice in the laboratory.

Sample Percent Question

13. Courtney sold a car for a friend for $6,000. Her friend gave her a $120 gift for helping with the sale. What percent of the sale was the gift?

Answer

1. 6,000 is the whole and 120 the part.
2. There are no pronouns, but there are words that stand for numbers. In the question at the end, the *sale* is 6,000 and the *gift* is 120.
3. The question is written out clearly: "What percent of 6,000 (sale) was 120 (gift)?"
4. "Was" is the verb. 120 is by itself on one side. It is the part, so it goes on top. 6,000 is near the *of* and is the whole, so it goes on the bottom.

    $$\frac{120}{6,000}$$

5. There is no percent so *x* goes over 100.

    $$\frac{x}{100}$$

6. The two equal each other.

    $$\frac{120}{6,000} = \frac{x}{100}$$

7. Solve.

    $$\frac{120 \times 100}{6,000} = \frac{\overset{2}{\cancel{120}} \times \overset{1}{\cancel{100}}}{\underset{1}{\cancel{\underset{\cancel{100}}{6,000}}}} = 2$$

8. The gift was 2% of the sale.

Sample Percent Change Question

A change problem is a little bit different than a basic percent problem. To solve it, just remember change goes over old: $\frac{change}{old}$.

14. The Handy Brush company made $500 million in sales this year. Last year, the company made $400 million. What was the percent increase in sales this year?

Answer

First of all, what was the change in sales? Yes, 100 million. You got that by subtracting the two numbers. Which number is the oldest? Last year is older than this year, so 400 is the oldest. Therefore, 100 goes over 400.

$$\frac{100}{400}$$

The percent is the unknown figure, so a variable is placed over 100 and the two are made equal to each other. Cross multiply and solve for *x*.

$$\frac{100}{400} = \frac{x}{100} \quad \frac{100 \times \cancel{100}}{\cancel{400}} = \frac{100}{4} = 25$$

The answer is 25%. Note that if you had put 100 over 500, your answer would have come out differently.

Sample Interest Question

15. How much interest will Jill earn if she deposits $5,000 at 3% interest for six months?

Answer

Interest is a percent problem with time added. The formula for interest is $I = PRT$. *I* is the interest. *P* is the principal, *R* is the rate or percent, and *T* is the time in years. To find the interest, you simply multiply everything together. Be sure to put the time in years. You may change the percent to a decimal, or place it over 100.

$5,000 (principal) × 0.03 (percent) × $\frac{1}{2}$ (year) = $75.

▶ Math 7: Algebra

Algebra is like a perfectly balanced scale. The object is to keep both sides balanced while isolating the part you need on one side of the scale. For example, suppose you know a novel weighs 8 ounces and you want to find out how much your thick phone book weighs. You have five novels on one side of the scale, and your phone book and two novels on the other side. They perfectly balance. By taking two novels off each side, your phone book is alone and perfectly balances with the three novels on the other side. Then you know that your phone book weighs 3 × 8, or 24 ounces.

Plugging in Numbers

There are several types of algebra problems you may see on the CBEST. The first consists of a formula, perhaps one you have never seen, such as $Y = t + Z - 3z$. You think, "I have never seen this..." and you are tempted to skip it. But wait... you read the question: What is Y if $t = 5$, $Z = 12$, and $z = 1$? All you do is plug in the numbers and do simple arithmetic.

$$Y = t + Z - 3z$$
$$Y = 5 + 12 - 3(1) = 14$$

Sample Question

1. Given the equation below, if $t = 5$ and $h = 7$, what is Q?

   $$Q = t^2 - 3h$$

Answer

You were right if you said 4.

$$Q = t^2 - 3h$$
$$Q = 5^2 - 3(7)$$
$$Q = 25 - 21 = 4$$

Solving an Equation

In the second type of question, you may actually be called upon to do algebra.

Three Success Steps for Algebra Problems

In order to make a problem less confusing, try the WHO method:
1. What numbers are on the same side as the variable? There are two sides of the equal sign, the right side and the left side.
2. How are the numbers and the variable connected?
3. The Opposite is what? The opposite of subtraction is addition.

Sample Algebra Question

2. Given the equation below, if $Q = 15$ and $h = 1$, what is the value of t?

   $$Q = t - 3h$$

Answer

First, plug in the numbers you know and do as much arithmetic as you can:

$$Q = t - 3h$$
$$15 = t - 3(1)$$
$$15 = t - 3$$

1. What numbers are on the same side as the variable? 3
2. How are the numbers and the variable connected? With a minus sign.
3. The Opposite is what? Addition.

With that, add 3 to both sides to get your answer:

$$\begin{array}{r} 15 = t - 3 \\ +3 \quad +3 \\ \hline 18 = t \end{array}$$

Practice

Try these problems. You can probably do them in your head, but it's a good idea to practice the algebra because the problems get harder later.

3. $3x = 21$ $x = 7$

4. $6 + x = 31$ $x = 25$

5. $x - 7 = 24$ $x = 31$

6. $\frac{x}{3} = 9$ $x = 27$

7. $\frac{1}{3}x = 5$ $x = 15$

Answers
3. $x = 7$
4. $x = 25$
5. $x = 31$
6. $x = 27$
7. $x = 15$

Other Operations You Can Use
The following are some other ways you can manipulate algebra on the CBEST.

Square Both Sides
When you're faced with a problem like $\sqrt{x} = 5$, you have to get x out from under the square root sign in order to solve it. The way to do this is to square both sides of the equation. Squaring is the opposite of a square root, and cancels it.

$$\sqrt{x} = 5$$
$$\sqrt{x}^2 = 5^2$$
$$x = 25$$

Take the Square Root of Both Sides
If the variable is squared, take the square root of both sides.

$$x^2 = 25$$
$$\sqrt{x^2} = \sqrt{25}$$
$$x = 5$$

Flip Both Sides
If the answer calls for x and the x ends up as a denominator, the answer is unacceptable as is, because the question called for x, not $\frac{1}{x}$. If you have gotten this far in a problem, you can find the answer easily by flipping both sides.

$$\frac{1}{x} = \frac{6}{7}$$
$$\frac{x}{1} = \frac{7}{6}$$
$$x = \frac{7}{6} \text{ or } 1\frac{1}{6}$$

Divide by a Fraction
To divide by a fraction, you take the reciprocal of the fraction and multiply.

$$\frac{3}{5}x = 15$$

Since the reciprocal of $\frac{3}{5}$ is $\frac{5}{3}$, multiply both sides by $\frac{5}{3}$:

$$\left(\frac{5}{3}\right)\frac{3}{5}x = 15\left(\frac{5}{3}\right)$$
$$x = \frac{15}{1}\left(\frac{5}{3}\right)$$

Reduce the fractions and multiply:

$$x = \frac{\cancel{15}^5}{1}\left(\frac{5}{\cancel{3}_1}\right) = 25$$

Practice
Solve for x:

8. $x^2 = 144$
9. $\sqrt{x} = 7$
10. $\frac{1}{x} = \frac{3}{4}$
11. $\frac{2}{3}x = 14$

Answers
8. 12
9. 49
10. $\frac{4}{3}$ or $1\frac{1}{3}$
11. 21

Multi-Step Problems

Now that you have mastered every algebraic trick you will need, let's juggle them around a little by doing multi-step problems. Remember the order of operations: Please Excuse My Dear Aunt Sally—Parentheses, Exponents, Multiply and Divide, Add and Subtract? That order was necessary when putting numbers together. In algebra, numbers are pulled apart to isolate one variable. In general, then, it is easier to reverse the order of operations—add and subtract, then multiply and divide, then take square roots and exponents. Here is an example:

$$35 = 4x - 3$$

In this problem, you would add the 3 to both sides first. There is nothing wrong with dividing the 4 first, but remember, you must divide the whole side like this:

$$\frac{35}{4} = \frac{4x - 3}{4} \text{ or } \frac{35}{4} = \frac{4x}{4} - \frac{3}{4}$$

As you can see, by adding first, you avoid working with fractions, making much less work for yourself:

$$35 = 4x - 3$$
$$\underline{+3 \qquad +3}$$
$$38 = 4x$$

Then divide both sides by 4 resulting in the answer:

$$\frac{\cancel{38}^{19}}{\cancel{4}_2} = \frac{4x}{4}$$
$$x = \frac{19}{2} = 9\frac{1}{2}$$

Practice

Try these:

12. $5y - 7 = 28$ $\quad y = \frac{35}{5} = 7$

13. $x^2 + 6 = 31$ $\quad x = \sqrt{25} = 5$

14. $\frac{4}{5}x - 5 = 15$ $\quad x = 25$

15. If $a - 2b = c$, what is a in terms of b and c?
    Hint: When a question calls for a variable in terms of other variables, manipulate the equation until that variable is on a side by itself.
    $a = c + 2b$

16. If $\frac{p}{3} + g = f$, what is p in terms of g and f?
    $p = 3(f - g)$

Answers

12. $y = 7$
13. $x = 5$
14. $x = 25$
15. $a = c + 2b$
16. $p = 3(f - g)$

Problems Involving Variables

Sometimes you'll find a problem on CBEST that has almost no numbers in it.

Sample Variable Question

17. John has 3 more than 10 times as many students in his choir class than Janet has in her special education class. If the number of students in John's class is v, and the number in Janet's class is s, which of the equations below does NOT express the information above?
    a. $v = 3 + 10s$
    b. $v - 3 = 10s$
    c. $\frac{v - 3}{10} = s$
    d. $10s - v = -3$
    e. $v + 3 = 10s$

Answer

After reading question 17, you're likely to come up with the equation in answer **a**. Since **a** is correct, it is not the right choice. Now manipulate the equation to see whether you can find an equivalent equation. If you subtract 3 from each side, answer **b** will result. From there, dividing both sides by 10, you come up with **c**. All those are equivalent equations. Choice **d** can be derived by using **b** and subtracting *v* from both sides. Choice **e** is not an equivalent and is therefore the correct answer.

Distance, Rate, and Time Problems

One type of problem made simpler by algebra are those involving distance, rate, and time. Your math review would not be complete unless you had at least one problem about trains leaving the station.

Three Success Steps for Distance, Rate, and Time Problems

1. First, write the formula. Don't skip this step! The formula for Distance, Rate, and Time is $D = R \times T$. Remember this by putting all the letters in alphabetical order and putting in the equal sign as soon as possible. Or think of the word *DIRT* where the *I* stands for *is*, which is always an equal sign.
2. Fill in the information.
3. Work the problem.

Sample Distance Problem

18. A train left the station near your home and went at a speed of 50 miles per hour for 3 hours. How far did it travel?
   a. 50 miles
   b. 100 miles
   (c.) 150 miles
   d. 200 miles
   e. 250 miles

Answer

Use the three Success Steps to work through the problem.

1. $D = R \times T$
2. $D = 50 \times 3$
3. $50 \times 3 = 150$

Practice

Try these:

19. How fast does a dirt bike go if it goes 60 miles every 3 hours?

20. How long does it take to go 180 miles at 60 miles per hour?

Answers

19. $R = 20$
20. $T = 3$

HOT TIP

Another way to look at the distance formula is

$$\frac{D}{R|T}$$

When you're working out a problem, cross out the letter that represents the value you need to find. What remains will tell you the operation you need to perform to get the answer: the horizontal line means divide and the vertical line means multiply. For example, if you need to find *R*, cross it out. You're left with *D* and *T*. The line between them tells you to divide, so that's how you'll find *R*. This is a handy way to remember the formula, especially on tests, but use the method that makes the most sense to you.

▶ Math 8: Averages, Probability, and Combinations

In this lesson, you'll have a chance to do sample average questions as well as problems on probability and on the number of possible combinations. They may be a little more advanced than those you did in school, but they will not be difficult for you if you master the information in this section.

Averages

You probably remember how you solved average problems way back in elementary school. You added up the numbers, divided by the number of numbers, and the average popped out. Here's this process in algebraic form:

$$\frac{\text{Sum of the Numbers}}{\text{Number of Numbers}} = \text{Average}$$

What makes CBEST average problems more difficult is that not all the numbers will be given for you to add. You'll have to find some of the numbers.

Four Success Steps for Average Problems

1. In order to use the formula above, draw the horizontal line that is under the sum and over the number of numbers in the average formula.
2. Write in all the information you know. Put the number of numbers under the line and the average beside the line. Unless you know the whole sum, leave the top of the line blank.
3. Multiply the number of numbers by the average. This will give you the sum of the numbers.
4. Using this sum, solve the problem.

Sample Average Question

1. Sean loved to go out with his friends, but he knew he'd be grounded if he didn't get 80% for the semester in his English class. His test scores were as follows: 67%, 79%, 75%, 82%, and 78%. He had two more tests left to go. One was tomorrow, but his best friend Jason had invited him to his birthday party tonight. If he studied very hard and got 100% on his last test, what could he get by with tomorrow and still have a chance at the 80%?
   a. 65%
   b. 72%
   c. 76.2%
   d. 79%
   e. 80.2%

Answer

Use the four Success Steps to solve the problem.

1. Draw the horizontal line: ————
2. Write in the information: $\frac{\quad}{7} = 80\%$
3. Multiply the *number of numbers* by the *average* to obtain the *sum of the numbers*: 7 × 80 = 560
4. 560 has to be the final *sum of the numbers*. So far, if you add up all the scores, Sean has a total of 381. With the 100 he plans to get on the last test, his total will be 481. Since he needs a sum of 560 for the average of the seven tests to come out 80, he needs 79 more points. The answer is **d**.

Sample Average Question

2. On an overseas trip, Jackie and her husband are allowed five suitcases that average 110 pounds each. They want to pack in all the peanut butter and mango nectar they can carry to their family in Italy. They weighed their first four suitcases and the weights were as follows: 135, 75, 90, and

120. How much weight are they allowed to stuff into their fifth bag?

Answer
1. Draw the horizontal line: ⎯⎯⎯⎯
2. Write in the information: $\frac{}{5} = 110$
3. Multiply the *number of numbers* by the *average* to obtain the *sum of the numbers*:
   $5 \times 110 = 550$.
4. Since the total weight they can carry is 550 lb. and they already have 420 lb. (135 + 75 + 90 + 120), the fifth suitcase can weigh as much as 550 − 420, or 130 lbs.

Frequency Charts

Some average problems on the CBEST use frequency charts.

Four Success Steps for Frequency Chart Questions

1. Read the question and look at the chart. Make sure you understand what the different columns represent.
2. If a question asks you to find the average, multiply the numbers in the first column by the numbers in the second column.
3. Add the figures you got by multiplying.
4. Divide the total sum by the sum of the left column. This will give you the average.

Sample Frequency Chart Question

3. The following list shows class scores for an easy Science 101 quiz. What is the average of the scores?

# of Students	Score
10	100
15	90
3	80
2	70

a. 28.5
b. 85
c. 91
d. 95
e. 100

Answer
Use the four Success Steps to solve the problem.

1. In this frequency chart, the test score is given on the right, and the number of students who received each grade is on the left: 10 students got 100, 15 got a 90, etc.
2. Multiply the number of students by the score, because to find the average, each student's grade has to be added individually:

   $10 \times 100 = 1,000$

   $15 \times 90 = 1,350$

   $3 \times 80 = 240$

   $2 \times 70 = 140$

3. Then add the multiplied scores:

   $1,000 + 1,350 + 240 + 140 = 2,730$

4. Then divide the total number of students, 30 (10 + 15 + 3 + 2), into 2,730 to get the average:

   $\frac{2,730}{30} = 91$.

CBEST MINI-COURSE

Other Average Problems

There are other kinds of averages besides the *mean,* which is usually what is meant when the word *average* is used:

- *Median* is the middle number in a range.
- *Mode* is the number that occurs most frequently.
- *Range* is the difference between the highest and lowest number.

Sample Median Question

4. What is the median of 6, 8, 3, 9, 4, 3, and 12?
   a. 2
   b. 6
   c. 9
   d. 10
   e. 12

Answer

To get a *median,* put the numbers in order—3, 3, 4, 6, 8, 9, 12—and choose the middle number: 6. If there are an even number of numbers, average the middle two (you probably won't have to do that on the CBEST).

Mode

The *mode* is the number used most frequently in a series of numbers. In the above example, the mode is 3 because 3 appears twice and all other numbers are used only once. Look again at the frequency table from the frequency chart sample question. Can you find the mode? More students (15) earned a score of 90 than any other score. Therefore the mode is 15.

Range

To obtain the *range,* subtract the smallest number from the largest number. The range in the median sample question is 12 – 3 or 9. The range in the frequency chart sample question is 100 – 70, or 30.

Probability

Suppose you put one entry into a drawing that had 700 entrants. What would be your chances of winning? 1 in 700 of course. Suppose you put in two entries. Your chances would then be 2 in 700, or reduced, 1 in 350. Probabilities are fairly simple if you remember the few tricks that are explained in this section.

Four Success Steps for Probability Questions

1. Make a fraction.
2. Place the total number of different possibilities on the bottom.
3. Place the number of the chances given on the top.
4. If the answers are in a:b form, place the numerator of the fraction first, and the denominator second.

Sample Probability Question

5. If a nickel were flipped thirteen times, what is the probability that heads would come up the thirteenth time?
   a. 1:3
   b. 1:2
   c. 1:9
   d. 1:27
   e. 1:8

Answer

Use the four Success Steps to solve the problem.
1. Form a fraction.
2. Each time a coin is flipped, there are 2 possibilities—heads or tails—so 2 goes on the bottom of the fraction. The thirteenth time, there are still going to be only two possibilities.
3. The number of chances given is 1. There is only one head on a coin. Therefore, the fraction is $\frac{1}{2}$.

"Thirteen times" is extra information and does not have a bearing on this case.

4. The answer is b, 1:2. The numerator goes to the left of the colon and the denominator to the right.

Sample Probability Question

6. A spinner is divided into 6 parts. The parts are numbered 1–6. When a player spins the spinner, what are the chances the player will spin a number less than 3?

Answer

Once again, use the four Success Steps.

1. Form a fraction.
2. Total number of possibilities = 6. Therefore, 6 goes on the bottom.
3. Two goes on top, since there are 2 numbers less than 3: 1 and 2.
4. The answer is $\frac{2}{6}$ or reduced $\frac{1}{3}$ = 1:3.

Combinations

Combination problems require the solver to make as many groups as possible given certain criteria. There are many different types of combination problems, so these questions need to be read carefully before attempting to solve them. One of the easiest ways to make combination problems into CBEST points is to make a chart and list in a pattern all the possibilities. The following sample question is a typical CBEST combination problem.

Sample Combination Question

7. Shirley had three pairs of slacks and four blouses. How many different combinations of one pair of slacks and one blouse could she make?
   a. 3
   b. 4
   c. 7
   d. 12
   e. 15

Answer

To see this problem more clearly, you may want to make a chart:

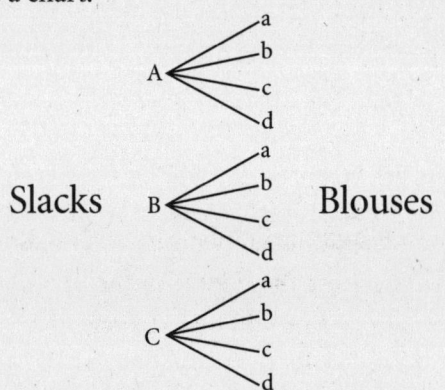

Each pair of slacks can be matched to 4 different blouses, making 4 different outfits for each pair of the 3 pairs of slacks, 3 × 4, making a total of 12 possible combinations.

Sample Combination Question

9. Five tennis players each played each other once. How many games were played?
   a. 25
   b. 20
   c. 15
   d. 10
   e. 5

Answer

This combination problem is a little trickier in that there are not separate groups of items as there were for the slacks and blouses. This question involves the same players playing each other. But solving it is not difficult. First, take the total number of players and subtract one: 5 − 1 = 4. Add the numbers from 4 down: 1 + 2 + 3 + 4 = 10. To learn how this works, take a look at the following chart:

Letter the five players from A to E:

- A plays B, C, D, and E (4 games)
- B has already played A, so needs to play C, D, E (3 games)
- C has already played A and B, so needs to play D, E (2 games)
- D has already played A, B, and C, so needs to play E (1 game)
- E has played everyone

Adding up the number of games played (1 + 2 + 3 + 4) gives a total of 10, choice **d**.

This same question might be asked on the CBEST using the number of games 5 chess players played or the number of handshakes that occur when 5 people shake hands with each other once.

Other Combination Problems

Although the above combination problems are the most common, other kinds of problems are possible. The best way to solve other combination problems is to make a chart. When you notice a pattern, stop and multiply. For example, if you're asked to make all the possible combinations of three letters using the letters A through D, start with A:

AAA	ABA	ACA	ADA
AAB	ABB	ACB	ADB
AAC	ABC	ACC	ADC
AAD	ABD	ACD	ADD

There seem to be 16 possibilities that begin with A, so probably there are 16 that begin with B and 16 that begin with C and D, so multiplying 16 × 4 will give you the total possible combinations: 64.

▶ Math 9: The Word Problem Game

The directions for the word problem game are simple: While carefully observing a word problem, find all the math words and numbers in the problem. Eliminate the nonessential words and facts in order to find your answer.

Operations in Word Problems

To prepare for the game, make five columns on a sheet of paper. Write one of these words on the top of each column: **Add, Subtract, Multiply, Divide, Equals**. Now try to think of five words that tell you to add, five that tell you to subtract, and so on. If you can think of five for each column, you win the first round. If you can't think of five, you can cheat by looking at the list below.

How did you do?

0 = keep studying
1–3 for each = good
4–6 for each = excellent
7+ for each = Why are you reading this book?

- **Add:** sum, plus, more than, larger than, greater than, and, increased by, added to, in all, altogether, total, combined with, together, lengthened by

CBEST MINI-COURSE

- **Subtract:** difference, minus, decreased by, reduced by, diminished by, less, take away, subtract, lowered by, dropped by, shortened by, lightened by, less, **less than, subtracted from, take from, deducted from.** Note: The words in bold are *backwardswords.* (See below.)
- **Multiply:** product, times, of, multiplied by, twice, thrice, squared, cubed, doubled, tripled, rows of, columns of
- **Divide:** quotient of, ratio of, halved, per, split, equal parts of, divided by, **divided into, reciprocal.** Note: The words in bold are *backwardswords.* (See below.)
- **Equals:** is, equal to, the same as, amounts to, equivalent to, gives us, represents

Backwardswords

Backwardswords are words in a word problem that tend to throw off test takers; they indicate the opposite of which the numbers appear in the problem. Only subtraction and division have *backwardswords*. Addition and multiplication come out the same no matter which number is written first: 2 + 6 is the same as 6 + 2, but 2 – 6 is not the same as 6 – 2. Using the numbers 10 and 7, notice the following translations:

Subtraction:
10 *minus* 7 is the same as 10 – 7
10 *take away* 7 is 10 – 7
10 *less* 7 is the same as 10 – 7
But 10 *less than* 7 is the opposite, 7 – 10
10 *subtracted from* 7 is also 7 – 10

Division:
10 *over* 7 is written $\frac{10}{7}$
The *quotient of* 10 and 7 is $\frac{10}{7}$
But 10 *divided into* 7 is written $\frac{7}{10}$
And the *reciprocal of* $\frac{10}{7}$ is $\frac{7}{10}$

HOT TIP
When setting up division problems in algebra, avoid using the division sign: ÷. Instead, use the division line: $\frac{3}{4}$.

Writing Word Problems in Algebraic Form

Four Success Steps for Converting Words to Algebra

In order to make an equation out of words use these steps:
1. Find the verb. The verb is always the = sign.
2. Write in the numbers.
3. Write in the symbols for the other code words. Be careful of backwardswords.
4. If necessary, add parentheses.

Sample Word Conversion Questions

The following are simple problems to rewrite in algebraic form. Using *N* for a number, try writing out the problems below. Remember to add parentheses as needed to avoid order of operation problems.

1. Three added to a number represents 6. $3 + N = 6$
2. Six subtracted from a number is 50. $N - 6 = 50$

Answers

Use the four Success Steps to find the answer to question 1.

1. "Represents" is the verb. Put in an equal sign: =
2. 3, 6, and *N* are the numbers: 3   *N* = 6
3. *Added* means +: 3 + *N* = 6
4. No parentheses are needed.

Follow the Success Steps for question 2.

124

1. "Is" is the verb. Put in an equal sign: =
2. 6, N, and 50 are the numbers: 6 N = 50.
3. *Subtracted from* means –, but it is a backwardsword: N – 6 = 50.
4. No parentheses are needed.

Practice

Underline the backwardswords, then write the equations.

3. A number subtracted from 19 is 7. $19 - N = 17$

4. 3 less a number is 5. $3 - N = 5$

5. 3 less than a number is 5. $N - 3 = 5$

6. 9 less a number is –8. $9 - N = -8$

7. A number taken from 6 is –10. $6 - N = -10$

8. 30 deducted from a number is 99. $N - 30 = 99$

9. The quotient of 4 and a number equals 2. $\frac{4}{N} = 2$

10. The reciprocal of 5 over a number is 10. $\frac{5}{N} > \frac{N}{5} = 10$

11. 6 divided into a number is 3. $\frac{N}{6} = 3$

Change the following sentences into algebraic equations.

12. The sum of 60 and a number all multiplied by 2 amounts to 128. $(60 + N)2 = 128$

13. Forty combined with twice a number is 46. $40 + 2N = 46$

14. $9 fewer than a number costs $29. $N - \$9 = \$29$

15. 7 feet lengthened by a number of feet all divided by 5 is equivalent to 4 feet. $\frac{(7+N)}{5} = 4$

16. 90 subtracted from the sum of a number and one gives us 10. $(N+1) - 9 = 10$

17. Half a number plus 12 is the same as 36. $\frac{N}{2} + 12 = 36$

Answers

3. subtracted from, $19 - N = 7$
4. $3 - N = 5$
5. less than, $N - 3 = 5$
6. $9 - N = -8$
7. taken from, $6 - N = -10$
8. deducted from, $N - 30 = 99$
9. $\frac{4}{N} = 2$
10. reciprocal of, $\frac{N}{5} = 10$
11. divided into, $\frac{N}{6} = 3$
12. $(60 + N)2 = 128$ or $2(60 + N) = 128$
13. $40 + 2N = 46$
14. $N - \$9 = \$29$
15. $\frac{7+N}{5} = 4$
16. $(N+1) - 90 = 10$
17. $\frac{N}{2} + 12 = 36$ or $\frac{1}{2}N + 12 = 36$

Words or Numbers?

Try these two problems and determine which is easier for you.

1. Three more than five times a number equals 23. $3 + 5(N) = 23$
2. Jack had three more than five times the number of golf balls than Ralph had. If Jack had 23 golf balls, how many did Ralph have? $3 + 5N = 23$

Answers: 1. $23 = 3 + 5N$
          2. $23 = 3 + 5N$

Did you notice that the two problems were the same, but the second one was more wordy? If question 1 was easier, you can work word problems more easily by eliminating non-essential words. If question 2 was easier, you can work out problems more easily by picturing actual situations. If they were both equally easy, then you have mastered this section. Go on to the section on two-variable problems, which is a little more difficult.

Practice
If you found wordy word problems difficult, here are some more to try:

18. Sally bought 6 less than twice the number of boxes of CDs that Raphael (R) bought. If Sally bought 4 boxes, how many did Raphael buy?

19. A 1-inch by 13-inch rectangle is cut off a piece of linoleum that was made up of three squares; each had N inches on a side. This left 62 square inches left to the original piece of linoleum. How long was each of the sides of the squares?

20. Six was added to the number of sugar cubes in a jar. After that, the number was divided by 5. The result was 6. How many sugar cubes were in the jar?

Answers
18. Sally = $2R - 6$. Substitute 4 for Sally: $4 = 2R - 6$
19. $(N^2 \times 3) - (1 \times 13) = 62$. N is the side of a square so the area of the square is N^2. There were three squares, so you have $3N^2$. 1×13 was taken away ($-$). Notice that the parentheses, while not strictly necessary if you follow the order of operations, will help you keep track of the numbers.
20. $\frac{6+N}{5} = 6$

Problems with Two Variables
In solving problems with two variables, you have to watch out for another backwards phrase: *as many as*.

Three Success Steps for Problems with Two Variables
When turning "as many as" sentences into equations, consider the following steps.
1. Read the problem to decide which variable is least.
2. Combine the number given with the least variable.
3. Make the combined number equal to the larger amount.

Sample Two-Variable Questions
The following equations require the use of two variables. Choose the answers from the following:

a. $2x = y$
b. $2y = x$
c. $2 + x = y$
d. $2 + y = x$
e. none of the above

21. Twice the number of letters Joey has equals the number of letters Tina has. Joey = x, Tina = y.

22. Tuli corrected twice as many homework assignments as tests. Homework = x, tests = y.

Answers
21. a. "Equals" is the verb. Joey or x is on one side of the verb, Tina or y is on the other. A straight rendering will give you the answer **a**, or $2x = y$, because Tina has twice as many letters. To check, plug in 6 for y. If Tina has 6 letters, Joey will have $6 \div 2$, or 12. The answer makes sense.

22. b. "Corrected" is the verb. Which did Tuli correct fewer of? Tests. You need to multiply 2 times the tests to reach the homework assignments. **Check:**

If there are 6 tests, then there are 12 homework assignments: 2 × 6 = 12. This answer makes sense.

Practice

Now that you are clued in, try the following using the same answer choices as above.

   a. $2x = y$
   b. $2y = x$
   c. $2 + x = y$
   d. $2 + y = x$
   e. none of the above

23. Sandra found two times as many conch shells as mussel shells. Conch = x, mussel = y.

24. Sharon walked two more miles today than she walked yesterday. Today = x, yesterday = y.

25. Martin won two more chess games than his brother won. His brother = x, Martin = y.

Answers
23. b.
24. d.
25. c.

▶ Math 10: The CA Approach to Word Problems

Of course, it helps to know the formula or method needed to solve a problem. But there are always those problems on the test that you don't recognize or can't remember how to do, and this may cause you a little anxiety. Even experienced math teachers experience that paralyzing feeling at times. But you shouldn't allow anxiety to conquer you. Nor should you jump into a problem and start figuring madly without a careful reading and analysis of the problem.

The CA SOLVE Approach

When approaching a word problem, you need the skills of a detective. Follow the CA SOLVE method to uncover the mystery behind a problem that is unfamiliar to you.

C Stands for Conquer

Conquer that queasy feeling—don't let it conquer you. To squelch it, try step *A*.

A Stands for Answer

Look at the **answers** and see if there are any similarities among them. Notice the form in which the answers are written. Are they all in cubic inches? Do they all contain pi? Are they formulas?

S Stands for Subject Experience

Many problems are taken from real life situations or are based on methods you already know. Ask: "Do I have any **experience** with this **subject** or with this type of problem? What might a problem about the subject be asking me? Can I remember anything that might relate to this problem?"

Eliminate experiences or methods of solving that don't seem to work. But be careful; sometimes sorting through your experiences and methods memory takes a long time.

O Stands for Organize the Facts

Here are some ways to **Organize** your data:

1. Look for clue words in the problem that tell you to add, subtract, multiply, or divide.
2. Try out each answer to see which one works. Look for answers to eliminate.
3. Think of formulas or methods that have worked for you in solving problems like this in the past. Write them down. There should be plenty of room on your test booklet for this.

HOT TIP

Don't try to keep a formula in your head as you solve the problem. Although writing does take time and effort, jotting down a formula is well worth it for three reasons: 1) A formula on paper will clear your head to work with the numbers; 2) You will have a visual image of the formula you can refer to and plug numbers into; 3) The formula will help you see exactly what operations you will need to perform to solve the problem.

L Stands for Live

Living the problem means pretending you're actually in the situation described in the word problem. To do this effectively, make up details concerning the events and the people in the problem as if you were part of the picture. This process can be done as you are reading the problem and should take only a few seconds.

V Stands for View

View the problem with different numbers while keeping the relationships between the numbers the same. Use the simplest numbers you can think of. If a problem asked how long it would take a rocket to go 1,300,000 miles at 650 MPH, change the numbers to 300 miles at 30 MPH. Solve the simple problem, and then solve the problem with the larger numbers the same way.

E Stands for Eliminate

Eliminate answers you know are wrong. You may also spend a short time checking your answer if there is time.

Sample Question

Solve this problem using the SOLVE steps described above.

1. There are 651 children in a school. The ratio of boys to girls is 4:3. How many boys are there in the school?
   a. 40
   b. 325
   c. 372
   d. 400
   e. 468

Answer

1. **Subject Experience:** You know that 4 and 3 are only one apart and 4 is more. You can conclude from this that boys are a little over half the school population. Following up on that, you can cut 651 in half and eliminate any answers that are under half. Furthermore, since there are three numbers in the problem and two are paired in a ratio, you can conclude that this is a ratio problem. Then you can think about what methods you used for ratio problems in the past.

2. **Organize:** The clue word *total* means *to add*. In the context in which it is used, it must mean girls plus boys equals 651. Also, since *boys* is written before *girls*, the ratio should be written *Boys:Girls*.

3. **Live:** Picture a group of three girls and four boys. Now picture more of these groups, so many that the total would equal 651.

4. **View:** If there were only 4 boys and 3 girls in the school, there would still be a ratio of 4 to 3. Think of other numbers that have a ratio of 4:3, like 40 and 30. If there were 40 boys and 30 girls, there would be 70 students in total, so the answer has to be more than 40 boys. Move on to 400 boys and 300 girls—700 total students. Since the total in the problem is 651, 700 is too large, but it is close, so

the answer has to be less than 400. This would narrow your choices to two.

5. **Eliminate:** Since you know from the step above that the number of students has to be less than 400, you can eliminate **d** and **e**. Since you know that the number of boys is more than half the school population, you can eliminate **a** and **b**. You are left with **c**, the correct answer.

Quick Tips and Tricks

Below is a miscellaneous list of quick tips to help you solve word problems.

Work From the Answers

On some problems, you can plug in given answers to see which one works in a problem. Start with choice **c**. Then if you need a larger number, go down, and if you need a smaller answer, go up. That way, you don't have to try them all. Consider the following problem:

1. One-fifth of what number is 30?
   a. 6
   b. 20
   c. 50
   d. 120
   e. 150

Try **c**: $\frac{1}{5}$ of 50 is 10. A larger answer is needed.

Try **d**: $\frac{1}{5}$ of 120 is 24. Not yet, but getting closer.

Try **e**: $\frac{1}{5}$ of 150 is 30—Bingo!

Problems with Multiple Variables

If there are so many variables in a problem that your head is spinning, put in your own numbers. Make a chart of the numbers that go with each variable so there is less chance for you to get mixed up. Then write your answer next to the given answer choices. Work the answers using the numbers in your chart until one works out to match your original answer. In doing this,

avoid the numbers 1 and 2 and using the same numbers twice. There may appear to be two or more right answers if you do.

Sample Multi-Variable Question

2. A man drove y miles every hour for z hours. If he gets w miles to the gallon of gas, how many gallons will he need?
   a. yzw
   b. $\frac{yz}{w}$
   c. $\frac{w}{yz}$
   d. $\frac{wy}{z}$
   e. $\frac{zw}{y}$

Answer

Picture yourself in the situation. If you drove 4 (y) miles every hour for 5 (z) hours, you would have driven 20 miles. If your car gets 10 (w) miles to the gallon, you would need 2 gallons. Since 2 is your answer, plug the numbers you came up with into the answer choices and see which one is correct. Choice **b** equals 2 and is therefore correct.

a. yzw $4 \times 5 \times 10 \neq 2$
b. $\frac{yz}{w}$ $\frac{4 \times 5}{10} = 2$
c. $\frac{w}{yz}$ $\frac{10}{4 \times 5} \neq 2$
d. $\frac{wy}{z}$ $\frac{10 \times 4}{5} \neq 2$
e. $\frac{zw}{y}$ $\frac{5 \times 10}{4} \neq 2$

Let the Answers Do the Math

When there is a lot of multiplication or division to do, you can use the answers to help you. Suppose you are asked to divide 9,765 by 31. The given answers are as follows:

a. 324
b. 316
c. 315
d. 314
e. 312

You know then that the answer will be a three-digit number and that the hundreds place will be 3. The tens place will either be 1 or 2, and more likely 1 because most of the answers have 1 in the tens place. Your division problem is practically worked out for you.

Problems with Too Much or Too Little

When you come across a problem that you think you know how to answer, but there seems to be a number left over that you just don't need in your equation, don't despair. It could very well be that the test writers threw in an extra number to throw you off. The key to not falling prey to this trick is to know your equations and check to make sure the answer you came up with makes sense.

When you come across a problem that doesn't seem to give enough information to calculate an answer, don't skip it. Read carefully, because sometimes a question asks you to set up an equation using variables, and doesn't ask you to solve the problem at all. If you are expected to actually solve a problem with what seems like too little information, experiment to discover how the information works together to lead to the answer. Try the CA tips.

More than One Way to Solve a Problem

Some questions ask you to find the only *wrong* way to solve a problem. Sometimes these are lengthy questions about children in a classroom who get the right answer the wrong way and the wrong answer the right way. In this type of question, do the computation yourself, and work from the answers. The choice that gives an answer different from the others has to be the wrong answer. Consider these choices:

a. 5% of 60
b. $\frac{5}{100} \times 60$
c. 0.05×60
d. $5 \times 60 \div 100$
e. 5×60

All of the answers compute to 3 except choice **e**, which turns out to be 300. Therefore, **e** must be the correct answer.

▶ Math 11: Logic and Venn Diagrams

You deserve a break after all your hard work on math problems. This lesson is shorter than the others; unless logic problems give you a lot of trouble, you can probably spend less than half an hour on this lesson.

If Problems

If problems are among the easiest problems on the test if you know how to work them. A genuine *if* problem begins with the word *if* and then gives some kind of rule. Generally, these problems mention no numbers. In order for the problem to be valid, the rule has to be true for *any* numbers you put in.

> **One Success Step for *If* Problems**
>
> Pick some numbers and try it out!

Sample *If* Question

The following is a typical *if* problem. Experiment with this problem to see how the answer is always the same no matter what measurements you choose to use.

CBEST MINI-COURSE

1. If the length and width of a rectangle are doubled, the area is
   a. doubled
   b. halved
   c. multiplied by 3
   d. multiplied by 4
   e. divided by 4

Answer
First of all, choose a length and width for your rectangle, like 2' by 3'. The area is 2 × 3, or 6. Now double the length and the width and find the area: 4 × 6 = 24. 24 is 4 times 6, so **d** must be the answer. Try a few different numbers for the original length and width to see how easy these types of questions can be.

Practice
Try another one:

2. If a coat was reduced 20% and then further reduced 20%, what is the total percent of discount off the original price?
   a. 28%
   b. 36%
   c. 40%
   d. 44%
   e. 50%

> **HOT TIP**
> When choosing numbers for *if* problems, choose small numbers. When working with percents, start with 100.

Answer
Since this question concerns percents, make the coat's beginning price $100. A 20% discount will reduce the cost to $80. The second time 20% is taken off, it is taken off $80, not $100. Twenty percent of 80 is 16. That brings the cost down to $64 (80 − 16 = 64). The original price of the coat, 100, minus 64 is 36. One hundred down to 64 is a 36% reduction. So two successive discounts of 20% equal not a 40%, but a 36% total reduction.

Venn Diagrams
Venn diagrams provide a way to think about groups in relationship to each other. Words such as *some, all,* and *none* commonly appear in these types of questions.

In Venn diagram problems, you are given two or more categories of objects. First, draw a circle representing one of the categories. Second, draw another circle representing the other category. Draw the second circle according to these rules:

1. If the question says that ALL of a category is the second category, place the second circle around the second category.

   Example: All pigs (p) are animals (a).

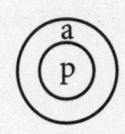

2. If the question says that SOME of a category is the second category, place the second circle so that it cuts through the first circle.

   Example: Some parrots (p) are talking birds (t).

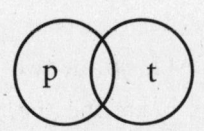

3. If the question says NO, meaning that none of the first category is in the second category, make the second circle completely separate from the first.

   Example: No cats (c) are fish (f).

CBEST MINI-COURSE

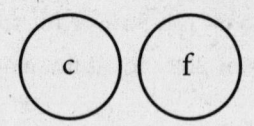

Sample Venn Diagram Question

3. All bipeds (B.) are two headed (T.H.). Which diagram shows the relationship between bipeds and two-headed?

a. [two separate circles labeled B. and T.H.]

b. [circle B. with triangle T.H. overlapping]

c. [rectangle labeled B. containing circle T.H.]

d. [square labeled T.H. containing triangle B.]

e. [two overlapping circles T.H. and B.]

Answer

The question says ALL, so the two-headed shape, in this case, a square, is around the triangle denoting bipeds. The answer is **d**.

More than Two Categories

Should there be more than two categories, proceed in the same way.

Example: Some candy bars (c) are sweet (s), but no bananas (b) are candy bars.

The sweet circle will cut through the candy bar circle. Since the problem did not specify where bananas and sweet intersect, bananas can have several positions. The banana circle can be outside both circles completely:

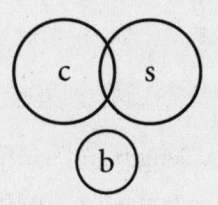

[diagram: overlapping c and s circles with b circle separate below]

The banana circle can intersect the sweet circle:

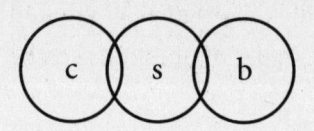

[diagram: three circles c, s, b with s overlapping both c and b]

Or the banana circle can be completely inside the sweet circle but not touching the candy bar shape:

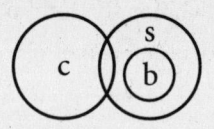

[diagram: c circle overlapping s circle, with b circle inside s]

HOT TIP

Even when there are no pictures of Venn diagrams in the answers, you can often solve this type of problem by drawing the diagram one way and visualizing all the possible positions of the circles given the facts in the problem.

132

▶ Writing 1: Outlining the Essay

You will be required to write two essays during your test time. One essay may be a persuasive essay, and the other a narrative or story essay. The persuasive essay question will ask your opinion, usually on a current or well-known issue. You will need to convince the reader of your side of the issue. The story essay question will often concern a person or event in your life that has influenced you in some way. You will need to communicate your experience to the reader in such a way that the reader will be able to understand and appreciate your experience. The evaluators are not concerned about whether or not the facts are correct—they are solely judging your writing ability.

Unlike math, writing is flexible. There are many different ways to convey the same meaning. You can pass the test with any logical arrangement of paragraphs and ideas that are "clearly communicated." Most CBEST and English instructors recommend a five-paragraph essay, which is an easy and acceptable formula. The five-paragraph essay assures that your ideas are logically and effectively arranged, and gives you a chance to develop three complete ideas. The longer and richer your essay, the better rating it will receive.

The first step in achieving such an essay is to come up with a plan or outline. You should spend the first four or five of the 30 minutes allowed in organizing your essay. This first writing lesson will show you how. The rest of the writing lessons will show you where to go from there.

Outlining the Persuasive Essay

Below are some tips on how to use your first four or five minutes in planning a persuasive essay, based on an essay topic similar to the one found in the diagnostic exam in Chapter 3.

Sample Persuasive Essay Question

1. In your opinion, should public schools require student uniforms?

Minute 1

During the first minute, read the question carefully and choose your side of the issue. If there is a side of the issue you are passionate about, the choice will be easy. If you know very little about a subject and do not have an opinion, just quickly choose a side. The test scorers don't care which side you take.

Minutes 2 and 3

Quickly answer as many of the following questions as apply to your topic. These questions can be adapted to either side of the argument. Jot down your ideas in a place on your test booklet that will be easily accessible as you write. Examples of how you might do this for the topic of school uniforms are provided here.

1. Do you know anyone who might feel strongly about the subject?
    Parents of school-age children, children, uniform companies, local children's clothing shops.
2. What reasons might they give for feeling the way they do?
    Pro: Parents will not have to worry about what school clothing to buy for their children. Children will not feel peer pressure to dress a certain way. Poorer children will not feel that their clothing is shabbier or less fashionable than that of the more affluent children. Uniform companies and fabric shops will receive business for the fine work they are doing.
    Con: Parents will not be able to dress their children creatively for school. Children will not have the opportunity to learn to dress and match their clothes very often. They will not be able to show off or talk about their new clothes. Clothing shops will lose money,

which may be bad for the economy of the town.

(Note that you can make a case for parents and children either way.)

3. If your side won the argument, who would benefit?

Uniforms may help keep discipline in the school. Lack of uniforms help children learn to make choices. And there are many other examples, on both sides.

4. If the opposing side won, who would be hurt?

Use the arguments from the opposite side and turn them around.

5. How much will it cost and who will pay? How will your side save money and the opposing side cost money?

Look at some of the pros and cons under number 2 above for some answers here.

6. Who might be an expert on the subject?

In this case, a teacher or school principal or a professor of education would make a good expert. It is helpful to quote at least one expert to show you know how to use quotation marks. You may make up the quote and the expert's name.

7. What might happen in your city, state, country and in the world should your side win? If your side was the law, what good might happen next and why? If the opposite side was the law, what evil might happen and why?

Here you take your pros and cons and extend them to the larger community. For instance, will imposing school uniforms lead to greater conformity among children? Is that a good or a bad thing?

8. How does your side affect, for the better, other current issues your readers might be passionate about; i.e., the environment, freedom of speech, and so on?

Will requiring uniforms preserve natural resources, since children will buy fewer clothes? Does requiring uniforms hinder children's (or parents') freedom of expression?

9. Should your side win, what senses—taste, smell, sight, touch, sound, and feelings—might be affected?

Think about the sight of hundreds of identically clad children versus that of hundreds of children in varied clothing, the feel of uniform fabric versus denim and T-shirts . . . or whatever fits your topic. If you can appeal to the five senses, you will have a more persuasive essay.

Minutes 4 and 5

When you have finished, organize your notes into three sub-topics. You may have three groups of people the proposal would affect. Under each, you would later write how each is affected, whether any of the groups would have to pay, and what else might happen to them. Alternately, you could have three topics such as local, state, and world that you can incorporate all your ideas into.

By the way, your essay doesn't absolutely have to have *just* three body paragraphs, though it shouldn't have *fewer* than three. It's just that three is a good, solid number of main points, so start practicing with three right from the start. You wouldn't want to be in the middle of your fourth body paragraph when time runs out.

For a persuasive essay, you should usually progress from your weakest point to your strongest one. If you were organizing, for example, under three groups of people, you might want to put the businesspeople first, the parents second, and the children last. It is easier for readers to be more passionate about children than about businesspeople. However, this is only by way of example. It could be that your businesspeople reasons affect the world, which will include the children as well as everyone else on earth. If you had three unrelated topics such as people, money, and the environment, you should start with the least persuasive argument, and end with the one you write about most convincingly.

> **HOT TIPS**
>
> Keep these tips in mind as you outline:
> - Make sure you stay on the topic you were given. If you write more about the environment than uniforms, you will be marked down.
> - Try to be realistic; do not exaggerate. Adopting uniforms at one school probably will not boost the global economy, have any significant impact on the national debt, eliminate sibling rivalry, or create lasting peace in the world. Instead of making such claims, you can use phrases such as *become more, help to,* or *work towards.* For example, you should not make an exaggerated claim like this: "Without uniforms, children will all become selfish." A more measured way to say the same thing is: "Without uniforms, children who take excessive pride in their looks might become even more self-centered."

Outlining the Narrative Essay

The process of outlining a narrative essay is similar to that of outlining a persuasive essay. You should still plan on taking the first four or five minutes for this process. The steps below will show you how to tackle a topic like this one:

Sample Narrative Essay Question

2. Describe an event from your elementary school years that has affected the way you live your life today.

Minute 1

In order to answer a question like this, you need to search your memory and pick out an event or a person that had a significant impact in your life. Although you can use a made-up person or event, it would not be to your advantage. A familiar person or event is easier to write about. You will be able to visualize the details and communicate them to your reader.

You should also try to choose an event that has had a significant impact, will grab your reader's attention, and make them feel or grow along with you. Writing about someone who inspired you to be a giving person or helped you overcome shyness is preferable to someone who taught you to avoid poison ivy or improve your penmanship. Something with a greater, more profound impact on your life is preferable to something trivial.

Minutes 2 and 3

Once you have chosen your topic, try to remember the events as they took place. Consider these questions:

1. What about you then was different than it is now?
2. Who were the principal actors?
3. How long did the situation last?
4. How did the event start, when did you first meet the person, or when were you first aware of what was happening?
5. How did you feel in the beginning?
6. How did the scene unfold?
7. What did you see, hear, taste, touch, and smell during the process?
8. What were the events that led up to the climax, and how did the climax take place?
9. How does the situation still affect you today?

Minutes 4 and 5

Place your thoughts in logical sequence on your paper. One logical sequence might be chronological order: Describe each of three parts of the event in detail and give your reactions, if necessary, as you go along. Alternately, if there are three actors, you might want to give each of them a paragraph of their own. Or you might want to write in the first paragraph about the event itself, in the second, talk about ways in which the situation affected you immediately, and in the third, explain how the situation affects you today. Any logical sequence will do. Jot the main ideas of your three sub-topics down in your test booklet and refer to them as you write. Try to limit your time to just five minutes each.

Practice

Try outlining the following essay topics using the hints above.

1. In the last three decades, environmental issues have received increasing amounts of attention. Teaching materials on this subject are abundant and some are even offered free to school districts. Given that some environmental issues should be covered, do you believe too much emphasis is being placed on environmental issues in our schools?
2. Many times in life there are choices to make. Sometimes people find themselves at a fork in life's road. Tell about such a time in your life and how you chose what road to take.

▶ Writing 2: Writing the Introduction

You have your outline. You know exactly what points you are going to make. It is time to write your introduction. The introduction can be the most fun of all the paragraphs of your essay. You will have the opportunity to be creative and to show off your parallel structure. Parallel structure will be explained later in this lesson.

> **HOT TIP**
> Leave margins on your paper. If you think you'll forget, bend your page over, without creasing it, and draw a light pencil line about one inch from the edge.
> Also, be sure to indent your paragraphs.

Your Outline

Let's say you decided to write in favor of requiring uniforms in public schools. (Remember, it doesn't matter which side you take. This is just an illustration.) Your outline on your scratch paper may look something like this:

Parents—Save money, can use hand-me-downs, save wear on good clothes, buying clothes easier, survey shows parents hate free dress days, less pressure from children and fewer fights over money for clothes.

Children—Poor children feel as well-dressed as peers, feel more of a sense of belonging, easier and faster to dress in morning, don't have to worry about what others think, more disciplined and calmer at school.

School staff—Experts say fewer fights at school, less bullying and teasing, more school loyalty among children so builds school community, parents less stressed so fewer calls for advice, frees officials to do other things like academics.

Conclusion: In the end, children and families benefit.

Three Parts of an Introduction

A surefire formula for a good introduction has three parts: an attention-grabber, an orientation for the reader, and a thesis statement (using parallel structure). The thesis statement is indispensable; you can play around with the other parts a bit.

Grab the Reader's Attention

This is your chance to be creative. The purpose of the first sentence or two of your introduction is to engage your reader.

You may start your introduction with a question or statement that engages the reader's imagination.

> How would your life change if you could wear a practical, comfortable uniform to work? Imagine a school auditorium full of alert children, all dressed neatly in blue and white uniforms, reciting the Pledge of Allegiance. Imagine these same children happily running out to play in their blue shorts and white oxford shirts, playing tag and flying on swings.

Orient the Reader

Whether or not you choose to use a "starter" like those above, you will need one or more sentences to orient your reader. Write as if your reader were an alien from outer space who knows nothing about your subject. You will need to introduce the topic and give some background information. Here's an example:

> Over 98% of our nation's schools have some kind of dress code for their students. Twenty percent of these codes designate a certain color and style of dress. Some of these uniform regulations even include specifics on shoes, socks, sweaters, and jackets. Over 1,000 schools each year are added to the ranks of those that have adopted stricter uniform policies for their children.

HOT TIP

It is perfectly all right to make up facts, figures, and quotes. The test makers want to know if you can write. They are not testing your knowledge of the subject.

But don't stew over a quote. It's important to get your ideas down on paper before you run out of time. If you can't think of something good right away, leave a line blank at the beginning of your essay so that you can put one in later if you have time.

For a persuasive essay, another kind of orientation states the other side of the argument briefly:

> Whether or not to dress public school children alike has been the subject of much controversy in recent decades. Opponents suggest that requiring uniforms will stifle children's ability to choose, squash necessary individuality, and infringe on the rights of children and families. Although there is some justification for these arguments, the benefits of uniforms far outweigh the disadvantages.

State Your Thesis

The third piece of your introduction includes a sentence stating your three main points in parallel form. The purpose of this sentence is to tell readers what you are going to tell them. The thesis sentence is taken from the three main points of your outline: parents, children, school staff. Put these in order from the least persuasive to the most persuasive. Look at your arguments for each topic and put last the one for which you can make the best case. Do you feel you can make the most convincing case for school staff and the least convincing case for parents? In that case, you should write about parents first, then children, and then staff.

The trick here is to put the three in parallel form. You can always use just the three plain words:

Adopting a school uniform policy will benefit parents, children, and school staff.

Alternatively, you can use any number of words in phrases or even whole sentences that summarize the ideas you are going to write about. This is not the place to give much detail, however, or you will have nothing to develop in the next paragraphs.

Uniform policies provide relief for parents, enhance self-esteem in children, and facilitate learning at school.

Putting It All Together

Here's one possible introduction, built out of the three pieces put together.

How would your life change if you could wear a practical, comfortable uniform to work? In many schools, uniform policies have been adopted. Over 98% of our nation's schools have some kind of dress code for their students. 20% of these codes designate a certain color and style of dress. Some of these uniform regulations even include specifics on shoes, socks, sweaters, and jackets. Over 1,000 schools each year are added to the ranks of those that have adopted stricter uniform policies for their children. Uniform policies provide relief for parents, enhance self-esteem in children, and facilitate learning at school.

The sentences in the introductory paragraphs need to fit together so that they flow. Notice that the sentence, "In many schools, uniform policies have been adopted," has been added to make a transition from the first sentence to the third. The first talks about work. The third gives statistics about schools. A transition from work to school is needed to put these two parts together.

Here's another possible introduction. In this case, no transitions were needed. Notice how it flows.

Imagine a school auditorium full of alert children, all dressed neatly in blue and white uniforms, reciting the Pledge of Allegiance. Imagine these same children happily running out to play in their blue shorts and white oxford shirts, playing tag and flying on swings. Whether or not to dress public school children alike has been the subject of much controversy in recent decades. Opponents suggest that requiring uniforms will stifle children's ability to choose, squash necessary individuality, and infringe on the rights of children and families. Although there is some justification for these arguments, the benefits of uniforms far outweigh the disadvantages. Adopting a uniform policy will benefit parents, children, and school staff.

Outlining a Narrative Essay

When writing the introduction to a narrative essay, use a sentence or two to engage the reader. Then give a little orientation by stating a few facts from your life that might help the reader understand what is to follow, or by restating the question. Then state your thesis.

Your orientation can go at least two ways. If the question asked you to describe a significant fork in the road, you might write:

- A brief description of your general situation at the time
- A general reflection on how people do occasionally or often come to forks in the road or how every day is full of forks and choices, but one significant one you remember is . . .

For your thesis statement you may choose to write three phrases such as:

My road to the fork was rocky, the fork was perplexing, but the road I took was paved with happiness.

In this case, your three paragraphs will be on:

1. The events preceding the fork
2. The decisions that were before you
3. The result of the path you chose

Note that if the question called for you to write about your reasons for choosing the fork, or to write in detail about each decision that faced you, you would need to adapt your outline to answer the question. If the question asked only for reasons, you would describe the fork briefly in the background sentences, and outline three reasons in your thesis statement. If it told you to describe the fork and give the reasons, then in your thesis sentence you might write two phrases on the fork and one on the reasons, or one on the fork and two on the reasons.

> **HOT TIP**
> There is no wrong way to organize your paragraphs and thesis statement, as long as you answer the question in some kind of logical arrangement.

Parallelism

Your thesis statement should use parallel form. Parallel writing serves to aid casual readers, impress test evaluators, and excite English teachers. The preceding sentence is an example of parallel writing—as were the sample thesis statements above. Parallel writing occurs when a series of phrases or sentences follow the same form. In the second sentence of this paragraph, there are three phrases that are parallel that are in the same form: verb, adjective, noun.

Verb	Adjective	Noun
aid	casual	readers
impress	test	evaluators
excite	English	teachers

Some say that John F. Kennedy won the presidency because the sparkling parallel structure of his speeches made him seem in control.

Parallelism Practice

Test and strengthen your skill at parallelism. Change each sentence to correct faulty parallelism.

1. Cathy bought herself a bracelet that had diamond charms, gold links, and one that had an adjustable clasp.
2. Simple, cheerful, and having trust, children are a joy to be around.
3. Being happy is more desirable than to be rich.
4. Succeeding as a teacher requires patience, caring, and having a tolerant attitude.
5. Tired, but with determination, the marathon runner kept practicing.
6. This district supports teachers by conducting inservices, supplying classroom materials, and sees that the salaries are increased each year.

Answers

1. Cathy bought herself a bracelet that had diamond charms, gold links, and an adjustable clasp.
2. Simple, cheerful, and trusting, children are a joy to be around.
3. Being happy is more desirable than being rich.
4. Succeeding as a teacher requires patience, caring, and tolerance.
5. Tired but determined, the marathon runner kept practicing.

6. This district supports teachers by conducting inservices, supplying classroom materials, and increasing salaries.

Introduction Practice
Try writing introductions for the following topics. You'll need to write a brief outline first. Be sure to use parallel structure.

7. Describe a time when you felt you took a significant step toward maturity.
8. Today's automobile insurance rates are higher for adults 16 to 30 than for older adults. Does this difference in rates represent an example of age discrimination?

▶ Writing 3: The Sandwich Paragraphs and the Last Slice

Once you have written your outline and your introduction, you need not concentrate so much on ideas; you already have them written down. In the body and conclusion of the essay, show off your style. Each of the three paragraphs after the introduction should contain a topic sentence and at least four supporting sentences. Your conclusion should restate your thesis and offer a few closing words.

Lesson Exercise
The sample sentences and paragraphs in this lesson contain mistakes in grammar, punctuation, diction, and even organization. See whether you can find all the errors, and try to correct them. You may need to simply rewrite some of the paragraphs as they might be pretty bad! Then compare your revisions to the ones you will find in Writing Sections 4 and 5. There are many ways to rewrite the paragraphs; maybe you'll find a better way than the ones given. If you can do that, you're sure to pass the writing portion of the CBEST.

TOPIC SENTENCE AND SUPPORTING SENTENCES
Each paragraph should have a topic sentence. Usually the topic sentence begins the paragraph and states the main idea of the paragraph in general. For each of the three paragraphs that will make up the body of your essay, one of the points from your outline will be used. That is why you made the outline. The subpoints you wrote down will be the subject of the rest of the sentences in the paragraph.

After composing the topic sentence, uphold and explain your main idea with supporting sentences. These sentences should be as detailed and descriptive as possible.

Go back to the uniform example and write some topic sentences and supporting sentences. Remember, the outline looked like this:

Parents—Save money, can use hand-me-downs, save wear on good clothes, buying clothes easier, survey shows parents hate free dress days, less pressure from children and fewer fights over money for clothes.

Children—Poor children feel as well dressed as peers, feel more of a sense of belonging, easier and faster to dress in morning, don't have to worry about what others think, more disciplined and calmer at school.

School staff—Experts say fewer fights at school, less bullying and teasing, more school loyalty among children so builds school community, parents less stressed so fewer calls for advice, frees officials to do other things, like academics. Principals and teachers love the uniform policy.

Conclusion: In the end, children and families benefit.

These were the thesis examples:

- Adopting a school uniform policy will benefit parents, children, and school staff.
- Uniform policies provide relief for parents, enhance self-esteem in children, and facilitate learning at school.

> **HOT TIP**
> When you write your CBEST essay, be sure to leave yourself plenty of room for revisions by double-spacing or leaving extra-wide margins.

Your first reason in favor of uniforms is that parents benefit. To make things easier, you can copy the first part of the thesis statement. This provides you with a transition (see below) as well as a topic sentence:

In my opinion a uniform policy will benefit parents.

Next, add your detailed reasons. Here is one possible way to write the first body paragraph. (Remember, the paragraphs in this lesson have mistakes in them. Can you correct them?)

In my opinion a uniform policy will benefit parents. Because they are all the same style and shape and usually very well made, children can use the hand-me-downs of older siblings or even used ones bought from another child. Parents they were also able to save money by buying fewer school clothes for their children. Children, who are often demanding, will have already agreed on what clothes their parents will need to buy so there will be fewer arguments over clothes for school their parents will need to buy. Children and teachers like it too. Parents are generally in favor of uniforms because you do not have to provide your children with a different matched set of clothes for each day. After buying uniforms the first year, more peace was reportedly experienced by 95% of the parents interviewed and many surveys reported that it saved them an average of $100–$200 in clothing costs.

Notice how this paragraph has used some statistics—completely made-up ones—to provide support for the topic sentence. When you are writing your narrative essay, you should usually organize the supporting sentences in chronological order, or in order of importance. Lots of descriptive detail and maybe even some conversation, when appropriate, will help support your main point and make your essay clear and compelling to your reader.

Now, how about a topic sentence for each of the other two body paragraphs?

Children benefit from a school uniform policy. Uniforms cost no extra money for teachers and administrators, yet the benefits are great.

These sentences are OK for now, but your essay needs transitions from one paragraph to another. The first topic from your thesis statement gave your first body paragraph an automatic transition from the introduction. Now you need something that will link the first body paragraph to the second, and the second to the third.

Transition Sentences

A transition sentence joins two paragraphs together in some way. Usually, an idea taken from one paragraph links with an idea in the second paragraph. This is done all in one sentence. Sometimes you can do this at the end of one paragraph to link it to the next, but often it's effective to build your transition right into your topic sentence, as you did with the first body paragraph.

For instance, take the topic sentence for your second body paragraph:

Children benefit from a school uniform policy.

How can you link parents, the subject of your first body paragraph, to children? Try something like this:

Not only are parents happy to see a uniform policy in place, but their children benefit as well.

Voilà, a transition that links together body paragraphs one and two.

You can also put your transition at the end of the previous paragraph, rather than at the beginning of the new one. For instance, you can put a sentence like this at the end of your paragraph on children to lead into the paragraph about teachers and administrators:

Children might be happy with the school uniform policy, but not as happy as their teachers and principals.

Now add the sub-points from your outline to your second and third body paragraphs. (Are you still looking for the mistakes in these paragraphs?)

Not only are parents happy to see a uniform policy in place, but their children benefit as well. If you were poor wouldn't you feel bad if you were not dressed as well as your peers. Children who dress differently are alienated from cliques at school and left to feel like outsiders and are teased unmercifully and end up losing a lot of self-esteem and so maybe they will grow up bitter and join gangs and use drugs and end up murdering someone. Dressing in uniform eliminates that problem. Instead you feel a sense of belonging. You are less distractd by cumparing your clothes to others so you are more apd to be relaxed and queiter in school. This enables them to learn more. Children might be happy with the school uniform policy but not as happy as their teachers and principals

Uniforms cost no extra money for teachers and administrators yet the benefits are great. There is less competition in school so there is less fights. The reason is because there is less bullying and teasing and there is a lot less complaints. Instead, principals and teachers were able to use uniforms to build school pride and loyalty. Administrators and teachers will be able to concentrate on what they love to do most teach instead of dealing with problems from children and parents.

HOT TIP

Write neatly! The scorers do not want to take time to stop and decipher your words. If a word appears illegible or spelled wrong (an *i* looks like an *e*), erase the letter or word neatly and write it again. If your handwriting is illegible, print.

The Conclusion

The concluding paragraph is one of the most difficult to compose. A good format to follow is to first restate your thesis, and then try for a "clincher," something that will leave your readers with a sense of closure, that they really have finished.

So in the first sentence or two, restate your thesis. Do not add any new ideas here. This is a good place to try out parallel form.

Adopting a uniform policy will lighten the burden of parents. It will promote cheerfulness and scholarship in children. Lastly, it will free the time and talents of teachers and administrators.

The concluding paragraph in a narrative essay could sum up the story.

I can look back now on that day long ago. I was at the crossroads. I knew I loved children and that my parents would be proud. I signed up for teacher's training.

The last sentence or two should contain the clincher. Its purpose is to end the paragraph gracefully and leave the reader with a sense of finality.

> **HOT TIP**
> Although you aren't required to write a title, it helps the judges to see that you are an organized and thoughtful person. Leave a few lines blank at the beginning of your essay, since you might not come up with a title until you're nearly finished. Make sure your title captures the main idea of your essay. "Uniforms, Boon or Bane?" would not be appropriate for an essay that mostly deals with the positive reasons for uniforms because it suggests there are two sides to the story. "In Praise of Uniforms" would be better.

The last sentence of a persuasive essay may be a call to action, a question, a prediction, or a personal comment. You might add one of these clinchers to the thesis summary on school uniforms:

What are we waiting for? We need to talk to our teachers, principals, and school boards, and give our children ALL the tools we can that are essential for their growth and development.

Since school uniforms do so much good, would you want your school to miss out?

For a narrative essay, this last sentence could state your opinion, or talk about someone, even yourself, who will never be the same. You might add one of these sentences about your decision to go into teacher training:

I am glad I did.
My world will never be the same.
I often wonder how many children's lives will be changed because of one decision on that one April day.

It can be difficult to write this last sentence or two, but you need to supply your readers with something that makes your essay memorable.

Once you have your ideas down on paper, it's important to see that they are clearly and correctly expressed—unlike the paragraphs found in this lesson. Go on to Writing 4 and Writing 5 to see how to make your sentence structure and word choice work for you.

▶ Writing 4: The Sentence Doctor

Even more important than a logical structure is the content of your essay. Generalizations need to be supported with exact and specific details, which you are free to make up. Your choice of words needs to be precise, your sentences varied, and your paragraphs unified. Your paragraphs should have connections between them so that your whole essay flows from one thought to another. Let us look at some of the sentence elements that make up good paragraphs.

Varied Sentence Structure

Within your paragraph, your sentences should be varied. It makes your essay more interesting and shows the test evaluators that you have mastered different sentence structures.

There are two types of sentence variation: sentence length and sentence structure. Sentence length should not be a problem. Put in some long sentences and some short ones. For varying the structure of a sentence, you might need to brush up on parts of speech and different types of clauses and phrases. If this is the case, go to your local curriculum department or school district office and check out a book on grammar, or check out some of the books on writing listed at the end of this chapter. The idea is not to be able to name all the different types of clauses, but only to be able to place some variety in your writing. The following exercise demonstrates a few examples of various sentence structures.

Practice with Varied Sentence Structures

Rewrite the sentences beginning with the part of speech indicated.

1. The hostess greeted her special guests graciously. (Adverb)
2. The proprietor, hard as nails, demanded the rent. (Adjective)
3. One must learn how to breathe to swim well. (Infinitive)
4. The white stallion leapt over the hurdles. (Preposition)
5. An octogenarian was playing with the children. (Participle)
6. The schools will not be state funded if they do not hire certified teachers. (Adverb clause)

For an additional exercise, try writing sentences that begin with these words:

After
Although
As
Because
Since

Unless
Where
Wherever
While

Answers

1. Graciously, the hostess greeted her special guests.
2. Hard as nails, the proprietor demanded the rent.
3. To swim well, one must learn how to breathe.
4. Over the hurdles leapt the white stallion.
5. Playing with the children was an octogenarian.
6. If they do not hire certified teachers, the schools will not be state-funded.

Dangling Clauses

When beginning your sentences with a clause, try to avoid dangling clauses. Dangling clauses mix up who's doing what:

If they do not hire certified teachers, funds will not be sent to the schools.

It sounds as if the funds were doing the hiring! Instead you should write:

If they do not hire certified teachers, the schools will not receive funding.

If you start off with a clause, make sure that the *who* or *what* referred to in the clause begins the next part of the sentence.

Look for dangling clauses in the first body paragraph from the last lesson. You should find two.

In my opinion, a uniform policy will benefit parents. Because they are all the same style and shape and usually very well made, children can use the hand-me-downs of older siblings or other children.

Parents they were also able to save money by buying fewer school clothes for their children. Children, who are often demanding, will have already agreed on what clothes their parents will need to buy so there will be fewer arguments over clothes for school their parents will need to buy. Children and teachers like it too. Parents are generally in favor of uniforms because you do not have to provide your children with a different matched set of clothes for each day. After buying uniforms the first year, more peace was reportedly experienced by 95% of the parents interviewed and many surveys reported that it saved them an average of $100 – $200 in clothing costs.

Did you find them? Look at the second sentence.

Because they are all the same style and shape and usually very well made, children can use the hand-me-downs of older siblings or other children.

What is the same style and shape? The sentence says the children are. Here is a corrected version:

Because they are all the same style and shape and usually very well made, uniforms can be passed down from an older child to a younger one, or even sold.

Now look at the last sentence of the paragraph.

After buying uniforms the first year, more peace was reportedly experienced by 95% of the parents interviewed and many surveys reported that it saved them an average of $100 – $200 in clothing costs.

Was it the peace that was buying the uniforms? Let's correct it:

On a recent survey, 95% of parents new to school uniforms attributed an increased feeling of peace to the adoption of the uniform policy. Parents also reportedly saved an average of $100-$200 on school clothes per child the first year.

Opinion Starters

There's a problem with the first sentence of that paragraph, too. Never start a sentence with "In my opinion" or "I think." If you didn't think it, you wouldn't be writing it. The first sentence of the first body paragraph should read simply:

A uniform policy will benefit parents.

Over and Over

Avoid redundancy. Try to keep your sentences as succinct as possible without losing meaning. Make every word and phrase count. Here's an example of a redundant sentence from the first body paragraph:

Children, who are often demanding, will have already agreed on what clothes their parents will need to buy so there will be fewer arguments over clothes for school their parents will need to buy.

The phrase "will need to buy" is in there twice. Get rid of it. "Children, who are often demanding" can be changed to "Demanding children." The words "for school" can be left out, because that's a given. So now you have a shorter, more effective sentence:

Demanding children will have already agreed on what clothes their parents will need to buy, so there will be fewer arguments.

> **HOT TIP**
>
> Make sure you have a quality eraser—unless you are perfect! Find an eraser that will erase pencil marks from newsprint without leaving smudges or tearing. Your essay paper will not be newsprint, but if an eraser can erase newsprint, it can erase anything. Avoid replacing a word with another by writing darker over the first word without erasing first. When you need to add a word, avoid "^" marks. Erase the words before and after the word you will put in, and put three words in place of two.

Sentence Stowaways and Sentence Order

Avoid writing sentences that are not on the same general topic as the rest of the paragraph. Did you notice the stowaway in the paragraph on parents? The sentence "Children and teachers like it too," does not belong in that paragraph.

The order of the sentences in your paragraph is just as important as the order of the paragraphs in your essay. If you are writing about money parents will save, put all the sentences on money together. Provide transitions for your sentences, just as you did with your paragraphs. You can join sentences with words such as *besides, second, lastly,* and so on, or you can put in sub-topic sentences:

Try rearranging the paragraph on parents in a logical order. You have two sub-topics: money and peace in the family. So add a sub-topic sentence to announce the first sub-idea:

First, uniforms would save parents money.

The fake survey you added at the end of the paragraph reports statistics on both money and peace, so that's a great way to tie the two topics together. The rest of the sentences should all fit under one of the two sub-topics. If you have something that doesn't fit, just leave it out. You don't have enough time to fool with it. Here's one way to provide a more logical organization:

A uniform policy will benefit parents. First, uniforms will save parents money. Parents will not have to provide their children with a different matched set of clothes for each day, so they will need to buy fewer school clothes for their children. Because uniforms are all the same style and shape and usually very well made, they can be passed down from an older child to a younger one, or even sold. On a recent survey, parents new to school uniforms reportedly saved a whopping $100-$200 on school clothes per child the first year. The survey also reported that 95% of parents attributed an increased feeling of peace to the adoption of the uniform policy. Children will have already agreed on what clothes their parents will need to buy, so there will be fewer arguments.

And On and On and On and On . . .

Before you move on to problems with words in the next lesson, take a look at a problem sentence from the second body paragraph on school uniforms.

Children who dress differently are alienated from cliques at school and left to feel like outsiders and are teased unmercifully and end up losing a lot of self-esteem and so maybe they will grow up bitter and join gangs and use drugs and end up murdering someone.

Do you see that there are two things wrong with this sentence? For one thing, it goes on and on and on. It should have been divided into at least two sentences.

Maybe you also noticed that the reasoning here is faulty. This is an exaggerated example of *slippery slope* reasoning: something causes something that leads to something else. In this example, the lack of uniforms leads to murder—this conclusion is neither logical nor believable. So let's just leave off that part and clean up the sentence structure.

> Children who dress differently are usually alienated from cliques at school and left to feel like outsiders. Often they are teased unmercifully.

What if you wanted to join those two sentences after all? You could do it with a semicolon; if you used a comma, you'd have a sentence fault called a *comma splice*. The same is true of the sentence you just read. For more on fixing your punctuation and word problems, go on to the next lesson.

▶ Writing 5: Finishing Touches

The scorers who read your essay will be on the lookout for precise wording and careful, accurate usage. This chapter will review some common errors.

Punctuation Deficit

A question mark goes at the end of a question. Use few, if any, exclamation points in your essay and always end your sentences with a period. There are many rules for using commas. Here are the most common places for a comma:

- At the end of long clauses
- Between lists of words
- Around appositives
- Between the sentences of a compound sentence
- Around non-essential words and clauses
- Wherever the meaning of the sentence would not be clear without one

If these rules aren't familiar, you can find details in the books listed at the end of this chapter.

As you proofread, check to see whether your essay flows well. If additional punctuation is necessary to get your point across, use it—but don't go overboard by throwing in commas where they are not necessary. Can you find the punctuation errors in the following paragraph?

> Not only are parents happy to see a uniform policy in place, but their children benefit as well. If you were poor wouldn't you feel bad if you were not dressed as well as your peers. Children who dress differently are usually alienated from cliques at school and left to feel like outsiders. Often they are teased unmercifully. Dressing in uniform eliminates that problem. Instead you feel a sense of belonging. You are less distractd by cumparing your clothes to others so you are more apd to be relaxed and queiter in school. This enables them to learn more. Children might be happy with the school uniform policy but not as happy as their teachers and principals

HOT TIP
Spend the last few minutes of exam time proofreading to see whether you included everything you had to say, whether you used the same verb tense and person throughout, and whether your words are clear. There is no time for big revisions, but check for such details as periods after sentences and spelling.

The second sentence is a question; it should have a question mark. Because the question doesn't start until after a phrase, the phrase should be set off by a comma.

> If you were poor, wouldn't you feel bad if you were not dressed as well as your peers?

There could be a comma after *Instead* at the beginning of the fifth sentence. This comma may not be necessary in some circumstances, but you are changing the flow of thought here, and you want the readers to know it.

Instead, you feel a sense of belonging.

The sixth sentence contains a compound sentence that should be set off with a comma. The last sentence could also use a comma to separate a long clause from the main sentence, particularly since you are once again switching gears. Lastly, don't let the fact that you're almost done make you forget to put a period at the end of the last sentence.

You are less distractd by cumparing your clothes to others, so you are more apd to be relaxed and queiter in school. This enables them to learn more. Children might be happy with the school uniform policy, but not as happy as their teachers and principals.

Identity Disorder

Keep the same person throughout the essay: *I* and *me* or *you*, or *they* and *them*. It is all right to address the reader with a question, but the facts and statements should match each other. In the paragraph below, the subject of the first and third sentences is "children." You need to continue to talk about children in the third person throughout the paragraph.

Not only are parents happy to see a uniform policy in place, but their children benefit as well. If you were poor, wouldn't you feel bad if you were not dressed as well as your peers? Children who dress differently are usually alienated from cliques at school and left to feel like outsiders. Often they are teased unmercifully. Dressing in uniform eliminates that problem. Instead, they feel a sense of belonging. They are less distractd by cumparing their clothes to others, so they are more apd to be relaxed and queiter in school.

The second sentence is not talking about children, but is addressing the reader, so it's OK to use *you* and *your*. The last two sentences talk about children, not about the reader, so those sentences should use *they* and *their*, not *you* and *your*.

Spelling Abnormality Disorder

You have to write quickly during the exam, but save a couple of minutes at the end to check your work for spelling errors. Often our minds go faster than our pencils, and left alone, our pencils make a lot of mistakes. Too bad there are no perfect pencils in this world! Did you find the misspelled words in the second body paragraph on school uniforms?

They are less distractd by cumparing their clothes to others so they are more apd to be relaxed and queiter in school.

Let's fix it:

They are less distracted by comparing their clothes to others so they are more apt to be relaxed and quieter in school.

Forked Tongue Disease

Be on the lookout for words or even sentences that might have two different meanings. Now that we've fixed the spelling errors in the sentence above, look again to see how it might be confusing. Does the sentence mean that comparing their clothes is less distracting? And what are they comparing their clothes to? To other people? There are too many meanings for this sentence. It needs to be revised.

Children do not need to compare their clothing with that of others, so they have fewer distractions.

Less than Insufficient Mistreatment

Remember to use problem words correctly. Avoid double negatives. If you must use them, make sure you are saying what you really mean. If you have time, you can brush up on other problem words such as *lay* and *lie*, *all together* and *altogether*, and so on. Discussions on these topics can be found in grammar books listed at the end of this chapter. Check the problem words in the following sentences from the third body paragraph.

There is less competition in school so there is less fights. The reason is because there is less bullying and teasing and there is a lot less complaints.

The word *fewer* refers to a quantity that can be counted.

There are fewer boys in the class.
There are fewer mistakes in this paragraph than in the last one.

"Less" refers to a quantity that cannot be counted, but might be able to be measured.

There is less water in that cup now that you drank from it.

In the sentence above, competition cannot be counted, so *less* is the right word. But the number of fights can be counted, so *fewer* should replace *less*. In the second sentence, the bullying and teasing in general are hard to count, so *less* is the right word. If the sentence was worded to read "incidences of teasing," then *fewer* would be used because incidences can be counted. Complaints can be counted so *fewer* should be used. *Fewer* takes the verb *are* and *less* takes the verb *is*.

You can also get rid of the redundant "The reason is because." Maybe you can show off some parallelism here. And why not name the actors in this sentence?

Because there is less competition in school, teachers and administrators report that there are fewer fights, less bullying, and fewer complaints from the students.

Tense All Over

Unless there is a very good reason for doing otherwise, the same tense should be used throughout your essay. You may use perfect tenses when appropriate, but try to avoid using future, past, and present in one paragraph. See whether you can find the tense mistakes in the following paragraph.

Uniforms cost no extra money for teachers and administrators yet the benefits are great. Because there is less competition in school, teachers and administrators report that there are fewer fights, less bullying, and fewer complaints from the students. Instead, principals and teachers were able to use uniforms to build school pride and loyalty. Administrators and teachers will be able to concentrate on what they love to do most, teach, instead of dealing with problems from children and parents.

The first part of the paragraph is in present tense. The past tense verb *were able* in the third sentence should be changed to the present *are able*. In the last sentence, the future tense *will be able* should be also be changed to the present *are able*.

Instead, principals and teachers are able to use uniforms to build school pride and loyalty. Administrators and teachers are able to concentrate on what they love to do most, teach, instead of dealing with problems from children and parents.

Sewing It Up

Notice how the few remaining problems with transitions have been cleaned up in this final version of the essay on school uniforms. The body paragraph on teachers and administrators ended with too strong a statement—no one will believe that school personnel will have *no* problems from children just because of uniforms—so that statement has been softened. This final version also has a title.

In Praise of School Uniforms

Imagine a school auditorium full of alert children, all dressed neatly in blue and white uniforms, reciting the Pledge of Allegiance. Imagine these same children happily running out to play in their blue shorts and white oxford shirts, playing tag and flying on swings. Whether or not to dress public school children alike has been the subject of much controversy in recent decades. Opponents suggest that requiring uniforms will stifle children's ability to choose, squash necessary individuality, and infringe on the rights of children and families. Although there is some justification for these arguments, the benefits of uniforms far outweigh the disadvantages. Adopting a uniform policy will benefit parents, children, and the school staff.

A uniform policy will benefit parents. Uniforms save parents money. Parents will not have to provide their children with a different matched set of clothes for each day, so fewer school clothes would be needed. Because uniforms are all the same style and shape and usually very well made, they can be passed down from an older child to a younger one, or even sold. On a recent survey, parents new to school uniforms estimated they saved up to $1,000 on school clothes per child the first year alone. The survey also reported that 95% of parents attributed an increased feeling of peace to the adoption of the uniform policy. Children will have already agreed on what clothes their parents will need to buy, so there will be fewer arguments on this often touchy subject.

Not only are parents happy to see a uniform policy in place, but their children benefit as well. If you were poor, wouldn't you feel badly if you were not dressed as well as your peers? Children who dress differently are usually alienated from cliques at school and left to feel like outsiders. Often they are teased unmercifully. Dressing in uniform eliminates that problem. Instead, uniformed children feel an increased sense of belonging that enables them to be more relaxed and quieter in school. Children do not need to compare their clothing with that of others, so they have fewer distractions during their learning time. Children like the policy because there is less nagging at home and dressing for school is much easier.

Parents and children are not the only ones who are better off with school uniforms. Teachers and administrators love them too. Uniforms cost no extra money, yet the benefits are great. Because there is less competition in school, teachers and administrators report that less time is spent mediating because there are fewer fights, less bullying, and fewer complaints from students. Administrators and teachers can use the time they save to do what they are paid to do—build school loyalty, form young minds, and teach basic skills. Teachers report a more peaceful classroom, and administrators report a more cooperative student body.

Adopting a uniform policy will lighten the burden of parents. It will promote cheerfulness and scholarship in children. Lastly, it will free the time and talents of teachers and administrators. What are we waiting for? We need to talk to our teachers, principals, and school boards, and give our children ALL the tools we can that will enhance their growth and development.

▶ More Help with Reading, Math, and Writing

If any or all of the three subjects covered in the mini-course are especially tough for you, you may want to consider doing some further reading. Following is a list of particularly useful books for preparing for the skills tested on CBEST.

Reading

- *501 Reading Comprehension Questions* (LearningExpress)
  Fast, focused practice to help you improve your skills
- *Read Better, Remember More* by Elizabeth Chesla (LearningExpress)
  A self-study book that helps you learn at your own pace, with varied exercises that make learning easy.
- *Reading Comprehension Success in 20 Minutes a Day* by Elizabeth Chesla (LearningExpress)
  A 20-step book that covers all the basics of reading well; especially useful for those preparing for exams like the CBEST.
- *Reading Success* (LearningExpress)
  Learn to understand everything you read—discover the meaning of new words, find the main idea, predict what will happen next, and much more!
- *10 Real SATs* by Cathy Claman (Editor) (College Board)
  Provides great test-taking tips as well as practice questions and answers.
- *Visual Communication* by Ned Racine (LearningExpress)
  Visual literacy is a growing area of assessment on standardized tests—find out here how to read maps, charts, diagrams, and schematics. Learn how to use and make use of visual communication!

Book List

The best way to improve your reading skills is to read as often as you can. Here is a list of well-known books that may interest you:

Angela's Ashes by Frank McCourt (Autobiography)
Black Boy by Richard Wright (Autobiography)
The Catcher in the Rye by J.D. Salinger (Coming of Age)
Dr. Jekyll and Mr. Hyde by Robert Louis Stevenson (Horror)
Frankenstein by Mary Shelley (Science Fiction)
Hiroshima by John Hershey (War)
The Hobbit by J.R.R. Tolkien (Fantasy)
Jurassic Park, The Lost World by Michael Crichton (Science Fiction)
The Last of the Mohicans by James Fenimore Cooper (Historical)
The Lives of a Cell by Lewis Thomas (Science/Medicine)
Moonlight Becomes You and other novels by Mary Higgins Clark (Detective)
Schindler's List by Thomas Keneally (Historical)
A Separate Peace by John Knowles (Coming of Age)
The Stand and other novels by Stephen King (Horror)
A Time to Kill, The Client by John Grisham (Thriller)

Math

- *Algebra the Easy Way,* 3rd ed. by Douglas Downing (Barron's)
    Covers all the basics of algebra; uses a continuous story to help make learning fun.
- *Algebra Success* (LearningExpress)
    Equations, inequalities, powers, and roots—master algebra now!
- *All the Math You'll Ever Need* by Steve Slavin (Wiley)
    A friendly guide for those seeking to brush up on mathematics and elementary algebra.
- *Essential Math/Basic Math for Everyday Use* by Edward Williams and Robert A. Atkins (Barron's)
    Emphasizes math applications in selected career areas.
- *Everyday Math for Dummies* by Charles Seiter (IDG).
    Like other books in the *For Dummies* series, this one features a fun presentation that will help you conquer math anxiety.
- *Geometry Success* (LearningExpress)
- *Math Builder* (LearningExpress)
- *Math the Easy Way,* 3rd ed. by Anthony Prindle and Katie Prindle (Barron's)
    Covers basic arithmetic, fractions, decimals, percents, word problems, and introduces algebra and geometry.
- *Math Essentials* by Steve Slavin (LearningExpress)
    If you have trouble with fractions, decimals, or percents, this book offers an easy, step-by-step review.
- *Math Smart: Essential Math for These Numeric Times* (Princeton Review)
    Covers all the basics of math using practice exercises with answers and explanations; good for studying math for the first time, or for review.
- *Math Success* (LearningExpress)
- *Mathematics Made Simple* by Abraham Sperling and Monroe Stuart (Doubleday)
    Targets students and others who want to improve their practical math skills.
- *1001 Math Problems* (LearningExpress)
    Fast, focused practice to help you improve your math skills!
- *Practical Math Success in 20 Minutes a Day* by Judith Robinovitz (LearningExpress)
    Provides review of basic math skills and easy-to-follow examples with opportunities for practice.
- *Visual Math* by Jessika Sobanski (LearningExpress)
    Specifically designed for the visual learner, this book explores shapes from many different perspectives. See how math makes sense!
- *501 Algebra Questions* (LearningExpress)
    Covers basic to advanced algebra skills.
- *501 Geometry Questions* (LearningExpress)
    Focused practice helps refine geometry skills.

Writing

- *1001 Pitfalls in English Grammar* (Barron's)
    Problem-solving approach to writing and grammar; very useful for nonnative speakers of English.
- *Better English* by Norman Lewis (Dell)
    Useful for general information; suited to both native and nonnative speakers of English.
- *Better Writing Right Now!* by Francine Galko (LearningExpress)
    Know the benchmarks that professionals use—learn how to make words work for you!
- *Grammar Essentials* by Judith Olson (LearningExpress)
    Gives a thorough review of all the rules of basic grammar; lots of exercises and examples make for a painless, and even fun, learning experience.

CBEST MINI-COURSE

- *English Made Simple* by Arthur Waldhorn and Arthur Ziegler (Made Simple Books)

    Designed for nonnative speakers of English; also good for native speakers with little training in grammar.

- *Errors in English and How to Correct Them* by Harry Shaw (HarperCollins)

    Addresses specific problems in both writing and grammar; useful for nonnative speakers of English.

- *501 Grammar and Writing Questions* (LearningExpress)

    Learn how to spot common grammar mistakes; compose correct sentences; organize clear, concise paragraphs; and much more!

- *Grammar* by James R. Hurford (Cambridge University Press)

    Thorough coverage of parts of speech, sentence structure, usage, punctuation, and mechanics; especially good for native speakers of English.

- *The Handbook of Good English* by Edward D. Johnson (Washington Square Press)

    Well-organized, comprehensive handbook for both grammar and writing.

- *Smart English* by Anne Francis (Signet)

    Thorough general-purpose handbook for both writing and grammar; good for nonnative speakers of English.

- *Write Better Essays* by Elizabaeth Chesla (LearningExpress)

    Your guide to top test scores, this book teaches the mechanics of good essay writing. It's like having a personal tutor!

- *Writing Skills Success in 20 Minutes a Day* by Judith Olson (LearningExpress)

    Covers all the basics of writing through step-by-step instruction and exercises; especially useful for those preparing for exams such as CBEST.

- *Writing Smart* by Marcia Lerner (Princeton Review)

    Good for general writing skills; well-organized so information is easy to find.

- *Writing Success* (LearningExpress)

CHAPTER 5 ▶ CBEST Practice Exam 1

CHAPTER SUMMARY
Here is another sample test based on the California Basic Educational Skills Test (CBEST). After working through the CBEST Mini-Course in Chapter 4, take this test to see how much your score has improved.

Like the real CBEST, the exam that follows consists of three sections: 50 questions on Reading, 50 questions on Mathematics, and two essay topics in the Writing section. For this exam, you should simulate the actual test-taking experience as closely as you can. Find a quiet place to work where you won't be disturbed. Tear out the answer sheet on the next page and find some number 2 pencils to fill in the circles with. Write your essays on a separate piece of paper. Allow yourself four hours for the exam: one and a half hours each for the reading and math sections and a half-hour each for the two essays. Set a timer or stopwatch, but do not worry too much if you go over the allotted time on this practice exam. You can work more on timing when you take the second practice exam in Chapter 6.

After the exam, use the answer key that follows it to see how you did and to find out why the correct answers are correct. As was the case for the diagnostic test, the answer key is followed by a section on how to score your exam.

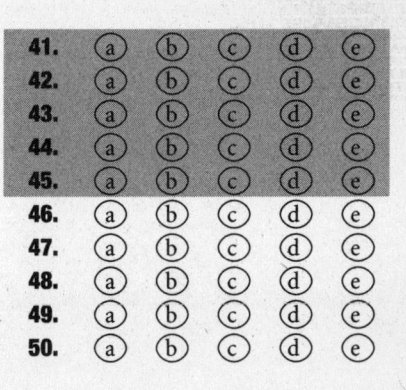

LEARNINGEXPRESS CALIFORNIA BASIC EDUCATIONAL SKILLS TEST ANSWER SHEET

Section 1: Reading Comprehension

1. ⓐ ⓑ ⓒ ⓓ ⓔ	21. ⓐ ⓑ ⓒ ⓓ ⓔ	41. ⓐ ⓑ ⓒ ⓓ ⓔ
2. ⓐ ⓑ ⓒ ⓓ ⓔ	22. ⓐ ⓑ ⓒ ⓓ ⓔ	42. ⓐ ⓑ ⓒ ⓓ ⓔ
3. ⓐ ⓑ ⓒ ⓓ ⓔ	23. ⓐ ⓑ ⓒ ⓓ ⓔ	43. ⓐ ⓑ ⓒ ⓓ ⓔ
4. ⓐ ⓑ ⓒ ⓓ ⓔ	24. ⓐ ⓑ ⓒ ⓓ ⓔ	44. ⓐ ⓑ ⓒ ⓓ ⓔ
5. ⓐ ⓑ ⓒ ⓓ ⓔ	25. ⓐ ⓑ ⓒ ⓓ ⓔ	45. ⓐ ⓑ ⓒ ⓓ ⓔ
6. ⓐ ⓑ ⓒ ⓓ ⓔ	26. ⓐ ⓑ ⓒ ⓓ ⓔ	46. ⓐ ⓑ ⓒ ⓓ ⓔ
7. ⓐ ⓑ ⓒ ⓓ ⓔ	27. ⓐ ⓑ ⓒ ⓓ ⓔ	47. ⓐ ⓑ ⓒ ⓓ ⓔ
8. ⓐ ⓑ ⓒ ⓓ ⓔ	28. ⓐ ⓑ ⓒ ⓓ ⓔ	48. ⓐ ⓑ ⓒ ⓓ ⓔ
9. ⓐ ⓑ ⓒ ⓓ ⓔ	29. ⓐ ⓑ ⓒ ⓓ ⓔ	49. ⓐ ⓑ ⓒ ⓓ ⓔ
10. ⓐ ⓑ ⓒ ⓓ ⓔ	30. ⓐ ⓑ ⓒ ⓓ ⓔ	50. ⓐ ⓑ ⓒ ⓓ ⓔ
11. ⓐ ⓑ ⓒ ⓓ ⓔ	31. ⓐ ⓑ ⓒ ⓓ ⓔ	
12. ⓐ ⓑ ⓒ ⓓ ⓔ	32. ⓐ ⓑ ⓒ ⓓ ⓔ	
13. ⓐ ⓑ ⓒ ⓓ ⓔ	33. ⓐ ⓑ ⓒ ⓓ ⓔ	
14. ⓐ ⓑ ⓒ ⓓ ⓔ	34. ⓐ ⓑ ⓒ ⓓ ⓔ	
15. ⓐ ⓑ ⓒ ⓓ ⓔ	35. ⓐ ⓑ ⓒ ⓓ ⓔ	
16. ⓐ ⓑ ⓒ ⓓ ⓔ	36. ⓐ ⓑ ⓒ ⓓ ⓔ	
17. ⓐ ⓑ ⓒ ⓓ ⓔ	37. ⓐ ⓑ ⓒ ⓓ ⓔ	
18. ⓐ ⓑ ⓒ ⓓ ⓔ	38. ⓐ ⓑ ⓒ ⓓ ⓔ	
19. ⓐ ⓑ ⓒ ⓓ ⓔ	39. ⓐ ⓑ ⓒ ⓓ ⓔ	
20. ⓐ ⓑ ⓒ ⓓ ⓔ	40. ⓐ ⓑ ⓒ ⓓ ⓔ	

Section 2: Mathematics

1. ⓐ ⓑ ⓒ ⓓ ⓔ	21. ⓐ ⓑ ⓒ ⓓ ⓔ	41. ⓐ ⓑ ⓒ ⓓ ⓔ
2. ⓐ ⓑ ⓒ ⓓ ⓔ	22. ⓐ ⓑ ⓒ ⓓ ⓔ	42. ⓐ ⓑ ⓒ ⓓ ⓔ
3. ⓐ ⓑ ⓒ ⓓ ⓔ	23. ⓐ ⓑ ⓒ ⓓ ⓔ	43. ⓐ ⓑ ⓒ ⓓ ⓔ
4. ⓐ ⓑ ⓒ ⓓ ⓔ	24. ⓐ ⓑ ⓒ ⓓ ⓔ	44. ⓐ ⓑ ⓒ ⓓ ⓔ
5. ⓐ ⓑ ⓒ ⓓ ⓔ	25. ⓐ ⓑ ⓒ ⓓ ⓔ	45. ⓐ ⓑ ⓒ ⓓ ⓔ
6. ⓐ ⓑ ⓒ ⓓ ⓔ	26. ⓐ ⓑ ⓒ ⓓ ⓔ	46. ⓐ ⓑ ⓒ ⓓ ⓔ
7. ⓐ ⓑ ⓒ ⓓ ⓔ	27. ⓐ ⓑ ⓒ ⓓ ⓔ	47. ⓐ ⓑ ⓒ ⓓ ⓔ
8. ⓐ ⓑ ⓒ ⓓ ⓔ	28. ⓐ ⓑ ⓒ ⓓ ⓔ	48. ⓐ ⓑ ⓒ ⓓ ⓔ
9. ⓐ ⓑ ⓒ ⓓ ⓔ	29. ⓐ ⓑ ⓒ ⓓ ⓔ	49. ⓐ ⓑ ⓒ ⓓ ⓔ
10. ⓐ ⓑ ⓒ ⓓ ⓔ	30. ⓐ ⓑ ⓒ ⓓ ⓔ	50. ⓐ ⓑ ⓒ ⓓ ⓔ
11. ⓐ ⓑ ⓒ ⓓ ⓔ	31. ⓐ ⓑ ⓒ ⓓ ⓔ	
12. ⓐ ⓑ ⓒ ⓓ ⓔ	32. ⓐ ⓑ ⓒ ⓓ ⓔ	
13. ⓐ ⓑ ⓒ ⓓ ⓔ	33. ⓐ ⓑ ⓒ ⓓ ⓔ	
14. ⓐ ⓑ ⓒ ⓓ ⓔ	34. ⓐ ⓑ ⓒ ⓓ ⓔ	
15. ⓐ ⓑ ⓒ ⓓ ⓔ	35. ⓐ ⓑ ⓒ ⓓ ⓔ	
16. ⓐ ⓑ ⓒ ⓓ ⓔ	36. ⓐ ⓑ ⓒ ⓓ ⓔ	
17. ⓐ ⓑ ⓒ ⓓ ⓔ	37. ⓐ ⓑ ⓒ ⓓ ⓔ	
18. ⓐ ⓑ ⓒ ⓓ ⓔ	38. ⓐ ⓑ ⓒ ⓓ ⓔ	
19. ⓐ ⓑ ⓒ ⓓ ⓔ	39. ⓐ ⓑ ⓒ ⓓ ⓔ	
20. ⓐ ⓑ ⓒ ⓓ ⓔ	40. ⓐ ⓑ ⓒ ⓓ ⓔ	

Section 1: Reading Comprehension

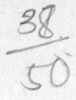

Answer questions 1–8 on the basis of the following passage.

(1) Produced in 1959, Lorraine Hansberry's play, *A Raisin in the Sun*, was a quietly revolutionary work that depicted African-American life in a fresh, new, and realistic way. The play made her the youngest American, the first African-American, and the fifth woman to win the New York Drama Critic's Circle Award for Best Play of the Year. In 1961, it was produced as a film starring Sydney Poitier and has since become a classic, providing inspiration for an entire generation of African-American writers.

(2) Hansberry was not only an artist but also a political activist and the daughter of activists. Born in Chicago in 1930, she was a member of a prominent family devoted to civil rights. Her father was a successful real-estate broker, who won an anti-segregation case before the Illinois Supreme Court in the mid-1930s, and her uncle was a Harvard professor. In her home, Hansberry was privileged to meet many influential cultural and intellectual leaders. Among them were artists and activists such as Paul Robeson, W.E.B. DuBois, and Langston Hughes.

(3) The success of *A Raisin in the Sun* helped gain an audience for her passionate views on social justice. It mirrors one of Hansberry's central artistic efforts, that of freeing many people from the smothering effects of stereotyping by depicting the wide array of personality types and aspirations that exist within one Southside Chicago family. *A Raisin in the Sun* was followed by another play, produced in 1964, *The Sign in Sidney Brustein's Window*. This play is about an intellectual in Greenwich Village, New York City, a man who is open-minded and generous of spirit who, as Hansberry wrote, "cares about it all. It takes too much energy not to care."

(4) Lorraine Hansberry died on the final day of the play's run on Broadway. Her early death, at the age of 34, was unfortunate, as it cut short a brilliant and promising career, one that, even in its short span, changed the face of American theater. After her death, however, her influence continued to be felt. A dramatic adaptation of her autobiography, *To Be Young, Gifted, and Black*, consisted of vignettes based on Hansberry's plays, poems, and other writings. It was produced Off-Broadway in 1969 and appeared in book form the following year. Her play, *Les Blancs*, a drama set in Africa, was produced in 1970; and *A Raisin in the Sun* was adapted as a musical, *Raisin*, and won a Tony award in 1973.

(5) Even after her death, her dramatic works have helped gain an audience for her essays and speeches on wide-ranging topics, from world peace to the evils of the mistreatment of minorities, no matter what their race, and especially for her works on the civil-rights struggle and on the effort by Africans to be free of colonial rule. She was a woman, much like the characters in her best-known play, who was determined to be free of racial, cultural, or gender-based constraints.

1. The writer of the passage suggests that Hansberry's political beliefs had their origins in her experience as
   a. the daughter of politically active parents.
   b. a successful playwright in New York.
   c. a resident of Southside Chicago.
   d. an intellectual in Greenwich Village.
   e. a civil rights activist.

2. The main purpose of the passage is to
   a. praise Lorraine Hansberry's writings and illustrate their artistic and political influence.
   b. summarize Lorraine Hansberry's best-known works.
   c. demonstrate that if one is raised in a well-educated family, such as Lorraine Hansberry's, one is likely to succeed.
   d. show Lorraine Hansberry's difficult struggle and ultimate success as a young female writer.
   e. persuade students to read *A Raisin In The Sun*.

3. Hansberry's father earned his living as
   a. a civil-rights worker.
   b. a banker.
   c. a real-estate broker.
   d. an artist and activist.
   e. an attorney.

4. Paragraph 3 suggests that Hansberry's main purpose in writing *A Raisin in the Sun* was to
   a. win her father's approval.
   b. break down stereotypes.
   c. show people how interesting her own family was.
   d. earn the right to produce her own plays.
   e. win a Best Play award.

5. By including paragraphs 4 and 5, the author most likely intended to show that
   a. the civil-rights struggle continued even after Hansberry died.
   b. Hansberry actually wrote more poems and essays than she did plays.
   c. *Raisin in the Sun* was more successful after Hansberry's death than it was before she died.
   d. Hansberry's work continued to influence people even after her death.
   e. Hansberry died unusually young.

6. According to the passage, how many women had won the New York Drama Critic's Circle Award for Best Play of the Year *before* Lorraine Hansberry did?
   a. none
   b. one
   c. four
   d. five
   e. six

7. As it is used in paragraph 3, the underlined phrase *wide array* most nearly means
   a. variety.
   b. gathering.
   c. arrangement.
   d. decoration.
   e. features.

8. According to the passage, which of the following dramatic works was based most directly on Hansberry's life?
   a. *A Raisin in the Sun*
   b. *Les Blancs*
   c. *The Sign in Sidney Brustein's Window*
   d. *To Be Young, Gifted, and Black*
   e. the musical *Raisin*

Answer question 9 on the basis of the following passage.

Moscow has a history of chaotic periods of war that ended with the destruction of a once largely wooden city and the building of a "new" city on top of the rubble of the old. The result is a layered city, with each tier holding information about a part of Russia's past. In some areas of the city, archaeologists have reached the layer from 1147, the year of Moscow's founding. Among the findings from the various periods of Moscow's history are carved bones, metal tools, pottery, glass, jewelry, and crosses.

infer – to conclude by reasoning from something known or assumed

9. From the passage, the reader can infer that
   a. the people of Moscow are more interested in modernization than in preservation.
   b. the Soviet government destroyed many of the historic buildings in Russia.
   c. Moscow is the oldest large city in Russia, founded in 1147.
   d. Moscow has a history of invasions, with each new conqueror razing past structures.
   e. Moscow has endured many periods of uprising and revolution.

Answer questions 10–13 on the basis of the following passage.

Heat reactions usually occur when large amounts of water and/or salt are lost through excessive sweating following strenuous exercise. When the body becomes overheated and cannot eliminate this excess heat, heat exhaustion and heat stroke are possible.

Heat exhaustion is generally characterized by clammy skin, fatigue, nausea, dizziness, profuse perspiration, and sometimes fainting, resulting from an inadequate intake of water and the loss of fluids. First aid treatment for this condition includes having the victim lie down, raising the feet 8–12 inches, applying cool, wet cloths to the skin, and giving the victim sips of salt water (1 teaspoon per glass, half a glass every 15 minutes), over the period of an hour.

Heat stroke is much more serious; it is an immediately life-threatening situation. The characteristics of heat stroke are a high body temperature (which may reach 106°F or more); a rapid pulse; hot, dry skin; and a blocked sweating mechanism. Victims of this condition may be unconscious, and first aid measures should be directed at cooling the body quickly. The victim should be placed in a tub of cold water or repeatedly sponged with cool water until his or her temperature is lowered sufficiently. Fans or air conditioners will also help with the cooling process. Care should be taken, however, not to overchill the victim once the temperature is below 102°F.

10. The most immediate concern of a person tending a victim of heat stroke should be to
    a. get salt into the victim's body.
    b. raise the victim's feet.
    c. lower the victim's pulse rate.
    d. have the victim lie down.
    e. lower the victim's temperature.

11. Which of the following is a symptom of heat exhaustion?
    a. unconsciousness
    b. excessive sweating
    c. hot, dry skin
    d. a weak pulse
    e. a rapid pulse

12. Heat stroke is more serious than heat exhaustion because heat stroke victims
    a. have too little salt in their bodies.
    b. cannot take in water.
    c. do not sweat.
    d. have frequent fainting spells.
    e. may have convulsions.

13. On the basis of the information in the passage, symptoms such as nausea and dizziness in a heat exhaustion victim indicate that the person most likely needs to
    a. be immediately taken to a hospital.
    b. be immersed in a tub of water.
    c. be given more salt water.
    d. sweat more.
    e. go to an air-conditioned place.

Answer questions 14 and 15 on the basis of the following passage.

Poet William Blake believed that true religion is revealed through art, not through nature. For Blake, it is through art also that eternity is revealed. One does not have to die to reach eternity; eternity is the moment of vision. It is only through the reordering of sense impressions by the creative imagination that we are able, as Blake says in his "Auguries of Innocence," "To see the World in a Grain of Sand / . . . And Eternity in an hour."

14. Which of the following would best describe what Blake meant by the words "To see the World in a Grain of Sand / . . . And Eternity in an hour?"
   a. a moment of mystical enlightenment
   b. conversion to Christianity
   c. a moment of artistic inspiration
   d. an hallucinatory experience
   e. a return to a state of being without sin

15. Which of the following defines Blake's view of "nature" as described in the passage?
   a. the raw stuff of which the world is made but which does not represent ultimate reality
   b. the work of God in a state of innocence before it is corrupted by human beings
   c. the world made up of base and corrupt material before it is changed by the perception of the artist at the "moment of vision"
   d. the temporal world that will perish, as opposed to the world of artistic vision that will last forever
   e. the real world as it is perceived by ordinary people, as opposed to the fantasy world of the artist

Answer questions 16–18 on the basis of the following passage.

Businesses today routinely keep track of large amounts of both financial and non-financial information. Sales departments keep track of current and potential customers; marketing departments keep track of product details and regional demographics; accounting departments keep track of financial data and issue reports. To be useful, all this data must be organized into a meaningful and useful system. Such a system is called a management information system, abbreviated MIS. The financial hub of the MIS is accounting.

Accounting is the information system that records, analyzes, and reports economic transactions, enabling decision-makers to make informed choices when allocating scarce economic resources. It is a tool that enables the user, whether a business entity or an individual, to make wiser, more informed economic choices. It is an aid to planning, controlling, and evaluating a broad range of activities. A financial accounting system is intended for use by both the management of an organization and those outside the organization. Because it is important that financial accounting reports be interpreted correctly, financial accounting is subject to a set of _____ guidelines called "generally accepted accounting principles" (GAAP).

16. This passage is most likely taken from
   a. a newspaper column.
   b. an essay about modern business.
   c. a legal brief.
   d. a business textbook.
   e. a business machine catalog.

17. The word that would fit most correctly into the blank in the final sentence is
   a. discretionary.
   b. convenient.
   c. instruction.
   d. austere.
   e. stringent.

18. According to the information in the passage, which of the following is LEAST likely to be a function of accounting?
   a. helping business people make sound judgments
   b. producing reports of many different kinds of transactions
   c. assisting with the marketing of products
   d. assisting companies in important planning activities
   e. providing information to potential investors

Answer questions 19 and 20 on the basis of the following passage.

The fictional world of Toni Morrison's novel *Sula*—the African-American section of Medallion, Ohio, a community called "the Bottom"—is a place where people, and even natural things, are apt to go awry, to break from their prescribed boundaries, a place where bizarre and unnatural happenings and strange reversals of the ordinary are commonplace. The very naming of the setting of *Sula* is a turning-upside-down of the expected; the Bottom is located high up in the hills. The novel is furthermore filled with images of mutilation, both psychological and physical. A great part of the lives of the characters, therefore, is taken up with making sense of the world, setting boundaries and devising methods to control what is essentially uncontrollable. One of the major devices used by the people of the Bottom is the seemingly universal one of creating a _____—in this case, the title character Sula—upon which to project both the evil they perceive outside themselves and the evil in their own hearts.

19. Based on the description of the setting of the novel *Sula*, which of the following adjectives would most likely describe the behavior of many of its residents?
   a. cowardly
   b. artistic
   c. unkempt
   d. arrogant
   e. eccentric

20. Which of the following words would BEST fit into the blank in the final sentence of the passage?
   a. victim
   b. hero
   c. leader
   d. scapegoat
   e. outcast

Answer questions 21–23 on the basis of the following passage.

Ever since human beings began their conscious sojourn on this planet, they have puzzled over the riddle of evil and debated its source. Two concepts have predominated in the debate. The first of these holds that evil is an active force, a force of darkness as substantial and powerful as that of light. In terms of the individual human being, this force might be seen as the "Shadow" side of the personality, the feared side that the individual may deny but that is still a real and integral part of her or him. The second of the two concepts holds that evil is essentially _____, the absence of good, that darkness is not a thing in itself but rather the absence of light. In terms of the individual human being, this doctrine says that evil arises from a lack, a deprivation, from what John A. Sanford calls "a mutilation of the soul."

21. Which of the following phrases would best fit into the blank in the third sentence of the passage?
   a. perplexing
   b. passive
   c. capricious
   d. ephemeral
   e. artificial

22. The main point of the passage is that
   a. human beings have long pondered the enigma of evil.
   b. evil may be viewed as either a natural force or a human characteristic.
   c. there are two long-debated, contradictory views of evil.
   d. human beings are not likely ever to solve the problem of evil.
   e. evil must be understood in order for good to be appreciated.

23. Which of the following, according to the passage, does an individual sometimes use to deal with the "Shadow" side of his or her personality?
   a. scorn
   b. love
   c. acceptance
   d. denial
   e. projection

Answer questions 24–26 on the basis of the following poem by Alfred Lord Tennyson.

The Eagle

He clasps the crag with crooked hands;
Close to the sun in lonely lands,
Ringed with the azure world he stands.

The wrinkled sea beneath him crawls;
He watches from his mountain walls,
And like a thunderbolt he falls.

24. Given the tone of the poem, and noting especially the last line, what is the eagle MOST likely doing in the poem?
   a. dying of old age
   b. hunting prey
   c. learning joyfully to fly
   d. keeping watch over a nest of young eagles
   e. battling another eagle

25. To which of the following do the words "azure world" most likely refer?
   a. a forest
   b. the sky
   c. the cliff
   d. nature
   e. God

26. In the second stanza, first line, to which of the following does the verb "crawls" refer?
   a. waves
   b. sea creatures
   c. sunlight on the water
   d. the eagle's prey
   e. the eagle itself

Answer questions 27 and 28 on the basis of the following index from a forest management textbook.

INDEX

fire protection, 51–55, 108, 115

forest conflicts: European, 8, 91–93, 116–117, 133–134, 186–188

forest destruction and ecological decline, 143; and fire, 31–35; and industrialization, 156–173; and railways 27–29; and scientific forestry, 60–61; and villagers, 107, 115–116; and World Wars, 42–43, 46–47

forest fires, 72, 87, 100–105, 124; and pasture, 48, 51–53, 115–118; arson, 51, 122, 126–130; *see also* fire protection

forest law: breaches of, 34–41, 49–52, 55, 70,

115–116, 121–123; *see also* forest conflicts

forest management: and agrarian economy, 104–105, 121, 186–189; and imperial needs, 28, 35; and slash-and-burn farming, 12–18, 48; and commercial orientation of, 30–32; peasant resistance to, 69–76, 89, 99–106

27. On the basis of the index, on which page would you be most likely to find information about the outlawed practice of burning forested areas to create fields for grazing small herds of livestock?
   a. page 89
   b. page 55
   c. page 107
   d. page 48
   e. page 51

28. On what cause of *forest destruction* does the author of the textbook focus most, from the evidence of the index?
   a. industrialization
   b. fire damage
   c. railroads
   d. ecological decline
   e. scientific forestry

Answer questions 29–31 on the basis of the following passage.

1) The Woodstock Music and Art Fair—better known to its participants and to history simply as "Woodstock"—should have been a colossal failure. 2) Just a month prior to its August 15, 1969 opening, the fair's organizers were informed by the council of Wallkill, New York, that permission to hold the festival was withdrawn. 3) Amazingly, not only was a new site found, but word got out to the public of the fair's new location. 4) At the new site, fences that were supposed to facilitate ticket collection never materialized, and all attempts at gathering tickets were abandoned. 5) Crowd estimates of 30,000 kept rising; by the end of the three days, some estimated the crowd at 500,000. 6) And then, on opening night, it began to rain. 7) Off and on, throughout all three days, huge summer storms rolled over the gathering. 8) In spite of these problems, most people think of Woodstock not only as a fond memory but as the defining moment for an entire generation.

29. Which of the following would be the most appropriate title for this passage?
   a. Woodstock as Metaphor
   b. Backstage at Woodstock
   c. Woodstock: From The Band to The Who
   d. Remembering Woodstock
   e. Woodstock: The Untold Story

30. Which of the following numbered sentences of the passage best represents an opinion rather than a fact?
   a. sentence 1
   b. sentence 2
   c. sentence 3
   d. sentence 4
   e. sentence 5

31. Why is the word "amazingly" used in sentence 3?
   a. because the time in which the move was made and information sent out was so short
   b. because the fair drew such an unexpectedly enormous crowd
   c. because there was such pressure by New York officials against holding the fair
   d. because the stormy weather was so unfavorable
   e. because ticket-taking was abandoned at the fair so anyone could come in

Answer questions 32–35 on the basis of the following passage.

Cuttlefish are intriguing little animals. The cuttlefish resembles a rather large squid and is, like the octopus, a member of the order of cephalopods. Although they are not considered the most highly evolved of the cephalopods, they are extremely intelligent. While observing them, it is hard to tell who is doing the observing, you or the cuttlefish, especially since the eye of the cuttlefish is very similar in structure to the human eye. Cuttlefish are also highly mobile and fast creatures. They come equipped with a small jet located just below the tentacles that can expel water to help them move. Ribbons of flexible fin on each side of the body allow cuttlefish to hover, move, stop, and start. _____
_____.

The cuttlefish is sometimes referred to as the "chameleon of the sea" because it can change its skin color and pattern instantaneously. Masters of camouflage, they can blend into any environment for protection, but they are also capable of the most imaginative displays of iridescent, brilliant color and intricate designs, which scientists believe they use to communicate with each other and for mating displays. However, judging from the riot of ornaments and hues cuttlefish produce, it is hard not to believe they paint themselves so beautifully just for the sheer joy of it. At the very least, cuttlefish conversation must be the most sparkling in all the sea.

32. Which of the following sentences, if inserted into the blank line, would best sum up the first paragraph and lead into the next?
   a. The cuttlefish can be cooked and eaten like its less tender relatives, the squid and octopus, but must still be tenderized before cooking in order not to be exceedingly chewy.
   b. On a scuba dive when you're observing cuttlefish, it is best to move slowly because cuttlefish have excellent eyesight and will probably see you first.
   c. Cuttlefish do not have an exoskeleton; instead, their skin is covered with chromataphors.
   d. The cuttlefish has ten arms, two of which are specialized feeders and its mouth is beak-like; this enables it to capture crustaceans with its powerful arms and crack shells with its strong mouth.
   e. By far their most intriguing characteristic is their ability to change their body color and pattern.

33. Which of the following is correct according to the information given in the passage?
   a. Cuttlefish are a type of squid.
   b. Cuttlefish use jet propulsion as one form of locomotion.
   c. The cuttlefish does not have an exoskeleton.
   d. Cuttlefish are the most intelligent cephalopods.
   e. Cuttlefish always imitate the patterns and colors of their environment.

34. Which of the following best outlines the main topics addressed in the passage?
   a. I. Explanation of why cuttlefish are intriguing
      II. Communication skills of cuttlefish
   b. I. Classification and difficulties of observing cuttlefish
      II. Scientific explanation of modes of cuttlefish communication
   c. I. Explanation of the cuttlefish's method of locomotion
      II. Description of color displays in mating behavior
   d. I. Comparison of cuttlefish with other cephalopods
      II. Usefulness of the cuttlefish's ability to change color
   e. I. General classification and characteristics of cuttlefish
      II. Uses and beauty of the cuttlefish's ability to change color

35. Which of the following best describes the purpose of the author of the passage?
   a. to prove the intelligence of cuttlefish
   b. to explain the communication habits of cuttlefish
   c. to produce a fanciful description of the "chameleon of the sea"
   d. to persuade scuba divers of the interest in observing cuttlefish
   e. to describe the "chameleon of the sea" informatively and entertainingly

Answer question 36 on the basis of the following passage.

A book proposal has three major functions. First, it should sell a publisher on the commercial potential of the as-yet-to-be-written book. Second, the writing in the proposal itself should convince the publisher that the author has the ability to write the book. Finally, the proposal should show that the author has the background necessary to write the book.

36. Which of the following is the best meaning of the word "background" as it is used in the passage?
   a. something behind the main event
   b. something in a subordinated position
   c. one's ability to do something
   d. events leading up to something
   e. facts to help explain something

Answer questions 37–40 on the basis of the following passage.

Off-site disposal of regulated medical wastes remains a viable option for smaller hospitals (those with less than 150 beds). However, some preliminary on-site processing, such as compaction or hydropulping, may be necessary prior to sending the wastes off-site.

Compaction reduces the total volume of solid wastes, often reducing transportation and disposal costs, but does not change the hazardous characteristics of the waste. However, compaction may not be economical if transportation and disposal costs are based on weight rather than volume. Hydropulping involves grinding the waste in the presence of an oxidizing fluid, such as hypochlorite solution. One advantage of hydropulping is that waste can be rendered innocuous and reduced in size within the same system. Disadvantages are the added operating burden, difficulty of controlling fugitive emission, and the difficulty of conducting microbiological tests to determine whether all organic matters and infectious organisms from the waste have been destroyed.

On-site disposal is a feasible alternative for hospitals generating two tons per day or more total of solid waste. Common treatment techniques include steam sterilization and incineration. Although other options are available, incineration is currently the preferred method for on-site treatment of hospital waste. A properly designed, maintained, and operated incinerator achieves a relatively high level of organism destruction. Incineration reduces the weight and volume of the waste as much as 95 percent and is especially appropriate for pathological wastes.

37. One disadvantage of the compaction method of waste disposal is that it
   a. cannot reduce transportation costs.
   b. reduces the volume of solid waste material.
   c. does not allow hospitals to confirm that organic matter has been eliminated.
   d. does not reduce the weight of solid waste material.
   e. cannot be done on-site.

38. The process that transforms waste from hazardous to harmless AND diminishes waste volume is
   a. sterilization.
   b. hydropulping.
   c. oxidizing.
   d. processing.
   e. compacting.

39. For hospitals that dispose of waste on their own premises, the optimum treatment method is
   a. incineration.
   b. compaction.
   c. sterilization.
   d. hydropulping.
   e. grinding.

40. According to the information in the passage, which of the following is one criterion used to determine whether waste will be disposed of on-site or off-site?
   a. number of patients the hospital serves
   b. amount of pathogens in the waste
   c. whether organisms can be properly destroyed
   d. whether or not the waste can be reduced
   e. whether or not the waste is regulated

Answer question 41 on the basis of the following passage.

The Sami are an indigenous people living in the northern parts of Norway, Sweden, Finland, and Russia's Kola peninsula. Originally, the Sami religion was animistic; that is, for them, nature and natural objects had a conscious life, a spirit. One was expected to move quietly in the wilderness and avoid making a disturbance out of courtesy to these spirits. Ghengis Khan is said to have declared that the Sami were one people he would never try to fight again. Since the Sami were not warriors and did not believe in war, they simply disappeared in times of conflict. They were known as "peaceful retreaters."

41. Based on the tone of the passage, which of the following words best describes the author's attitude toward the Sami people?
   a. admiring
   b. pitying
   c. contemptuous
   d. patronizing
   e. perplexed

Answer question 42 on the basis of the following passage.

Electronic mail (e-mail) has been in widespread use for more than a decade. E-mail simplifies the flow of ideas, connects people from distant offices, eliminates the need for meetings, and often boosts productivity. But e-mail should be carefully managed to avoid unclear and inappropriate communication. E-mail messages should be concise and limited to one topic. When complex issues need to be addressed, phone calls are still best.

42. The paragraph best supports the statement that e-mail
   a. is not always the easiest way to connect people from distant offices.
   b. has changed considerably since it first began a decade ago.
   c. causes people to be unproductive when it is used incorrectly.
   d. is most effective when it is wisely managed.
   e. should be used mainly for unimportant messages.

Answer question 43 on the basis of the following passage.

More and more office workers telecommute from offices in their own homes. The upside of telecommuting is both greater productivity and greater flexibility. Telecommuters produce, on average, 20% more than if they were to work in an office, and their flexible schedule allows them to balance both their family and work responsibilities.

43. The paragraph best supports the statement that telecommuters
   a. have more family responsibilities than workers who travel to the office.
   b. get more work done in a given time period than workers who travel to the office.
   c. produce a better quality work product than workers who travel to the office.
   d. are more flexible in their personal lives than workers who travel to the office.
   e. would do 20% more work if they were to work in an office.

Answer question 44 on the basis of the following passage.

Fax machines have made it possible for information to be transmitted to distant locations within minutes, but what about confidential information? Are faxes always secure? To avoid having faxes misdirected, arrange for authorized persons to receive and transmit confidential messages. Always phone the recipient about an incoming confidential fax, and make contact a second time to make sure the fax was received.

44. The paragraph best supports the statement that
   a. the majority of faxes contain confidential information.
   b. faxes should not be sent if the information is confidential.
   c. fax machines should be locked up in secure offices.
   d. precautions should be taken before a confidential fax message is sent.
   e. a fax is more timely than other office transmission systems.

Answer question 45 on the basis of the following passage.

Keeping busy at important tasks is much more motivating than having too little to do. Today's employees are not afraid of responsibility. Most people are willing to take on extra responsibility in order to have more variety on their jobs. And, along with more responsibility should come the authority to carry out some important tasks independently.

45. The paragraph best supports the statement that
   a. variety on the job helps increase employee motivation.
   b. employees like responsibility more than authority.
   c. to avoid boredom, many people do more work than their jobs require of them.
   d. today's employees are demanding more independence than ever before.
   e. office jobs in the past have carried little responsibility.

Answer questions 46–50 on the basis of the following passage.

A government report addressing concerns about the many implications of prenatal and newborn genetic testing outlined policy guidelines and legislative recommendations intended to avoid involuntary and ineffective testing and to protect confidentiality.

The report recommended that all such screening be voluntary. Citing results of two different voluntary newborn screening programs, the report said these programs can achieve compliance rates equal to or better than those of mandatory programs. State health departments might be wise to eventually mandate the offering of tests for diagnosing treatable conditions in newborns; however, careful pilot studies for conditions diagnosable at birth need to be done first.

Although the report asserted that it would prefer that all screening be voluntary, it did note that if a state elects to mandate newborn screening for a particular condition, the state should do so only if there is strong evidence that a newborn would benefit from effective treatment at the earliest possible age. Newborn screening is the most common type of genetic screening today. More than four million newborns are tested annually so that effective treatment can be started in a few hundred infants.

Obtaining informed consent—a process that would include educating participants, not just processing documents—would enhance voluntary participation. When offered testing, parents should receive comprehensive counseling, which should be nondirective. Relevant medical advice, however, is recommended for treatable or preventable conditions.

46. Based on the passage, for which of the following would the government report LEAST likely recommend mandated genetic testing?
   a. contagious diseases
   b. untreatable conditions
   c. fatal diseases
   d. disabling diseases
   e. carrier diseases

47. According to the passage, how many infants are treated for genetic disorders as a result of newborn screening?
   a. dozens
   b. hundreds
   c. thousands
   d. millions
   e. It is not possible to tell from the information in the passage.

48. One intention of the policy guidelines was to
  a. implement compulsory testing.
  b. minimize patient concerns about quality control.
  c. endorse the expansion of screening programs.
  d. rule out testing for minor genetic disorders.
  e. preserve privacy in testing.

49. According to the report, states should implement mandatory infant screening only
  a. if the compliance rate for voluntary screening is low.
  b. for mothers who are at high risk for genetic disease.
  c. after meticulous research is undertaken.
  d. to avoid the abuse of sensitive information.
  e. if fatal disorders are suspected.

50. According to the passage, the most prevalent form of genetic testing is conducted
  a. on high-risk populations.
  b. on adults.
  c. on fetuses prior to birth.
  d. on infants shortly after birth.
  e. on mothers shortly after they give birth.

▶ **Section 2:** Mathematics

Use the information below to answer question 1.

If Linda purchases an item that costs $30 or less, she will pay with cash.
If Linda purchases an item that costs between $30 and $70, she will pay with a check.
If Linda purchases an item that costs $70 or greater, she will use a credit card.

1. If Linda recently paid for a certain item using a check, which of the following statements could be true?
  a. The item costs $20.
  b. The item costs $80.
  c. If the item had cost $20 more, she would have paid with cash.
  d. The item costs at least $70.
  e. The item costs more than $25.

2. What is 56.73647 rounded to the nearest hundredth?
  a. 100
  b. 57
  c. 56.7
  d. 56.74
  e. 56.736

3. Which of the following is between $\frac{1}{3}$ and $\frac{1}{4}$?
  a. $\frac{1}{2}$
  b. $\frac{1}{5}$
  c. $\frac{2}{3}$
  d. $\frac{2}{5}$
  e. $\frac{2}{7}$

4. The population of Smithtown increases at a rate of 3% annually. If the population is currently 2,500, what will the population be at the same time next year?
   a. 2,530
   b. 2,560
   c. 2,575
   d. 2,800
   e. 3,000

Use the graph below to answer questions 5 and 6.

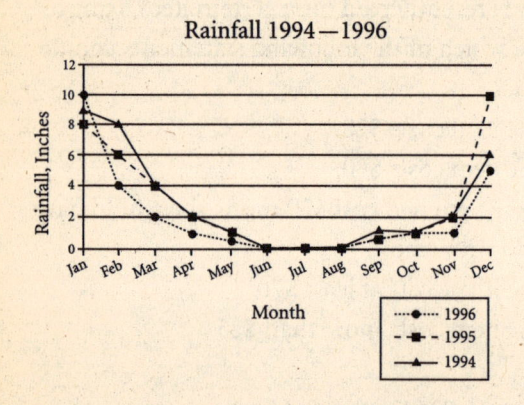

Rainfall 1994—1996

5. What month in 1995 had the most rainfall?
   a. January
   b. February
   c. March
   d. November
   e. December

6. What was the average (mean) rainfall in February for the three years?
   a. 4 inches
   b. 5 inches
   c. 6 inches
   d. 7 inches
   e. 8 inches

7. The Chen family traveled 75 miles to visit relatives. If they traveled $43\frac{1}{3}$ miles before they stopped at a gas station, how far was the gas station from their relatives' house?
   a. $31\frac{2}{3}$ miles
   b. $32\frac{2}{3}$ miles
   c. 35 miles
   d. $38\frac{1}{3}$ miles
   e. $43\frac{1}{3}$ miles

8. Julie counts the cars passing her house, and finds that 2 of every 5 cars are foreign. If she counts for an hour, and 60 cars pass, how many of them are likely to be domestic?
   a. 12
   b. 24
   c. 30
   d. 36
   e. 40

Use the table and the information below to answer question 9.

A recent survey polled 2,500 people about their reading habits. The results are as follows:

| SURVEY REGARDING READING HABITS ||
Books per month	Percentage
0	13
1–3	27
4–6	32
> 6	28

9. How many people surveyed had read books in the last month?
   a. 325
   b. 700
   c. 1,800
   d. 1,825
   e. 2,175

10. A certain university has 36,042 total students. Of these students, 16,534 are male. Approximately how many more women attend the university than men?
    a. 1,500
    b. 2,000
    c. 3,000
    d. 4,000
    e. 4,500

11. A rectangular tumbling mat for a gym class is 5 feet wide and 7 feet long. What is the area of the mat?
    a. 12 square feet
    b. 22 square feet
    c. 24 square feet
    d. 35 square feet
    e. 42 square feet

12. A machine on a production line produces parts that are not acceptable by company standards 4% of the time. If the machine produces 500 parts, how many will be defective?
    a. 4
    b. 8
    c. 10
    d. 16
    e. 20

13. A certain congressional district has about 490,000 people living in it. The largest city in the area has 98,000 citizens. Which most accurately portrays the portion of the population made up by the city in the district?
    a. $\frac{1}{5}$
    b. $\frac{1}{4}$
    c. $\frac{2}{9}$
    d. $\frac{3}{4}$
    e. $\frac{4}{5}$

14. A recipe calls for $1\frac{1}{4}$ cups of flour. If Larry wants to make $2\frac{1}{2}$ times the recipe, how much flour does he need?
    a. $2\frac{3}{4}$
    b. $3\frac{1}{8}$
    c. $3\frac{1}{4}$
    d. $3\frac{5}{8}$
    e. $4\frac{1}{4}$

15. Thirty percent of the high school is involved in athletics. If 15% of the athletes play football, what percentage of the whole school plays football?
    a. 4.5%
    b. 9.0%
    c. 15%
    d. 30%
    e. 45%

16. Twenty percent of the people at a restaurant selected the dinner special. If 40 people did not select the special, how many people are eating at the restaurant?
    a. 10
    b. 20
    c. 40
    d. 50
    e. 60

17. John's Market sells milk for $2.24 per gallon. Food Supply sells the same milk for $2.08 per gallon. If Mitzi buys 2 gallons of milk at Food Supply instead of John's, how much will she save?
a. $0.12
b. $0.14
c. $0.32
d. $0.38
e. $0.42

18. Fifty-four students are to be separated into six groups of equal size. How many students are in each group?
a. 8
b. 9
c. 10
d. 11
e. 12

Use the information below to answer question 19.

Textbooks are to be ordered in the following quantities:

History: 24 books at $20 each
Math: 20 books at $30 each
Science: 15 books at $25 each

19. What is the total cost of the textbooks?
a. $1455
b. $1495
c. $1500
d. $1510
e. $1550

20. A small town emergency room admits a patient on August 3 at 10:42 P.M. and another patient at 1:19 A.M. on August 4. How much time has elapsed between admissions?
a. 1 hour 19 minutes
b. 1 hour 37 minutes
c. 2 hours 23 minutes
d. 2 hours 37 minutes
e. 3 hours 23 minutes

21. Nationwide, in one year there were about 21,500 residential fires associated with furniture. Of these, 11,350 were caused by smoking materials. About what percent of the residential fires were smoking related?
a. 47%
b. 49%
c. 50%
d. 51%
e. 53%

22. Jerry was $\frac{1}{3}$ as young as his grandfather 15 years ago. If the sum of their ages is 110, how old is Jerry's grandfather?
a. 80
b. 75
c. 65
d. 60
e. 50

23. Solve for x in the following equation: $\frac{1}{3}x + 3 = 8$.
a. 33
b. 15
c. 11
d. 3
e. $\frac{11}{3}$

Use the diagram below to answer question 24.

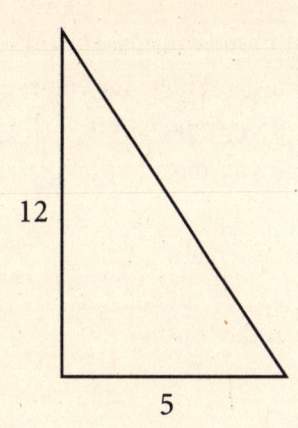

24. What is the perimeter of the figure shown above?
 a. 17
 b. 20
 c. 30
 d. 40
 e. 60

Use the diagram below to answer question 25.

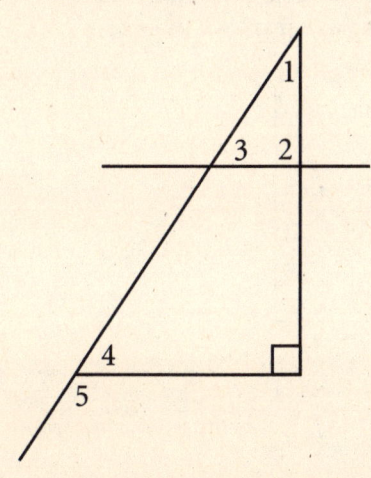

25. In the diagram above, if angle 1 is 30 degrees, and angle 2 is a right angle, what is the measure of angle 5?
 a. 30 degrees
 b. 60 degrees
 c. 120 degrees
 d. 140 degrees
 e. 150 degrees

Use the diagram below to answer question 26.

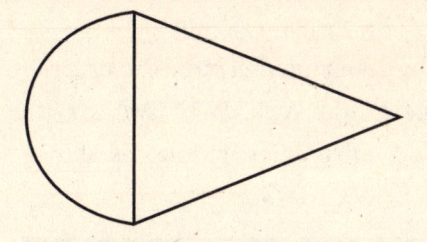

26. In the diagram, a half-circle is laid adjacent to a triangle. What is the total area of the shape, if the radius of the half-circle is 3 and the height of the triangle is 4?
 a. $6(\pi + 4)$
 b. $6\pi + 12$
 c. $6\pi + 24$
 d. $\frac{9\pi}{2} + 12$
 e. $\frac{9}{2}\pi + 24$

Use the table below to answer question 27.

DISTANCE TRAVELED FROM CHICAGO WITH RESPECT TO TIME

Time (hours)	Distance from Chicago (miles)
1	60
2	120
3	180
4	240

27. A train moving at a constant speed leaves Chicago for Los Angeles at time $t = 0$. If Los Angeles is 2,000 miles from Chicago, which of the following equations describes the distance from Los Angeles at any time t?
 a. $D(t) = 60t - 2,000$
 b. $D(t) = 60t$
 c. $D(t) = 2,000 - 60t$
 d. $D(t) = \frac{2,000}{60t}$
 e. $D(t) = 2,000 + 60t$

175

Use the table and the information below to answer question 28.

Felipe is planning to get an Internet service in order to have access to the World Wide Web. Two service providers, A and B, offer different rates as shown below.

INTERNET SERVICE RATES

Provider	Free Hours	Base Charge	Hourly Charge
A	17.5	$20.00	$1.00
B	20	$20.00	$1.50

28. If Felipe plans on using 25 hours of Internet service per month, which of the following statements is true?
   a. Provider A will be cheaper.
   b. Provider B will be cheaper.
   c. The answer cannot be determined from the information given.
   d. The answer cannot be determined but could be if no hours were free.
   e. The providers will cost the same per month.

29. Anne has two containers for water: a rectangular plastic box with a base of 16 square inches, and a cylindrical container with a radius of 2 inches and a height of 9 inches. If the rectangular box is filled with water 9 inches from the bottom, and Anne pours the water into the cylinder without spilling, which of the following will be true?
   a. The cylinder will overflow.
   b. The cylinder will be exactly full.
   c. The cylinder will be filled to an approximate level of 10 inches.
   d. The cylinder will be filled to an approximate level of 8 inches.
   e. The cylinder will be filled to an approximate level of 6 inches.

Use the information below to answer question 30.

Roger, Lucy, Mike, and Samantha are cousins. They all practice unique sports: One enjoys skiing, one enjoys fishing, one enjoys tennis, and one enjoys volleyball. Use the statements below to answer the question that follows.
   I. The cousin who fishes is female.
   II. Roger and Lucy hate sports with balls.
   III. Samantha is older than the cousin who fishes.

30. Who likes to fish?
   a. Roger
   b. Mike
   c. Samantha
   d. Lucy
   e. The answer cannot be determined from the information given.

31. Triangles RST and MNO are similar. What is the length of line segment MO?

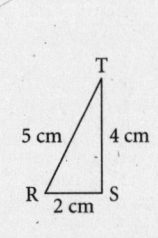

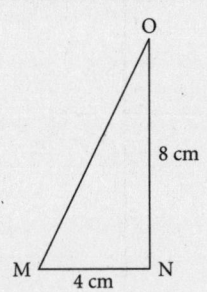

   a. 5 cm
   b. 10 cm
   c. 20 cm
   d. 32 cm
   e. 40 cm

32. Which number sentence is true?
   a. $4.3 < 0.43$
   b. $0.43 < 0.043$
   c. $0.0043 > 0.43$
   d. $0.00043 > 0.043$
   e. $0.043 > 0.0043$

33. Which of the following means $5n + 7 = 17$?
 a. 7 more than 5 times a number is 17
 b. 5 more than 7 times a number is 17
 c. 7 less than 5 times a number is 17
 d. 12 times a number is 17
 e. 17 divided by a number is 5

Use the diagram to answer item 34.

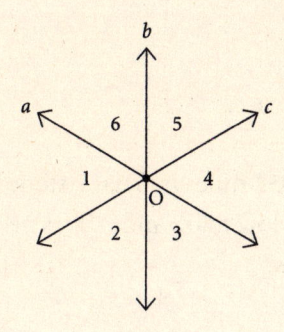

34. In the diagram, lines *a*, *b*, and *c* intersect at point O. Which of the following are NOT adjacent angles?
 a. $\angle 1$ and $\angle 6$
 b. $\angle 1$ and $\angle 4$
 c. $\angle 4$ and $\angle 5$
 d. $\angle 2$ and $\angle 3$
 e. All of the angles are adjacent.

35. What is the value of *y* when $x = 3$ and $y = 5 + 4x$?
 a. 6
 b. 9
 c. 12
 d. 17
 e. 20

36. The radius of a circle is 13. What is the approximate area of the circle?
 a. 81.64
 b. 530.66
 c. 1,666.27
 d. 169
 e. 175.66

Use the diagram to answer item 37.

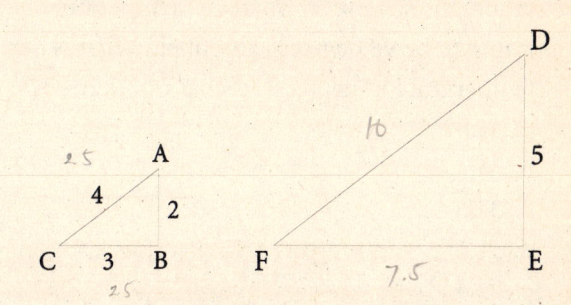

37. If the two triangles in the diagram are similar, with angle *A* equal to angle *D*, what is the perimeter of triangle *DEF*?
 a. 12
 b. 21
 c. 22.5
 d. 24.75
 e. 25.0

38. Which of these angle measures form a right triangle?
 a. 45 degrees, 50 degrees, 85 degrees
 b. 40 degrees, 40 degrees, 100 degrees
 c. 20 degrees, 30 degrees, 130 degrees
 d. 40 degrees, 40 degrees, 40 degrees
 e. 40 degrees, 50 degrees, 90 degrees

39. What is another way to write $3\sqrt{12}$?
 a. $12\sqrt{3}$
 b. $6\sqrt{3}$
 c. $2\sqrt{10}$
 d. 18
 e. 36

40. Third grade student Stephanie Wink goes to the school nurse's office, where her temperature is found to be 98 degrees Fahrenheit. What is her temperature in degrees Celsius? $C = \frac{5}{9}(F - 32)$
   a. 35.8
   b. 36.7
   c. 37.6
   d. 31.1
   e. 22.4

41. Three high schools can serve a town of 105,000 people. How many people could be served by 4 high schools?
   a. 130,000
   b. 135,000
   c. 140,000
   d. 145,000
   e. 150,000

42. A recipe serves four people and calls for $1\frac{1}{2}$ cups of broth. If you want to serve six people, how much broth do you need?
   a. 2 cups
   b. $2\frac{1}{4}$ cups
   c. $2\frac{1}{3}$ cups
   d. $2\frac{1}{2}$ cups
   e. $2\frac{3}{4}$ cups

43. Plattville is 80 miles west and 60 miles north of Quincy. How long is a direct route from Plattville to Quincy?
   a. 100 miles
   b. 110 miles
   c. 120 miles
   d. 140 miles
   e. 160 miles

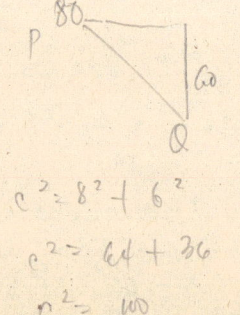

44. Which of the following brands is the least expensive?

Brand	W	X	Y	Z
Price	0.21	0.48	0.56	0.96
Weight in ounces	6	15	20	32

   a. W
   b. X
   c. Y
   d. Z
   e. They are equal in price.

45. A salesman drives 2,052 miles in 6 days, stopping at 2 towns each day. How many miles does he average between stops?
   a. 171
   b. 342
   c. 513
   d. 684
   e. 1,026

46. A school cafeteria manager spends $540 on silverware. If a place setting includes 1 knife, 1 fork, and 2 spoons, how many place settings did the manager buy?
   a. 90
   b. 108
   c. 135
   d. 180
   e. There is not enough information to solve this problem.

47. An office uses 2 dozen pencils and $3\frac{1}{2}$ reams of paper each week. If pencils cost 5 cents each and a ream of paper costs $7.50, how much does it cost to supply the office for a week?
   a. $7.55
   b. $12.20
   c. $26.25
   d. $27.45
   e. $38.25

48. What is the estimated product when 157 and 817 are rounded to the nearest hundred and multiplied?
  a. 160,000
  b. 180,000
  c. 16,000
  d. 80,000
  e. 123,000

Use the following information to answer question 49.

Mr. James Rossen is just beginning a computer consulting firm and has purchased the following equipment:

- 3 telephone sets, each costing $125
- 2 computers, each costing $1,300
- 2 computer monitors, each costing $950
- 1 printer costing $600
- 1 answering machine costing $50

49. Mr. Rossen is reviewing his finances. What should he write as the total value of the equipment he has purchased so far?
  a. $3,025
  b. $3,275
  c. $5,400
  d. $5,525
  e. $6,525

50. Body mass index (BMI) is equal to weight in kilograms/(height in meters)^2. A man who weighs 64.8 kilograms has a BMI of 20. How tall is he?
  a. 1.8 meters
  b. 0.9 meters
  c. 2.16 meters
  d. 3.24 meters
  e. 1.62 meters

▶ **Section 3:** Essay Writing

Carefully read the two essay-writing topics that follow. Plan and write two essays, one on each topic. Be sure to address all points in the topic. Allow about 30 minutes for each essay.

Topic 1

In his play, *The Admirable Crighton*, J. M. Barrie wrote, "Courage is the thing. All goes if courage goes."

Write an essay about a time in your life when you had the courage to do something or face something difficult, or when you feel you fell short. What did you learn from the experience?

Topic 2

Recently American students are said to have fallen behind in the sciences, and some educators believe it is because American teachers are conducting science classes ineffectively.

Write an essay in which you suggest ways science classes could be conducted so as to more effectively challenge high school and college students.

▶ Answers and Explanations

Section 1: Reading Comprehension

1. **a.** The first paragraph speaks of Hansberry's being raised as the daughter of political activists. Choices **b, d,** and **e** are related to her beliefs but are not depicted as the origin of those beliefs. The passage does not say that Hansberry herself ever lived in Southside Chicago (choice **c**).

2. **a.** The passage begins and ends with praise of Hansberry's works and influence. Hansberry's works are summarized (choice **b**) but this is not the main purpose of the passage. Choice **c** is not necessarily true and is not in the passage. Lorraine Hansberry may have had a *difficult struggle* (choice **d**), but the struggle is not shown in the passage. The author tells about Hansberry's plays, but does not try to persuade students to read them (choice **e**).

3. **c.** See the third sentence of paragraph 2. Her father definitely worked in the cause of civil rights (choice **a**), but he did not earn his living that way (choice **e**). There was no mention of her father's being either a banker (choice **b**) or an artist (choice **d**).

4. **b.** This correct answer is clearly stated in the second sentence of paragraph 3. There is no support for the other choices.

5. **d.** Both paragraphs focus on how much Hansberry's work continued to be an influence even after she died. In paragraph 4: *Her influence continued to be felt*, and in paragraph 5, *Even after her death, her dramatic works have helped gain an audience for...* Choices **a** and **e** may be true, but this is not the main purpose of the paragraphs. There is no support for choices **b** or **c**.

6. **c.** See the second sentence of the first paragraph. She was the *fifth* woman to win the award, which means there were *four* women before her.

7. **a.** Choice **a** is the most logical choice, given the context of the sentence. It is illogical to describe personality types and aspirations as a gathering, arrangement, decoration, or feature (choices **b, c, d,** and **e**).

8. **d.** See paragraph 4, which describes *To Be Young, Gifted, and Black* as a dramatic adaptation of an autobiography. Choices **a** and **e** are wrong because there is no support for the idea that *Raisin* is Hansberry's family. *Les Blancs* is set in Africa, which rules out choice **b**. *The Sign in Sidney Brustein's Window* is about a man, which rules out choice **c**.

9. **d.** Answer **d** is the most accurate conclusion because the first sentence speaks of *periods of war*. The other choices, whether true or false, are not addressed in the selection.

10. **e.** This is stated in the last paragraph: *...first aid measures should be directed at cooling the body quickly*. The other responses—except for choice **c**, which does not appear in the passage—are first aid treatments for heat exhaustion victims.

11. **b.** This is clearly stated in the first sentence of the second paragraph. Choices **a, c,** and **e** are symptoms of heat stroke. Choice **d** is not mentioned.

12. **c.** Heat stroke victims have a *blocked sweating mechanism*, as stated in the third paragraph. Choice **a** is a symptom of heat exhaustion. Choices **b, d,** and **e** are not in the passage.

13. **c.** The second paragraph states that for the symptoms of heat exhaustion—which include *nausea* and *dizziness*—first aid treatment includes *giving the victim sips of salt water*. The other choices relate to heat stroke.

14. **a.** According to the passage, Blake believed that, *through art* (that is, *through the reordering of sense impression by the creative imagination*) *true religion is revealed*. Artistic inspiration (choice **c**) might be involved, but the words *religion* and *moment of vision* point towards a mystical experience, rather than a primarily artistic one. There is no mention in the passage of *Christianity* or *sin* (choices **b** and **e**) and no hint that the author views Blake's *moment of vision* as a false perception (*hallucinatory experience*, choice **d**).

15. **a.** The passage's tone and word choice (*true religion* and *eternity . . . revealed* through art) indicate that the world at *the moment of vision* is reality. There is no hint in the passage that nature represents a state of innocence for Blake (choice **b**)—the contrary is implied. The idea that nature is made up of *base and corrupt material* or that it will *perish* (choices **c** and **d**) are not in the passage. There is no evidence that Blake thought of the world of the artist as *fantasy* (choice **e**).

16. **d.** The passage contains objective information about accounting such as one might find in a textbook. There is nothing new or newsworthy in it (choice **a**). The passage does not contain the significant amount of personal opinion one would expect to find in an essay (choice **b**). It does not deal with matters that might involve litigation (choice **c**). It is not brief enough for a business machine catalog and does not contain language suitable to advertising (choice **e**).

17. **e.** The final sentence emphasizes the importance of correct interpretation of financial accounting. Choice **a** is wrong, because something so important would not be discretionary (optional). Choice **b** may be true, but it is not as important for guidelines to be convenient as it is for them to rigorous. *Instruction* is another word for *guidelines;* therefore, choice **c** is redundant. Choice **d** is wrong because the word *austere* connotes sternness; people may be stern, but inanimate entities, such as guidelines, cannot be.

18. **c.** Choices **a**, **b**, and **d** are all listed in the passage as functions of accounting. In addition, the passage notes that accounting can benefit entities outside the company, such as those mentioned in **e**. On the other hand, the second sentence of the passage speaks of a *marketing department*, separate from the *accounting department*.

19. **e.** The passage says of the people who live in "the Bottom" that they are *apt to go awry*, to *break from their natural boundaries*. A person who is *eccentric* is quirky or odd. Nowhere in the passage is it implied that the people are *cowardly, artistic, unkempt*, or *arrogant* (choices **a**, **b**, **c**, and **d**).

20. **d.** A *scapegoat* is one who is forced to bear the blame for others or upon which the sins of a community are heaped. Choices **b** and **c** are wrong because nowhere in the passage is it implied that Sula is a hero or leader, or even that "the Bottom" has such a personage. Sula may be a *victim* (choice **a**), or an *outcast* (choice **e**) but a community does not necessarily *project evil* onto a victim or an outcast the way they do onto a scapegoat.

21. **b.** The first side of the debate says that evil is an *active force* so the opposing side would see evil as just the opposite, something *passive*. Choice **a** is reflected in the first sentence: human beings are *puzzled* (therefore perplexed) by evil, but their being puzzled is not one of the two *concepts* of evil discussed in the passage. Choices **c**, **d**, and **e** are not reflected in the passage.

22. **c.** The whole passage is a description of the debate between two concepts of evil. Choice **a** is mentioned in the passage but only by way of introduction to the description of the debate. Choices **b**, **d**, and **e** are not in the passage.

23. **d.** The fourth sentence states that the "Shadow" side of the personality is something *the individual may deny*. The other choices are not in the passage.

24. **b.** The eagle, who *watches from his mountain walls* and falls *like a thunderbolt*, is depicted as too alert and dynamic to be dying (choice **a**). There is really no joy depicted in the poem nor any sense that this is a baby eagle (choice **c**), and there is no mention of baby birds he might be watching over (choice **d**). There is no other eagle mentioned in the poem (choice **e**). Saying that the eagle *watches* and then falls *like a thunderbolt* implies alertness and striking, so the most logical choice is that the eagle is hunting.

25. **b.** The word *azure* means blue and is often used to describe the sky. Neither a forest nor cliffs are azure (choices **a** and **c**), and neither God nor nature is mentioned as an entity in the poem (choices **d** and **e**).

26. **a.** It is the *wrinkled sea* that *crawls* in the first line of the second stanza of the poem.

27. **e.** Page 89 (choice **a**) deals with *peasant resistance*; page 55 (choice **b**) with *fire protection*; page 107 (choice **c**) with *villagers*; page 48 (choice **d**) with *slash-and-burn farming*. All might pertain somewhat to the question, but the index lists page 51 (choice **e**) under the topics of both *pasture* and *arson* (which is illegal burning), so it is the best choice.

28. **a.** Although there are more entries in the index having to do with fire, arson, and fire protection, the greatest number of pages listed under the topic of forest destruction is *industrialization*—18 pages.

29. **d.** The titles in choices **b**, **c**, and **e** all imply that the passage will provide information which it does not. Choice **a** is not logical given the content of the passage; choice **d** is the most accurate choice because the passage deals mainly with remembering the fair.

30. **a.** Sentence 1 (choice **a**) contains the phrase *should have been a colossal failure*, which is an opinion of the author. The other choices are sentences that provide factual information about Woodstock.

31. **a.** The sentence preceding and leading into sentence 3 speaks of the very brief time—a month—that the organizers of the fair had to find a new site and get information out. Choices **b**, **d**, and **e** are incorrect because they could not have been known about at the time the fair was moved. Choice **c** is incorrect because there is no indication in the passage that New York officials tried to stop the fair's moving or information getting out.

32. **e.** Choice **e** sums up the first paragraph, which is essentially a list of the cuttlefish's characteristics, by declaring which is the most interesting characteristic, and the sentence introduces the subject of the second paragraph—the ability of the cuttlefish to change color. Choice **a** adds information not in keeping with the tone or focus of the passage. Choice **b** basically repeats information in the first paragraph but does not introduce the next one. Choice **c** uses but does not explain scientific language, which is out of keeping with the general informational style of the passage. Choice **d** adds to the list of characteristics in the first paragraph without summing it up.

33. **b.** The passage describes the cuttlefish's use of a water jet to move. Choice **a** is incorrect because the passage only describes cuttlefish as *resembling* squid. Choice **c** is a true characteristic, but is not mentioned in the passage. Choice **d** is incorrect because the passage never describes cuttlefish as the *most* intelligent cephalopod. Choice **e** is not true, based on the information in the passage.

34. **e.** Choice **e** covers the most important ideas in the two paragraphs. All the other choices choose more minor details from the paragraphs as the main subjects.

35. **e.** Choice **e** includes both the informational content and light tone of the passage. Choices **a** and **b** describe too scientific an aim for the content and tone. Choice **c** does not include the informational content of the passage. Choice **d** assumes a particular audience for the passage which is neither named nor implied in any of the passage's content.

36. **c.** Any of the choices may be a definition of *background*; however, the context of the passage indicates that the word refers to the education and training of the proposed author—that is, the author's ability to write the book.

37. **d.** See the second sentence of the second paragraph. Compaction may well reduce transportation costs (choice **a**) according to the first sentence of the second paragraph. That it reduces the volume of waste (choice **b**) is an advantage, not a disadvantage. Compaction is not designed to eliminate organic matter, so confirming that it has been eliminated (choice **c**) is not an issue. Compaction is done on-site (refuting choice **e**), as asserted in the first paragraph.

38. **b.** See sentence four of the second paragraph. The effects of sterilization of waste (choice **a**) is not included in the passage. Oxydizing (choice **c**) is simply a part of the process of hydropulping. Processing (choice **d**) is the general category that includes all the methods of disposing of medical wastes. While compacting (choice **e**) does change the volume of the waste, it is not appropriate for eliminating hazardous materials.

39. **a.** See the last sentence of the third paragraph, which states that *incineration is . . . the preferred method for on-site treatment*. The other choices take place off-site.

40. **a.** The first sentence states that off-site disposal is appropriate for hospitals *with less than 150 beds*, which implies fewer patients. Choices **b**, **c**, and **d** are mentioned with regard to both off-site and on-site disposal. The first sentence of the passage indicates that all the waste discussed in the passage is regulated (choice **e**).

41. **a.** To depict the Sami, the author uses words that point to their gentleness, which is an admirable quality: They move *quietly*, display *courtesy* to the spirits of the wilderness, and were known as *peaceful retreaters*. There is nothing pitying, contemptuous, or patronizing in the language, and nothing in the passage indicates that the author is perplexed—the description of the Sami is clear and to the point.

42. **d.** The correct answer is implied by the statement in the third sentence that carefully managed e-mail results in effective communication. Choice **a** is wrong because the opposite is true. Choice **b** is wrong because even though e-mail is more widespread, it has not necessarily *changed considerably*. Choices **c** and **e** are not indicated in the paragraph.

43. **b.** This choice is correct because the third sentence states that telecommuters produce 20% more than their on-location counterparts. Choice **a** is not mentioned in the paragraph. Choice **c** is wrong because more productivity does not necessarily mean better quality. Choices **d** is not mentioned, and choice **e** is refuted in the final sentence.

44. **d.** The last two sentences point to the need for precautions when sending a fax. There is no indication in the paragraph that choice **a** is true. Choice **b** is incorrect because the paragraph indicates that, with caution, confidential faxes can be

sent. Choice c is not mentioned. Choice d is vague because it does not define *timely*; at any rate, a phone call will arrive more quickly than a fax.

45. a. The answer is stated in the first sentence. Choices b, d, and e are not mentioned in the paragraph. Choice c is attractive, but it is incorrect because the paragraph is talking about more responsibility and independence, not necessarily more work.

46. b. See the first sentence of the third paragraph, which asserts that states should mandate genetic testing *only if there is strong evidence that a newborn would benefit from effective treatment at the earliest possible age.*

47. b. See the last sentence of the third paragraph, which states that *effective treatment can be started in a few hundred infants.*

48. e. The first paragraph says that the report addressed concerns about *protecting confidentiality.*

49. c. The last sentence of the second paragraph states that *careful pilot studies . . . need to be done first.*

50. d. See the third paragraph: *Newborn screening is the most common type of genetic screening today.*

Section 2: Mathematics

1. e. Because Linda pays with a check only if an item costs more than $30, the item must have cost more than $25.

2. d. The hundredth is the second digit to the right of the decimal point. Because the third decimal is 6, the second is rounded up to 4.

3. e. Find the answer using the following equations: $\frac{1}{3} = 0.333$; $\frac{1}{4} = 0.25$; $\frac{2}{7} = 0.286$. $\frac{2}{7}$ is between the other two fractions.

4. c. 3% is equal to 0.03, so multiply 2,500 times 0.03 and then add the result to 2,500, for a total of 2,575.

5. e. From the line chart, 1995 is represented by the line with squares at each month. In December 1995, there was 10 inches of rainfall, the most that year.

6. c. The mean is the sum of the values divided by the number of values. Add 8 + 6 + 4 = 18 inches, and then divide by 3 to get 6 inches.

7. a. If the gas station is $43\frac{1}{3}$ miles from their house, and their relatives live 75 miles away, the numbers are subtracted. $75 - 43\frac{1}{3} = 31\frac{2}{3}$.

8. d. If 2 of 5 cars are foreign, 3 of 5 are domestic. $\frac{3}{5}$ (60 cars) = 36 cars.

9. e. 13% had not read books; therefore, 87% had. 87% is equal to 0.87. 0.87 × 2,500 = 2175 people.

10. c. To estimate quickly, the numbers can be rounded to 36,000 and 16,500. 36,000 students minus 16,500 male students is equal to 19,500 female students. 19,500 women minus 16,500 men is equal to 3,000 more women than men.

11. d. The area is width times length, in this case, 5 times 7, or 35 square feet.

12. e. 4% is equal to 0.04. 500 × 0.04 = 20.

13. a. Rounding to close numbers helps. This is approximately 100,000 divided by 500,000, which is 0.20 or $\frac{1}{5}$.

14. b. $2\frac{1}{2} = 2.5$. $1\frac{1}{4} = 1.25$. $2.5 \times 1.25 = 3.125$ or $3\frac{1}{8}$.

15. a. Multiply the percentages by one another (30% = 0.30; 15% = 0.15). 0.30 × 0.15 = 0.045 or 4.5%.

16. d. If 20% are not eating the special, 80% are. 80% = 40 people. 40 divided by 0.80 = 50 people total.

17. c. To find the answer, work this equation: ($2.24 − $2.08) × 2 = $0.32.

18. b. 54 divided by 6 is 9.

19. a. 24 history books at $20 each are $480. 20 math books at $30 each are $600. 15 science books at $25 each are $375. $480 + $600 + 375 = $1455.

20. d. Between 10:42 and 12:42, two hours have elapsed. From 12:42 to 1:00, another 18 minutes have elapsed (60 – 42 = 18). Then from 1:00 to 1:19, there is another 19 minutes. 2 hours + 18 minutes + 19 minutes = 2 hours, 37 minutes.

21. e. Division is used to arrive at a decimal, which can then be rounded to the nearest hundredth and converted to a percentage: 11,350 divided by 21,500 = 0.5279. 0.5279 rounded to the nearest hundredth is 0.53, or 53%.

22. b. This uses two algebraic equations to solve for the age. Jerry (J) and his grandfather (G) have a sum of ages of 110 years. Therefore, J + G = 110. Jerry was one-third as young as his grandfather 15 years ago. Therefore, J – 15 = $\frac{1}{3}$(G – 15). Solve the first equation for J: J = 110 – G. Now substitute this value of J into the second equation: 110 – G – 15 = $\frac{1}{3}$(G – 15). Solve for G: 95 – G = $\frac{1}{3}$ G –5; 100 = $\frac{4}{3}$ G; G = 75.

23. b. $\frac{1}{3}x$ + 3 = 8. In order to solve the equation, all numbers need to be on one side and all x values on the other. Therefore, $\frac{1}{3}x$ = 5; x = 15.

24. c. In order to find the perimeter, the hypotenuse of the triangle must be found. This comes from recognizing that the triangle is a 5-12-13 triangle, or by using the Pythagorean theorem. 5 + 12 + 13 = 30.

25. c. If angle 1 is 30 degrees, angle 3 must be 60 degrees by right triangle geometry. Because the two lines are parallel, angles 3 and 4 must be congruent. Therefore, to find angle 5, angle 4 must be subtracted from 180 degrees. This is 120 degrees.

26. d. Because the radius of the hemisphere is 3, and it is the same as half the base of the triangle, the base must be 6. Therefore, the area of the triangle is $\frac{1}{2}bh$ = 12. The area of the circle is πr^2 which is equal to 9π. Therefore, the half-circle's area is $\frac{9\pi}{2}$. Adding gives $\frac{9\pi}{2}$ + 12.

27. c. The speed of the train is 60 miles per hour, obtained from the table. Therefore, the distance from Chicago would be equal to 60t. However, as the train moves on, the distance decreases from Los Angeles, so there must be a function of –60t in the equation. At time t = 0, the distance is 2,000 miles, so the function is 2,000 – 60t.

28. e. The cost for 25 hours for both providers must be found. For A, the base charge is $20, plus 7.5 hours at $1 per hour. This is $27.50. For B, the base charge is $20, plus 5 hours at $1.50. This is also $27.50. Therefore, they will cost the same.

29. a. The amount of water held in each container must be found. The rectangular box starts with 16 square inches times 9 inches = 144 cubic inches of water. The cylindrical container can hold 3.14(4)(9) cubic inches of water, which is approximately 113 cubic inches. Therefore, the container will overflow.

30. d. This problem can be solved using only statements I and III. Since the cousin who fishes is female, either Lucy or Samantha likes to fish. Statement III eliminates Samantha, which leaves Lucy.

31. b. The dimensions of triangle MNO are double those of triangle RST. Line segment RT is 5 cm; therefore line segment MO is 10 cm.

32. e. The farther to the right the digits go, the smaller the number.

33. a. The expression 5n means 5 times n. The addition sign before the 7 indicates the phrase *more than*.

34. b. Angles 1 and 4 are the only ones NOT adjacent to each other.

35. d. Substitute 3 for x in the expression 5 + 4x to determine that y equals 17.

36. b. The formula for finding the area of a circle is A = πr^2. First, square the radius: 13 times 13

equals 169. Then multiply by the approximate value of π, 3.14, to get 530.66.

37. **c.** *DE* is 2.5 times greater than *AB*; therefore, *EF* is 7.5 and *DF* is 10. Add the three numbers together to arrive at the perimeter.

38. **e.** This is the only choice that includes a 90 degree angle.

39. **b.** The square root of 12 is the same as the square root of 4 times 3, which is the same as the square root of 4 times the square root of 3. The square root of 4 is 2. So 3 times the square root of 12 is the same as 3 times 2 times the square root of 3, or 6 times the square root of 3.

40. **b.** Use the formula beginning with the operation in parentheses: 98 minus 32 equals 66. Then multiply 66 by $\frac{5}{9}$, first multiplying 66 by 5 to get 330. 330 divided by 9 is 36.66667, which is rounded up to 36.7.

41. **c.** The ratio of 105,000 : 3 is equal to the ratio of $x : 4$, or $\frac{105,000}{3} = \frac{x}{4}$, where x is the population served by four schools. Solve for x by multiplying 4 times 105,000 and then dividing by 3 to get 140,000.

42. **b.** $1\frac{1}{2}$ cups equals $\frac{3}{2}$ cups. The ratio is 6 people to 4 people, which is equal to the ratio of x to $\frac{3}{2}$. By cross multiplying, we get $6(\frac{3}{2})$ equals $4x$, or 9 equals $4x$. Dividing both sides by 9, we get $\frac{9}{4}$, or $2\frac{1}{4}$ cups.

43. **a.** The distance between Plattville and Quincy is the hypotenuse of a right triangle with sides of length 80 and 60. The length of the hypotenuse equals the square root of (80^2 plus 60^2), which equals the square root of (6400 plus 3600), which equals the square root of 10,000, which equals 100 miles.

44. **c.** You can find the price per ounce of each brand, as follows:

Brand	W	X	Y	Z
Price in cents per ounce:	$\frac{21}{6} = 3.5$	$\frac{48}{15} = 3.2$	$\frac{56}{20} = 2.8$	$\frac{96}{32} = 3.0$

It is then easy to see that Brand Y, at 2.8 cents per ounce, is the least expensive.

45. **a.** 2,052 miles divided by 6 days equals 342 miles per day. 342 miles divided by 2 stops equals 171 miles.

46. **e.** There is not enough information to solve this problem. The price of one piece of silverware is needed to find the solution.

47. **d.** First find the total price of the pencils: (24 pencils)($0.05) equals $1.20. Then find the total price of the paper: (3.5 reams)($7.50 per ream) equals $26.25. Next, add the two totals together: $1.20 and $26.25 equals $27.45.

48. **a.** 157 is rounded to 200; 817 is rounded to 800. 200 times 800 equals 160,000.

49. **d.** It is important to remember to include all three telephone sets ($375 total), both computers ($2,600 total), and both monitors ($1,900 total) in the total value for the correct answer of $5525.

50. **a.** Substituting known quantities into the formula yields $20 = \frac{64.8}{x^2}$. Next, you must multiply through by x^2 to get $20x^2 = 64.8$ and then divide through by 20 to get $x^2 = 3.24$. Now take the square root of both sides to get $x = 1.8$.

Section 3: Essay Writing

Following are the criteria for scoring CBEST essays.

A "4" essay is a coherent writing sample that addresses the assigned topic and is aimed at a specific audience. Additionally, it has the following characteristics:

- A main idea and/or a central point of view that is focused; its reasoning is sound

- Points of discussion that are clear and arranged logically
- Assertions that are supported with specific, relevant detail
- Word choice and usage that is accurate and precise
- Sentences that have complexity and variety, with clear syntax; paragraphs that are coherent (minor mechanical flaws are acceptable)
- Style and language that are appropriate to the assigned audience and purpose

A "3" essay is an adequate writing sample that generally addresses the assigned topic, but may neglect or only vaguely address one of the assigned tasks; it is aimed at a specific audience. Generally, it has the following additional characteristics:

- A main idea and/or a central point of view and adequate reasoning
- Organization of ideas that is effective; the meaning of the ideas is clear
- Generalizations that are adequately, though unevenly, supported
- Word choice and language usage that are adequate; mistakes exist but these do not interfere with meaning
- Some errors in sentence and paragraph structure, but not so many as to be confusing
- Word choice and style that are appropriate to a given audience

A "2" essay is an incompletely formed writing sample that attempts to address the topic and to communicate a message to the assigned audience but is generally incomplete or inappropriate. It has the following additional characteristics:

- A main point, but one which loses focus; reasoning that is simplistic

- Ineffective organization that causes the response to lack clarity
- Generalizations that are only partially supported; supporting details that are irrelevant or unclear
- Imprecise language usage; word choice that distracts the reader
- Mechanical errors; errors in syntax; errors in paragraphing
- Style that is monotonous or choppy

A "1" essay is an inadequately formed writing sample that only marginally addresses the topic and fails to communicate its message to, or is inappropriate to, a specific audience. Additionally, it has the following characteristics:

- General incoherence and inadequate focus, lack of a main idea or consistent point of view; illogical reasoning
- Ineffective organization and unclear meaning throughout
- Unsupported generalizations and assertions; details that are irrelevant and presented in a confusing manner
- Language use that is imprecise, with serious and distracting errors
- Many serious errors in mechanics, sentence syntax, and paragraphing

Following are examples of scored essays for Topics 1 and 2. (There are some deliberate errors in all the essays, so that you can tell how much latitude you have.)

TOPIC 1

Pass—Score = 4

Courage and cowardice seem like absolutes. We are often quick to label other people, or ourselves, either "brave" or "timid," "courageous," or "cowardly." However, one bright afternoon on a river deep in the wilds of the Ozark mountains, I learned that these qualities are as changable as mercury.

During a cross-country drive, my friend Nina and I decided to stop at a campsite in Missouri and spend the afternoon on a float trip down Big Piney River, 14 miles through the wilderness. We rented a canoe and paddled happily off.

Things went fine—for the first seven or eight miles. We gazed at the overhanging bluffs, commented on the wonderful variety of trees (it was spring, and the dogwood was in bloom), and marveled at the clarity of the water. Then, in approaching a bend in the river (which we later learned was called "Devil's Elbow") the current suddenly swept us in toward the bank, underneath the low-hanging branches of a weeping willow. The canoe tipped over and I was pulled under, my foot caught for just a few seconds on the submerged roots of the willow. Just as I surfaced, taking my first frantic gulp of air, I saw the canoe sweeping out, upright again, but empty, and Nina frantically swimming after it.

I knew I should help but I was petrified and hung my head in shame as I let my friend brave the treacherous rapids and haul the canoe back onto the gravel bar, while I stood by cravenly.

Then came the scream. Startled, I glanced up to see Nina, both hands over her eyes, dash off the gravel bar and back into the water. I gazed down into the canoe to see, coiled in the bottom of it, the unmistakeable, black-and-brown, checkerboard-patterned form of a copperhead snake. It had evidently been sunning itself peacefully on the weeping willow branch when we passed by underneath.

I don't know exactly why, but the supposedly inborn terror of snakes is something that has passed me by completely. I actually find them rather charming in a scaly sort of way.

Nina was still screaming, "Kill it!" But I was calm in a way that must have seemed smug. "We're in *its* home, it's not in ours," I informed her. And gently I prodded it with the oar until it reared up, slithered over the side of the canoe, and raced away—terrified, itself—into the underbrush.

Later that night, in our cozy, safe motel room, we agreed that we each had cold chills thinking about what might have happened. Still, I learned something important from the ordeal. I know that, had we encountered only the rapids, I might have come away ashamed, labeling myself a coward, and had we encountered only the snake, Nina might have done the same. And I also know that neither of us will ever again be quite so apt to brand another person as lacking courage. Because we will always know that, just around the corner, may be the snake or the bend in the river or the figure in the shadows or something else as yet unanticipated, that will cause our own blood to freeze.

Marginal Pass—Score = 3

Courage can be shown in many ways and by many kinds of people. One does not have to be rich, or educated, or even an adult to show true courage.

For example, a very heartbreaking thing happened in our family. It turned out all right but at the time it almost made us lose our faith. However, it also taught us a lesson regarding courage. In spite of his father's and my repeated warnings, my son Matt went ice-fishing with some friends and fell through the ice into the fridgid water beneath. He is prone to do things that are dangerous no matter how many times he's told. Fortunately there were grown-ups near and they were able to throw him a life line and pull him to safety. However, when they got him onto shore they discovered he was unconsious. There were vital signs but they were weak, the paramedics pronounced him in grave danger.

He is his little sisters (Nan's) hero. He is 16 and she is 13, just at the age where she admires everything he does. When they took him to the hospital she insisted on going that night to see him, and she insisted on staying with me there. My husband thought we should insist she go home, but it was Christmas vacation for her so there was no real reason. So we talked it over and she stayed. She stayed every night for the whole week just to be by Matt's side. And when he woke up she was there. Her smiling face the was first thing he saw.

In spite of the fact she was just a child and it was frightning for her to be there beside her brother she loves so much, and had to wonder, every day if he would die, she stayed. So courage has many faces.

Marginal Fail—Score = 2
Courage is not something we are born with. It is something that we have to learn.

For example when your children are growing up you should teach them courage. Teach them to face lifes challanges and not to show there fear. For instance my father. Some people would say he was harsh, but back then I didnt think of it that way. One time he took me camping and I had a tent of my own. I wanted to crawl in with him but he said there was nothing to be afriad of. And I went to sleep sooner than I would have expect. He taught me not to be afriad.

There are many reasons for courage. In a war a solder has to be couragous and a mother has to be no less couragous if she is rasing a child alone and has to make a living. So, in me it is totally alright to be afriad as long as you face your fear. I have been greatful to him ever since that night.

Sometimes parents know what is best for there kids even if at the time it seems like a harsh thing. I learned not to show my fear that night, which is an important point to courage. In everyday life it is important to learn how to be strong. If we dont learn from our parents, like I did from my father, then we have to learn it after we grow up. But it is better to learn it, as a child. I have never been as afriad as I was that night, and I learned a valuble lesson from it.

Fail—Score = 1
Courage is important in a battle and also ordinary life. In a war if your buddy depends on you and you let him down he might die. Courage is also important in daly life. If you have sicknes in the famly or if you enconter a mugger on the street you will need all the courage you can get. There are many dangers in life that only courage will see you through.

Once, my apartment was burglerised and they stole a TV and micro-wave. I didnt have very much. They took some money to. I felt afraid when I walked in and saw things moved or gone. But I call the police and waited for them inside my apartment which was brave and also some might say stupid! But the police came and took my statement and also later caught the guy. Another time my girlfreind and I were in my apartment and we looked out the window and there was somebody suspisious out in front. It turned out to be a false alarm but she was scard and she said because I was calm it made her feel better. So courage was important to me, in my relationship with my girlfreind.

So courage is importand not only in war but also in life.

Topic 2
Pass—Score = 4
The best way for teachers to boost their students' science test scores is to stop worrying quite so much about the scores and start being concerned about making the students excited by science.

Before ever asking students to memorize facts, the teacher should demonstrate a scientific process or, better, teach the students how to experiment for themselves, allowing them to apprehend the process with their senses before trying to fix it in their intellect. For example, the teacher might pass around an ant farm in the class room and let the students observe the little critters skittering behind the glass, going about their complex, individual tasks, before asking the student to read that ants have a rigid social structure, just as people do. If possible, it would be even better to take them on a field trip to observe a real ant-hill or to see how other kinds of real animals behave, say on a farm or in a zoo. The teacher might allow the students to create a chemical reaction in a beaker—taking care of course that they don't blow themselves up—before asking them to memorize the formula.

When I was small, I had first-hand experience with this kind of teaching. My father built a telescope (a painstaking project that should only be taken on out of love because it is a very difficult, intricate task—I recall that even he swore a lot during that period!). The telescope had a clock at its base that kept it fixed on the moon or stars rather than turning as the earth turns. When my father switched off the clock, I remember watching through the eyepiece, fascinated at how quickly the stars drifted out of my field of vision—it took only seconds—and even more fascinated to realize that what I was seeing was *us* floating so swiftly through space. He told me the magical names of the geological formations on the moon, such as the crater called "The Sea of Tranquility." When I looked through the lens, the pock-marked silvery disc of the moon seemed as close as the hills behind our suburban house.

After that, I became interested in the statistics such as the rate of the rotation of the earth, the geophysical facts behind the making of the craters that form the moon's laughing face, in a way I never would have if the facts had been the starting point of a lecture.

This approach should be begun, not in high school or college, but in grade school or even in kindergarten. The facts are important, of course— without them, we can have no real understanding. But curiosity is as vital to learning as the ability to memorize—perhaps more so. Because curiosity will keep students learning long after they've passed their final test in school.

Marginal Pass—Score = 3

Science is important for many reasons, but especially because today's world is based on technology. If other countries get ahead of us in science the consequences may be dire. So it is extremely important for our students to excell.

> *dire — dreadful; terrible.*

The first and best way to teach science is to make the student see the practical application of it. For example, if the teacher is teaching botony, she might explain the medical uses of plants. Or if teaching physics, she might show a diagram of a rocket ship. Field trips are a good idea, as well, perhaps to a factory that makes dolls. The point is to make it practical and interesting to boys and girls alike.

When I was in high school I had a teacher named Mr. Wiley who let us mix things in jars and watch the results. Sometimes they were unexpected! Such as a kind of mushroom we planted that was poisonous and reminded us of the horror movies we all loved in those days. Mr. Wiley made it interesting in a personal way, so that it wasn't just dry facts. And he told us the practical uses, such as this particular kind of mushroom is used in the making of certain insect poison.

In this day and age it is important for all of us to know something about science because it affects all aspects of our lives, but for young people it is vital. Their livelihoods—and even their lives—may depend on that knowledge.

Marginal Fail—Score = 2

Science is a necesary skill because it can effect each one of us, such as the making of the hydrogen bomb or finding a cure for AIDS. It is responsable for TV, cars, and a host of other items we take for granted. So we all depend on it and need to learn it.

The best way to teach science is to have a good textbook and also good equiptment in the classroom. If the equiptment is poor there is no way they are going to learn it, which is why the poorer schools are behind the richer ones and also behind other countries. Its the most important factor in the classroom today.

Another way to teach science is through field trips and vidio-tapes. There are many tapes in the library and every school should have a good vidio system. Also a good library is importent. And there are many places to take the class that they would find intresting.

When I was in school I thought science was boring. I wish I had learned more about it because I think it would make me a better teacher someday as well as better understand the world of technology. If we don't understand technology we are at it's mercy, and it is something we rely on to get us through our lives. Without science we would have no technilogical advances. If other countries are ahead of us it is our own fault for not putting science as a priority.

Fail—Score = 3

Science is importnt and we should teach it to our students in the right way. A scientist coming in to talk would be one way. Also experimints that the students can do. The reason it is important, is other countrys are ahead of us and we may have a war. Then if there tecnoligy is better they will take us over. So it is dangerous not to have students that know alot about science.

If we teach our children to relay too much on science and technoligy what will happen if it fails. If the computers fail we are in serious trouble. There is still no cure for cancer and our products cause polution. So science is important and our students should learn but it isnt everything and they should learn that they should study other things to, like how to make a good living for there family. And religion also knows things science can never know.

If we teach science in the right way our country will be better off as well as our children when they are caught up to the new melinnium.

▶ Scoring

Once again, in order to evaluate how you did on this practice exam, start by scoring the three sections of the CBEST—Reading Comprehension, Mathematics, and Essay Writing—separately. You will recall that Reading Comprehension and Mathematics are scored the same way: First find the number of questions you got right out of the 50 questions in each section, then use the table below to check your math and find percentage equivalents for several possible scores.

Number of questions right	Approximate percentage
50	100%
46	92%
43	86%
39	78%
35	70%
32	64%
28	56%
25	50%

As previously stated, you will need a score of at least 70 percent on both the Reading Comprehension section and the Mathematics section to be certain to pass those portions of the CBEST. (Remember that the scores are converted from raw scores to scaled scores, so the actual number you receive on the real CBEST will *not* be "70"; however, for the purpose of finding out if you passed these practice exams, a percentage will work fine.) Besides achieving a score of 70 percent on the Reading Comprehension and Mathematics sections, you must receive a passing score on the Essay Writing section of the CBEST, which will be evaluated by especially-trained readers. The criteria are outlined in detail in the Answers section above, but generally the essays are scored as follows:

4 = Pass (an excellent and well-formed essay)

3 = Marginal Pass (an average and adequately-formed essay)

2 = Marginal Fail (a partially-formed but substandard essay)

1 = Fail (an inadequately-formed essay)

The best way to see how you did on your essays for this second practice exam is to give your essays and the scoring criteria to a teacher and ask him or her to score your essays for you.

You have probably seen improvement between your first practice exam score and this one; but if you didn't improve as much as you'd like, following are some options:

- **If you scored below 60%,** you should seriously consider whether you're ready for the CBEST at this time. A good idea would be to take some brush-up courses, either at a university or community college nearby or through correspondence, in the areas you feel less sure of. If you don't have time for a course, you might try private tutoring.

- **If your score is in the 60 to 70% range,** you need to work as hard as you can to improve your skills. The LearningExpress books *Reading Comprehension Success in 20 Minutes a Day* and *Practical Math Success in 20 Minutes a Day* or other books from your public library will undoubtedly help. Also, reread and pay close attention to all the advice in Chapters 2 and 4 of this book in order to improve your score. It might also be helpful to ask friends and family to make up mock test questions and quiz you on them.

- **If your score is between 70 and 90%,** you could still benefit from additional work by going back

to Chapter 4 and by brushing up your reading comprehension and general math skills before the exam.
- **If you scored above 90%,** that's great! This kind of score should make you a good candidate for a teaching job. Don't lose your edge, though; keep studying right up to the day before the exam.

Keep in mind that what's much more important than your scores, for now, is how you did on each of the basic skills tested by the exam. Using the advice above, diagnose your strengths and weaknesses so that you can concentrate your efforts as you prepare for the exam. Your percentage scores in conjunction with the LearningExpress test preparation guide in Chapter 2 of this book will help you revise your study plan if need be. After your study plan is revised, turn again to the CBEST Mini-Course in Chapter 4, which covers each of the basic skills tested on the CBEST.

If you didn't score as well as you would like, ask yourself the following: Did I run out of time before I could answer all the questions? Did I go back and change my answers from right to wrong? Did I get flustered and sit staring at a difficult question for what seemed like hours? If you had any of these problems, once again, be sure to go over the LearningExpress Test Preparation System in Chapter 2 again to learn how to avoid them.

After working on your reading, writing, and math skills, take the second practice exam in Chapter 6 to see how much you've improved.

CHAPTER 6
CBEST Practice Exam 2

CHAPTER SUMMARY
This is the third of the three practice tests in this book based on the California Basic Educational Skills Test (CBEST). Use this test to see how much you've improved.

Like the previous CBEST exams in this book, this one is divided into three sections of the same types as the real exam—the Reading Comprehension section, consisting of 50 multiple-choice questions; the Mathematics section, consisting of 50 multiple-choice questions; and the Essay Writing section, consisting of two topics on which you are to write essays.

For this exam, you should simulate the actual test-taking experience as closely as you can. Work in a quiet place, away from interruptions. Tear out the answer sheet on the next page, and use your number 2 pencils to fill in the circles. (As you did for the other two exams, write your essays on a separate piece of paper.) Use a timer or stopwatch and allow yourself four hours for the exam: one-and-a-half hours each for the reading and math sections and a half-hour each for the two essays.

After the exam, again use the answer key that follows it to see your progress on each section and to find out why the correct answers are correct and the incorrect ones incorrect. Then use the scoring section at the end of the exam to see how you did overall.

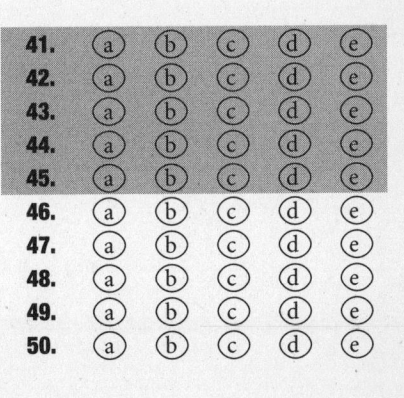

LEARNINGEXPRESS CALIFORNIA BASIC EDUCATIONAL SKILLS TEST ANSWER SHEET

Section 1: Reading Comprehension

(Answer bubbles 1–50, options a, b, c, d, e)

Section 2: Mathematics

(Answer bubbles 1–50, options a, b, c, d, e)

▶ Section 1: Reading Comprehension

Answer questions 1–8 on the basis of the following passage.

(1) Milton Hershey was born near the small village of Derry Church, Pennsylvania, in 1857. It was a modest beginning that did not foretell his later popularity. Milton only attended school through the fourth grade; at that point, he was apprenticed to a printer in a nearby town. Fortunately for all chocolate lovers, Milton did not excel as a printer. After a while, he left the printing business and was apprenticed to a Lancaster, Pennsylvania, candy maker. It was apparent he had <u>found his calling in life</u> and, at the age of eighteen, he opened his own candy store in Philadelphia. In spite of his talents as a candy maker, the shop failed after six years.

(2) Milton Hershey's fans today may be surprised to learn that his first candy success came with the manufacture of caramel. After the failure of his Philadelphia store, Milton headed for Denver, where he learned the art of caramel making. There he took a job with a local manufacturer who insisted on using fresh milk in making his caramels; Milton saw that this made the caramels especially tasty. After a time in Denver, he once again attempted to open his own candy-making businesses, in Chicago, New Orleans, and New York City. Finally, in 1886, he went to Lancaster, Pennsylvania, where he raised the money necessary to try again. This company—the Lancaster Caramel Company—made Milton's reputation as a master candy maker.

(3) In 1893, Milton attended the Chicago International Exposition, where he saw a display of German chocolate-making implements. Captivated by the equipment, he purchased it for his Lancaster candy factory and began producing chocolate, which he used for coating his caramels. By the next year, production had grown to include cocoa, sweet chocolate, and baking chocolate. The Hershey Chocolate company was born in 1894 as a <u>subsidiary</u> of the Lancaster Caramel Company. Six years later, Milton sold the caramel company, but retained the rights, and the equipment, to make chocolate. He believed that a large market of chocolate consumers was waiting for someone to produce reasonably priced candy. He was right.

(4) Milton Hershey returned to the village where he had been born, in the heart of dairy country, and opened his chocolate-manufacturing plant. With access to all the fresh milk he needed, he began producing the finest milk chocolate. The plant that opened in a small Pennsylvania village in 1905 is today the largest chocolate factory in the world. The confections created at this facility are favorites in the U.S. and internationally.

(5) The area where the factory is located is now known as Hershey, Pennsylvania. Within the first decades of its existence, the town thrived, as did the chocolate business. A bank, a school, churches, a department store, even a park and a trolley system all appeared in short order. Soon, the town even had a zoo. Today, a visit to the area reveals the Hershey Medical Center, Milton Hershey School, and Hershey's Chocolate World, a theme park where visitors are greeted by a giant Reese's Peanut Butter Cup. All of these things—and a huge number of happy chocolate lovers—were made possible because a caramel maker visited the Chicago Exposition of 1893!

CBEST PRACTICE EXAM 2

1. The writer's main purpose in this passage is to
   a. recount the founding of the Hershey Chocolate Company.
   b. describe the process of manufacturing chocolate.
   c. compare the popularity of chocolate to other candies.
   d. explain how apprenticeships work.
   e. persuade readers to visit Hershey, Pennsylvania.

2. As it is used in paragraph 1, the underlined phrase *found his calling in life* most nearly means
   a. became educated.
   b. discovered a vocation.
   c. was a talented person.
   d. called on other people to help him.
   e. had good luck.

3. Which of the following statements is supported by information in the passage?
   a. Chocolate is popular in every country in the world.
   b. The Hershey Chocolate Company's factory is near Derry Church, Pennsylvania.
   c. Chocolate had never been manufactured in the United States before Milton Hershey did it.
   d. The Hershey Chocolate Company is run by Milton Hershey's children.
   e. The Hershey Chocolate Company has branches in Chicago, New Orleans, and New York City.

4. Which of the following words best describes Milton Hershey's character, as he is presented in the passage?
   a. defective
   b. determined
   c. carefree
   d. cautious
   e. greedy

5. According to the passage, Milton Hershey first began to produce chocolate in order to
   a. make cocoa and baking chocolate.
   b. save his caramel company from bankruptcy.
   c. make chocolate-covered caramels.
   d. attend the Chicago International Exposition.
   e. found a new town.

6. Which of the following best defines the underlined word *subsidiary* as used in paragraph 3?
   a. a company that is in financial trouble
   b. a company founded to compete with another company
   c. a company that is not incorporated
   d. a company controlled by another company
   e. a company owned by one person

7. The passage implies that Hershey opened his first chocolate company in
   a. Chicago.
   b. Denver.
   c. Philadelphia.
   d. Lancaster.
   e. Derry Church.

8. The author most likely included the information in paragraph 5 in order to show that
   a. Hershey's chocolate factory was so successful that a whole town was built around it.
   b. people all over the world have become tourists in Hershey, Pennsylvania.
   c. Hershey's chocolate factory has now become a successful theme park.
   d. Hershey moved back to the town where he was born.
   e. the Hershey Chocolate Company manufactures both chocolate and caramel.

Answer questions 9–10 on the basis of the following passage.

An ecosystem is a group of animals and plants living in a specific region and interacting with one another and with their physical environment. Ecosystems include physical and chemical components, such as soils, water, and nutrients, that support the organisms living there. These organisms may range from large animals to microscopic bacteria. Ecosystems also can be thought of as the interactions among all organisms in a given habitat; for instance, one species may serve as food for another. People are part of the ecosystems where they live and work. Human activities can harm or destroy local ecosystems unless actions such as land development for housing or businesses are carefully planned to conserve and sustain the ecology of the area. An important part of ecosystem management involves finding ways to protect and enhance economic and social well-being while protecting local ecosystems.

9. What is the main idea of the passage?
   a. An ecosystem is a community that includes animals, plants, and microscopic bacteria.
   b. Human activities harm or destroy local ecosystems, no matter how careful we may be.
   c. In managing the ecology of an area, it is important to protect both human interests and the interests of other members of local ecosystems.
   d. People should remember that they are a part of the ecosystems where they live and work.
   e. Ecosystems include both living and non-living things.

10. An ecosystem can most accurately be defined as a
    a. geographical area.
    b. community.
    c. habitat.
    d. protected environment.
    e. region.

Answer questions 11–12 on the basis of the following passage.

The city has distributed standardized recycling containers to all households; the containers are marked with directions that read: "We would prefer that you use this new container as your primary recycling container. Additional recycling containers may be purchased from the city."

11. According to the directions, each household
    a. may only use one recycling container.
    b. must use the new recycling container.
    c. should use the new recycling container.
    d. must buy a new recycling container.
    e. should pick up the new recycling container.

12. According to the directions, which of the following is true about the new containers?
    a. The new containers are better than other containers.
    b. Households may use only the new containers for recyclable items.
    c. The new containers hold more than the old containers did.
    d. Households may use other containers besides the new ones if they wish.
    e. Additional containers can be delivered at no charge.

Answer questions 13–16 on the basis of the following passage.

In Ralph Waldo Emerson's view, although individual consciousness will eventually be lost, every living thing is part of the blessed Unity, part of the transcendent "over-soul" which is the universe. And so, in the main body of his philosophy, Emerson accepts the indifference of Nature to the individual life, and does not struggle against it. His acceptance of Nature as tending toward overall unity and good in spite of her indifference to the individual is curiously and ironically akin to the Puritan acceptance of the doctrine of

Divine Election. In his "Personal Narrative" Jonathan Edwards writes that he finally has "a delightful conviction" of the doctrine of God's sovereignty, of God's choosing according to His divine and arbitrary will, "whom he would to eternal life, and rejecting whom he pleased...." He writes that the doctrine had formerly seemed _____ to him; however, it had finally come to seem "exceedingly pleasant, bright, and sweet." In "Fate," Emerson writes that "Nature will not mind drowning a man or a woman, but swallows your ship like a grain of dust," but that "the central intention of Nature [is] harmony and joy. Let us build altars to the Beautiful Necessity...."

13. Which of the following statements would LEAST effectively support the view of both Emerson and Edwards toward the nature of the universe?
    a. God notices the fall of a sparrow.
    b. God is all-powerful and all-wise.
    c. The universe is a harmonious place.
    d. Nature is beautiful and good.
    e. One should accept the universal plan.

14. Which of the following best describes the main idea of the passage?
    a. As philosophers reflecting on the nature of the universe, Ralph Waldo Emerson and Jonathan Edwards are ironically akin to one another.
    b. Ralph Waldo Emerson believes that nature is indifferent to individuals; on the other hand, Jonathan Edwards believes God makes decisions about individuals, but based on His desires.
    c. Ralph Waldo Emerson believes in a world ruled by the transcendent oversoul of Nature, whereas Jonathan Edwards believes in a world ruled by a sovereign God.
    d. Ralph Waldo Emerson believes that individual consciousness will be lost after death, whereas Jonathan Edwards believes that the soul will go to heaven or hell.
    e. Ralph Waldo Emerson's acceptance of Nature's indifference to the individual is ironically similar to Jonathan Edwards' acceptance of the doctrine of Divine Election.

15. Which of the following terms best defines the doctrine of Divine Election as discussed in the passage?
    a. God's power
    b. the soul's redemption
    c. eternal damnation
    d. predestined salvation
    e. a state of grace

16. In the context of the passage, which of the following words would best fit in the blank?
    a. loving
    b. just
    c. horrible
    d. imperious
    e. satisfying

Answer question 17 on the basis of the following passage.

Authentic Dhurrie rugs are hand-woven in India. Today, they are usually made of wool, but they are descendants of cotton floor- and bed-coverings. In fact, the name Dhurrie comes from the Indian word *dari*, which means threads of cotton. The rugs are noted for their soft colors and their varieties of design and make a stunning focal point for any living room or dining room.

17. Which of the following is the most likely intended audience for the passage?
    a. people who are planning a trip to India
    b. people studying traditional Indian culture
    c. people who are studying Indian domestic customs
    d. people learning to operate a rug loom
    e. people who enjoy interior decorating

Answer questions 18 and 19 on the basis of the following passage.

A healthy diet with proper nutrition is essential for maintaining good overall health. Since vitamins were discovered earlier in this century, people have routinely been taking vitamin supplements for this purpose. The Recommended Dietary Allowance (RDA) is a frequently used nutritional standard for maintaining optimal health. The RDA specifies the recommended amount of a number of nutrients for people of both sexes and in many different age groups. The National Research Council's Committee on Diet and Health has proposed a definition of the RDA to be that amount of a nutrient which meets the needs of 98 percent of the population.

The RDA approach _____. First, it is based on the assumption that it is possible to accurately define nutritional requirements for a given group. However, individual nutritional requirements can vary widely within each group. The efficiency with which a person converts food intake into nutrients can also vary widely. Certain foods when eaten in combination actually prevent the absorption of nutrients. For example, spinach combined with milk reduces the amount of calcium available to the body from the milk. Also, the RDA approach specifies a different dietary requirement for each age and sex; however, it is clearly unrealistic to expect a homemaker to prepare a different menu for each family member. Still, although we cannot rely solely upon RDA to ensure our overall long-term health, it can be a useful guide so long as its limitations are recognized.

18. Which of the following would best fit in the blank in the first sentence of paragraph two?
    a. is based on studies by respected nutritionists
    b. has a number of shortcomings
    c. has been debunked in the last few years
    d. is full of holes
    e. is constantly being refined

19. With which of the following would the author most likely agree?
    a. The RDA approach should be replaced by a more realistic nutritional guide.
    b. The RDA approach should be supplemented with more specific nutritional guides.
    c. In spite of its flaws, the RDA approach is definitely the best guide to good nutrition.
    d. The RDA approach is most suitable for a large family.
    e. The RDA approach is too complicated for most consumers.

Answer questions 20–22 on the basis of the following passage.

It has been more than twenty-five years since the National Aeronautic and Space Administration (NASA) last sent a craft to land on the moon. The Lunar Prospector took off in January of 1998, in the first moon shot since astronauts last walked on the moon in 1972. This time, the moon-traveller is only a low-cost robot, who will spend a year on the surface of the moon, collecting minerals and ice.

Unlike the moon shots of the 1960s and 1970s, Lunar Prospector does not carry a camera, so the American public will not get to see new pictures of the moon's surface. _____. Scientists are anxious for the results of one exploration in particular—that done by the neutron spectrometer. Using this instrument, Prospector will examine the moon's poles, searching for signs of water ice. There has long been *speculation* that frozen water from comets may have accumulated in craters at one of the moon's poles and may still be there, as this pole is permanently shielded from the sun. The neutron spectrometer seeks out the hydrogen atoms in water and can detect the presence of as little as one cup of water in a cubic yard of soil.

20. Which sentence, if inserted into the blank line in the second paragraph, would be most consistent with the writer's purpose and intended audience?
    a. You won't, therefore, be able to see if the surface of the moon has changed much in thirty years.
    b. Instead, Prospector carries instruments that will map the make-up of the entire surface of the moon.
    c. I don't believe that new pictures would prove very interesting, anyway.
    d. However, the topography of the lunar terrain retains a mundane familiarity that is not consistent with the nature of NASA's *raison d'etre* and will contribute little to advancements *vis a vis* missions such as Sojourner.
    e. Entertainment of the public does not justify the enormous cost of space exploration.

21. Which of the following is the best meaning of the word "speculation" as it is used in the second paragraph of the passage?
    a. a theory
    b. an investment
    c. a vision
    d. an image
    e. a process

22. Which of the following kinds of publications would most likely contain this passage?
    a. an astrophysics text book
    b. a history text book
    c. a collection of personal essays
    d. a general circulation magazine
    e. an internal NASA memo

Answer questions 23–26 on the basis of the following passage.

O'Connell Street is the main thoroughfare of Dublin City. Although it is not a particularly long street, Dubliners will tell the visitor proudly that it is the widest street in all of Europe. This claim usually meets with protests, especially from French tourists, claiming the Champs Elysees of Paris as Europe's widest street. But the witty Dubliner will not relinquish bragging rights easily and will trump the French visitor with a fine distinction: the Champs Elysees is a *boulevard;* O'Connell is a *street.*

Divided by several important monuments running the length of its center, the street is named for Daniel O'Connell, an Irish patriot. _____
_____. O'Connell stands high above the unhurried crowds of shoppers, business people, and students on a sturdy column, surrounded by four serene angels seated at each corner of the monument's base. Further up the street is the famous General Post Office that the locals affectionately call "the GPO." During the 1916 rebellion, the GPO was taken over and occupied by the Irish rebels to British rule, sparking weeks of armed combat in the city's center. To this day, the angels of O'Connell's monument bear the marks of the fighting: one sits reading calmly, apparently unaware of the bullet hole dimpling her upper arm; another, reaching out to stroke the ears of a huge bronze Irish wolfhound, has survived what should be a mortal wound to her heart.

23. Which of the following would be the best title for this passage?
    a. Dublin's Famous Monuments
    b. The Irish Take Pride in Their Capital City
    c. The Widest Street in Europe
    d. Sights and History on Dublin's O'Connell Street
    e. Tourism in Dublin

24. Which sentence, if inserted in the blank space above, would be the most correct and contribute the most pertinent information to that paragraph?
- a. His monument stands at the lower end of the road, the end closest to the river Liffey that bisects Dublin.
- b. Other monuments along the street include statues to Charles Parnell, Anna Livia Plurabelle, and James Joyce.
- c. Dublin tourist buses leave from this site every twenty minutes.
- d. Daniel O'Connell was an important Irish nationalist, who died before the 1916 rebellion.
- e. We can see his monument standing in lower O'Connell Street facing the Liffey River.

25. What is the best definition for the word "trump" as it is used in the first paragraph of the passage?
- a. to trumpet loudly, to blare or drown out
- b. to trample
- c. to get the better of by using a key or hidden resource
- d. to devise a fraud, to employ trickery
- e. to use a particular suit of cards

26. With which of the following statements about the people of Dublin would the author of the passage most likely agree?
- a. They are proud of their history but lack industry.
- b. They are playful and tricky.
- c. They are rebellious and do not like tourists.
- d. They are witty and relaxed.
- e. They are unaware of their history.

Answer questions 27–29 on the basis of the following passage.

In 1899, Czar Nicholas II of Russia invited the nations of the world to a conference at The Hague. This conference—and a follow-up organized by Theodore Roosevelt in 1907—*ushered in* a period of vigorous growth in international law. This growth was in response to several factors, not least of which was the increasing potential for destruction of modern warfare. The recently concluded Civil War in the United States made this potential clear.

During this growth, the subjects of international law were almost exclusively restricted to the relationships that countries had with one another. Issues of trade and warfare dominated both the disputes and the agreements of the period. _____, the developments of this period paved the way for further expansion of international law, which has occurred in the last several years. _____, organizations such as the United Nations and the International Court of Justice are greatly concerned not only with the way countries deal with one another, but the ways in which they treat their own citizens.

27. Which words or phrases, if inserted in order into the blanks in the passage, would help the reader understand the sequence of the author's ideas?
- a. Therefore; In addition
- b. However; Now
- c. Furthermore; Yet
- d. Even if; On the other hand
- e. As a result; Meanwhile

205

28. According to the passage, what was the impact of the U.S. Civil War on the development of international law?
   a. It encouraged the United States to join the international community.
   b. It allowed armaments manufacturers to test new weapons.
   c. It diminished the influence of the United States internationally.
   d. It resulted in the suspension of agriculture exports from Southern states.
   e. It highlighted the increasing destructive capabilities of modern warfare.

29. Which of the following is the best meaning of the phrase *ushered in* as it is used in the passage?
   a. escorted
   b. progressed
   c. guarded
   d. heralded
   e. conducted

Answer questions 30–32 on the basis of the following passage.

   Emperor Charlemagne of the Franks was crowned in 800 A.D. The Frankish Empire at that time extended over what is now Germany, Italy, and France. Charlemagne died in 814, but his brief reign marked the dawn of a distinctly European *culture*. The artists and thinkers that helped create this European civilization drew on the ancient texts of the Germanic, Celtic, Greek, Roman, Hebrew, and Christian worlds.
   _____.
   These mores in turn laid the groundwork for the laws, customs, and even attitudes of today's Europeans.

30. According to the passage, for how many years was Charlemagne Emperor of the Franks?
   a. fourteen years
   b. fifteen years
   c. thirteen years
   d. sixteen years
   e. twelve years

31. Which of the following is the best meaning of the word "culture" as it is used in the passage?
   a. the fashionable class
   b. a community of inter-related individuals
   c. a partnership
   d. a group of loosely associated outsiders
   e. an organized group with a common goal

32. Which sentence, if inserted into the blank line in the passage, would be most consistent with the writer's purpose and intended audience?
   a. In order to understand these traditions as prototype, one must be familiar with the issues surrounding the transference of rites from generation to generation.
   b. Cultural traditions function to identify members of a culture to one another and, also, to allow the individual to self-identify.
   c. Many of the traditions of these cultures remained active in Frankish society for centuries.
   d. When tradition is lacking or is not honored by the younger generation in a society, there is danger that the culture will be lost.
   e. I don't think it is necessary to discuss the origin of these traditions; it will only muddy the water.

Answer questions 33 and 34 on the basis of the following index.

Freedom of Expression, 217–290
    Text of the First Amendment, 217
    Suppression of Message Content, 217–272
        Cohen v. California, 219–220
        Marketplace of Ideas, 221–225
            Abrams v. United States, 223
        Unprotected Categories, 225–259
            Chaplin v. New Hampshire, 226
            Obscenity, 232–239
                Miller v. California, 233–235
            Advocating (Imminent) Illegal Behavior, 239–242
                Schenck v. Ohio, 240
            Defamation, 242–246
                New York Times v. Sullivan, 243–245
            Fighting Words, 247–252
                Feiner v. New York, 249
            Mere rationality analysis, 252–260
                Brandenburg v. Ohio, 256–259
        Outside the Unprotected Categories, 260–272
            Regulations Presumed Unconstitutional, 260–263
                Metromedia, Inc. v. San Diego, 261–263
            Government's Interest, 264–272
                Chicago Police Department v. Mosley, 266–267
                Significance, 267
                    Widmar v. Vincent, 268–269
                Narrowly Drawn, 270–272
                    Boos v. Barry, 270–271
    Incidental Interference with Expression, 273–290
        Time, Place, and Manner, 274–277
            Clark v. Community for Creative Non-Violence, 275–276
        Forum, 278–283
            Hague v. CIO, 281–283
            Public, 279
            Not Public, 280
        Government's Interest, 283–290
            Schneider v. State, 284–286
            Significance, 286–287
            Narrowly Drawn, 287–289
            Available Alternatives, 289–290

33. On which pages should one look to find information about the categories of unprotected speech?
    a. 217–220
    b. 221–225
    c. 225–259
    d. 260–272
    e. 273–290

34. Which of the following best describes the organizational pattern used in the section of the book dealing with suppression of message content?
    a. by the types of publications involved
    b. by the courts that heard the cases
    c. by the dates of the court decisions
    d. by the forum in which the speech took place
    e. by the category of the content of the speech

Answer question 35 on the basis of the following passage.

    Ratatouille is a dish that has grown in popularity worldwide over the last few years. Essentially, ratatouille is a vegetable stew, which usually features eggplant, zucchini, tomato, peppers, and garlic, chopped, mixed together, sauteed briefly, and finally, cooked slowly over low heat. As the vegetables cook slowly, they make their own broth, which may be extended with a little tomato paste. The name *ratatouille* comes from the French word *touiller*, meaning to stir or mix together.

35. According to the information presented in the passage, what should one do immediately after chopping the vegetables?
    a. saute them
    b. mix them together
    c. cook them slowly over low heat
    d. add tomato paste
    e. add garlic

Answer questions 36 and 37 on the basis of the following passage.

When the current measure used to calculate poverty levels was introduced in 1963, the poverty line for a family of two adults and two children was about $3,100. In 1992, there were 36.9 million people, or 14.5% of the U.S. population, with incomes below the poverty line. A proposed new way of measuring poverty levels would include for the first time the effects of work-related expenses such as transportation costs and child care costs on families' available income.

The largest effect of the new measure would be a decrease in the percentage of people in families receiving cash welfare who fall under the poverty line, and an increase in the percentage of people in working families who fall under it. People in families receiving cash welfare would make up 30% of the poor under the new measure, compared with 40% under the current measure. In contrast, people in working families would make up 59% of the poor under the new measure, compared with 51% under the current measure.

36. According to the 1963 standards, the current number of poor working families is approximately what proportion of the population?
   a. 30%
   b. 60%
   c. 40%
   d. 59%
   e. 51%

37. One difference between the current and proposed measures is the fact that
   a. the proposed measure identifies fewer working poor.
   b. the current measure identifies fewer working poor.
   c. the proposed measure disregards expenses for basic needs.
   d. the current measure includes more people with health insurance.
   e. the current measure ignores the completely destitute.

Answer questions 38–41 on the basis of the following poem by Emily Dickinson.

> A narrow fellow in the grass
> Occasionally rides;
> You may have met him—did you not?
> His notice sudden is.
> The grass divides as with a comb,
> A spotted shaft is seen,
> And then it closes at your feet
>   And opens further on.
>
> He likes a boggy acre,
> A floor too cool for corn,
> Yet when a boy, and barefoot,
> I more than once at noon
> Have passed, I thought, a whip-lash
> Unbraiding in the sun,
> When, stooping to secure it,
>   It wrinkled, and was gone.

Several of nature's people
I know and they know me;
I feel for them a transport
Of cordiality;
But never met this fellow,
Attended or alone,
Without a tighter breathing
And zero at the bone.

38. Who or what is the "fellow" in this poem?
   a. a whip-lash
   b. a weed
   c. a snake
   d. a gust of wind
   e. a boy

39. The phrase "Without a tighter breathing / And zero at the bone" most nearly indicates
   a. fright.
   b. cold.
   c. grief.
   d. awe.
   e. relief.

40. The phrase "nature's people" means
   a. nature-lovers.
   b. children.
   c. animals.
   d. neighbors.
   e. grain.

41. The speaker of this poem is most likely
   a. an adult woman.
   b. an adult man.
   c. a young girl.
   d. a young boy.
   e. Emily Dickinson.

Answer questions 42–45 on the basis of the following passage.

By using tiny probes as neural prostheses, scientists may be able to restore nerve function in quadriplegics and make the blind see or the deaf hear. Thanks to advanced techniques, a single, small, implanted probe can stimulate individual neurons electrically or chemically and then record responses. Preliminary results suggest that the microprobe telemetry systems can be permanently implanted and replace damaged or missing nerves.

The tissue-compatible microprobes represent an advance over the typical aluminum wire electrodes used in studies of the cortex and other brain structures. Researchers accumulate much data using traditional electrodes, but there is a question of how much damage they cause to the nervous system. Microprobes, which are about as thin as a human hair, cause minimal damage and disruption of neurons when inserted into the brain.

In addition to recording nervous system impulses, the microprobes have minuscule channels that open the way for delivery of drugs, cellular growth factors, neurotransmitters, and other neuroactive compounds to a single neuron or to groups of neurons. Also, patients who lack certain biochemicals could receive doses via prostheses. The probes can have up to four channels, each with its own recording/stimulating electrode.

42. One similar feature of microprobes and wire electrodes is
   a. a minimal disturbance of neurons.
   b. the density of the material.
   c. the capacity for multiple leads.
   d. the substance from which they are made.
   e. their ability to generate information.

43. Which of the following best expresses the main idea of the passage?
a. Microprobes require further technological advances before they can be used in humans.
b. Wire electrodes are antiquated as a means for delivering neuroactive compounds to the brain.
c. Microprobes have great potential to help counteract neural damage.
d. Technology now exists that may enable repair of the nervous system.
e. Use of wire electrodes is being replaced by use of wire electrodes.

44. All of the following are mentioned in the passage as potential uses for prostheses EXCEPT
a. transportation of medication.
b. induction of physical movement.
c. compensation for damaged nerves.
d. transportation of growth factor.
e. removal of biochemicals from the cortex.

45. The initial function of microprobe channels is to
a. create pathways.
b. disrupt neurons.
c. replace ribbon cables.
d. study the brain.
e. induce sight and hearing in the blind and deaf.

Answer questions 46 and 47 on the basis of the following passage.

Greyhound racing is the sixth most popular spectator sport in the United States. Over the last decade a growing number of racers have been adopted to live out their retirement as household pets, once their racing career is over.

Many people hesitate to adopt a retired racing greyhound because they think only very old dogs are available. Actually, even champion racers only work until they are about three and a half years old. Since greyhounds usually live to be 12-15 years old, their retirement is much longer than their racing careers.

People worry that a greyhound will be more nervous and active than other breeds and will need a large space to run. These are false impressions. Greyhounds have naturally sweet, mild dispositions, and while they love to run, they are sprinters rather than distance runners and are sufficiently exercised with a few laps around a fenced-in backyard everyday.

Greyhounds do not make good watchdogs, but they are very good with children, get along well with other dogs (and usually cats as well), and are very affectionate and loyal. They are intelligent, well-behaved dogs, usually housebroken in only a few days. A retired racing greyhound is a wonderful pet for almost anyone.

46. Based on the tone of the passage, the author's main purpose is to
a. teach prospective owners how to transform their racing greyhound into a good pet.
b. show how the greyhound's nature makes it equally good as racer and pet.
c. encourage people to adopt retired racing greyhounds.
d. objectively present the pros and cons of adopting a racing greyhound.
e. argue in favor of banning Greyhound racing.

47. According to the passage, adopting a greyhound is a good idea for people who
 a. do not have children.
 b. live in apartments.
 c. do not usually like dogs.
 d. are retired.
 e. already have another dog or a cat.

Answer question 48 on the basis of the following passage.

Rhesus monkeys use facial expressions to communicate with each other and to enforce social order. For example, the "fear grimace," although it looks ferocious, is actually given by a _____ monkey who is intimidated by a _____ member of the group.

48. Which pair of words or phrases, if inserted into the blanks in sequence, makes the most sense in the writer's context?
 a. calm . . . aggressive
 b. dominant . . . subordinate
 c. confident . . . fearless
 d. subordinate . . . dominant
 e. high-ranking . . . low-ranking

Answer questions 49 and 50 on the basis of the following table.

DISTRIBUTION OF OCCUPATIONS OF 200 ADULT MALES IN THE BAIDYA CASTE MADARIPUR VILLAGE, BENGAL, 1914

Occupation	Number
Farmers	02
Government service, clerks	44
Landowners	08
Lawyers	06
Newspapers and presses	05
No occupation	25
Not recorded	08
Students	68
Teachers	11
Trade and commerce	23

49. The largest number of men in the Baidya caste of Madaripur are involved in which field?
 a. education
 b. agriculture
 c. government
 d. publishing
 e. trade

50. What percentage of the Baidya caste men are employed in the legal profession?
 a. 12%
 b. 0.3%
 c. 6%
 d. 3%
 e. 1.2%

▶ **Section 2:** Mathematics

1. Roger earned $24,355 this year, and $23,000 the year before. To the nearest $100, what did Roger earn in the past two years?
   a. $47,300
   b. $47,350
   c. $47,355
   d. $47,360
   e. $47,400

Use the information below to answer question 2.

A cafeteria has three different options for lunch.
For $2, a customer can get either a sandwich or two pieces of fruit.
For $3, a customer can get a sandwich and one piece of fruit.
For $4, a customer can get either two sandwiches, or a sandwich and two pieces of fruit.

2. If Jan has $6 to pay for lunch for her and her husband, which of the following is not a possible combination?
   a. three sandwiches and one piece of fruit
   b. two sandwiches and two pieces of fruit
   c. one sandwich and four pieces of fruit
   d. three sandwiches and no fruit
   e. one sandwich and three pieces of fruit

Use the table below to answer question 3.

PRODUCTION OF FARM-IT TRACTORS FOR THE MONTH OF APRIL

FACTORY	APRIL OUTPUT
Dallas	450
Houston	425
Lubbock	
Amarillo	345
TOTAL	1780

3. What was Lubbock's production in the month of April?
   a. 345
   b. 415
   c. 540
   d. 550
   e. 560

Use the pie chart to answer question 4.

Sales For 1997

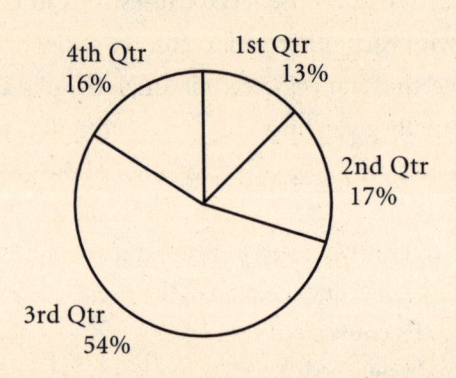

4. The chart shows quarterly sales for Cool-Air's air-conditioning units. Which of the following combinations contributed 70% to the total?
   a. 1st and 2nd quarters
   b. 1st and 3rd quarters
   c. 2nd and 3rd quarters
   d. 2nd and 4th quarters
   e. 3rd and 4th quarters

5. Rashaard went fishing six days in the month of June. He caught 11, 4, 0, 5, 4, and 6 fish respectively. On the days that Rashaard fished, what was his average catch?
   a. 4
   b. 5
   c. 6
   d. 7
   e. 8

6. An average of 90% is needed on five tests to receive an A in a class. If a student received scores of 95, 85, 88, and 84 on the first four tests, what score will the student need to achieve on the fifth test to get an A?
   a. 90
   b. 92
   c. 94
   d. 96
   e. 98

7. A bag of jellybeans contains 8 black beans, 10 green beans, 3 yellow beans, and 9 orange beans. What is the probability of selecting either a yellow or an orange bean?
   a. $\frac{1}{10}$
   b. $\frac{2}{5}$
   c. $\frac{4}{15}$
   d. $\frac{3}{10}$
   e. $\frac{1}{3}$

8. What is the perimeter of a pentagon with three sides of 3 inches, and the remaining sides 5 inches long?
   a. 19 inches
   b. 9 inches
   c. 14 inches
   d. 12 inches
   e. 24 inches

9. What is the result of multiplying 11 by 0.032?
   a. 0.032
   b. 0.0352
   c. 0.32
   d. 0.352
   e. 3.20

10. If a school buys three computers at a, b, and c dollars each, and the school gets a discount of 90%, which expression would determine the average price paid by the school?
    a. $\frac{0.9 \times a + b + c}{3}$
    b. $\frac{(a+b+c)}{0.9}$
    c. $(a+b+c) \times 0.9$
    d. $\frac{(a+b+c)}{3}$
    e. $\frac{3 \times (a+b+c)}{0.9}$

11. Roger wants to know if he has enough money to purchase several items. He needs three heads of lettuce, which cost $.99 each, and two boxes of cereal, which cost $3.49 each. He uses the expression $(3 \times \$0.99) + (2 \times \$3.49)$ to calculate how much the items will cost. Which of the following expressions could also be used?
    a. $3 \times (\$3.49 + \$.99) - \$3.49$
    b. $3 \times (\$3.49 + \$.99)$
    c. $(2 + 3) \times (\$3.49 + \$.99)$
    d. $(2 \times 3) + (\$3.49 \times \$.99)$
    e. $3 \times (\$3.49 + \$.99) + \$3.49$

12. Rosa finds the average of her three most recent golf scores by using the following expression, where a, b, and c are the three scores: $\frac{a+b+c}{3} \times 100$. Which of the following would also determine the average of her scores?
    a. $(\frac{a}{3} + \frac{b}{3} + \frac{c}{3}) \times 100$
    b. $\frac{\frac{a+b+c}{3}}{100}$
    c. $(a+b+c) \times \frac{3}{100}$
    d. $\frac{a \times b \times c}{3 + 100}$
    e. $\frac{a+b+c}{3+100}$

213

13. What is $\frac{2}{3}$ divided by $\frac{5}{12}$?
   a. $1\frac{3}{5}$
   b. $1\frac{5}{18}$
   c. $1\frac{7}{36}$
   d. $1\frac{5}{6}$
   e. $1\frac{2}{3}$

14. A 15 cc dosage of a medication must be increased by 20 percent. What is the new dosage?
   a. 17 cc
   b. 18 cc
   c. 20 cc
   d. 30 cc
   e. 35 cc

15. City High School basketball coach Donna Green earns $26,000 a year. If she receives a 4.5% salary increase, how much will she earn?
   a. $26,110
   b. $26,450
   c. $27,170
   d. $27,260
   e. $29,200

16. In the Pinebrook school district last year, 220 students were vaccinated for measles, mumps, and rubella. Of those, 60 percent reported that they had had flu at some time in their lives. How many students had not had the flu previously?
   a. 36
   b. 55
   c. 88
   d. 126
   e. 132

17. Of the 1,125 teachers in a study of bilingual education, 135 speak fluent Spanish. What percentage of the group of teachers in the study speaks fluent Spanish?
   a. 12 percent
   b. 7.3 percent
   c. 8.3 percent
   d. 9.3 percent
   e. 14 percent

Answer questions 18–20 by referring to the following chart, which gives the causes of major home fires.

MAJOR CAUSES OF HOME FIRES IN THE PREVIOUS 4-YEAR PERIOD

Cause (% of Total)	Fires Civilian Deaths (% of Total)
Heating equipment 161,500 (27.5%) (16.8%)	770
Cooking equipment 104,800 (17.8%) (7.7%)	350
Incendiary, suspicious 65,400 (11.1%) (13.6%)	620
Electrical equipment 45,700 (7.8%) (9.6%)	440
Other equipment 43,000 (7.3%) (5.3%)	240
Smoking materials 39,300 (6.7%)	1,320 (28.9%)

Appliances, air conditioning
36,200 (6.2%)   120
(2.7%)

Exposure and other heat
28,600 (4.8%)   191
(4.2%)

Open flame
27,200 (4.6%)   130
(2.9%)

Child play
26,900 (4.6%)   370
(8.1%)

Natural causes
9,200 (1.6%)   10
(0.2%)

18. What is the percentage of the total fires caused by electrical equipment and other equipment combined?
  a. 7.8%
  b. 14.9%
  c. 15.1%
  d. 29.9%
  e. 30.0%

19. Of the following causes, which one has the highest ratio of total fires to percentage of deaths?
  a. heating equipment
  b. smoking materials
  c. exposure and other heat
  d. child play
  e. natural causes

20. The snack machine in the teachers' lounge accepts only quarters. Candy bars cost 25¢, packages of peanuts cost 75¢, and cans of cola cost 50¢. How many quarters are needed to buy two candy bars, one package of peanuts, and one can of cola?
  a. 8
  b. 7
  c. 6
  d. 5
  e. 4

21. All of the rooms on the top floor of a government building are rectangular, with 8-foot ceilings. One room is 9 feet wide by 11 feet long. What is the combined area of the four walls, including doors and windows?
  a. 99 square feet
  b. 160 square feet
  c. 320 square feet
  d. 72 square feet
  e. 288 square feet

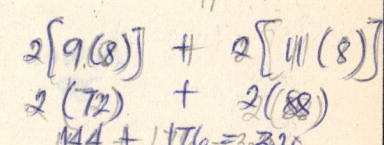

22. A child has a temperature of 40 degrees C. What is the child's temperature in degrees Fahrenheit? $F = \frac{9}{5}C + 32$.
  a. 100 degrees F
  b. 101 degrees F
  c. 102 degrees F
  d. 103 degrees F
  e. 104 degrees F

Answer question 23 on the basis of the following information.

Mr. Richard Tupper is purchasing gifts for his family. He stops to consider what else he has to buy. A quick mental inventory of his shopping bag so far reveals the following:

- 1 cashmere sweater valued at $260
- 3 diamond bracelets, each valued at $365
- 1 computer game valued at $78
- 1 cameo brooch valued at $130

Later, having coffee in the Food Court, he suddenly remembers that he has purchased only 2 diamond bracelets, not 3, and that the cashmere sweater was on sale for $245.

23. What is the total value of the gifts Mr. Tupper has purchased so far?
 a. $833
 b. $975
 c. $1,183
 d. $1,198
 e. $1,563

Answer questions 24–25 on the basis of the following list.

Here is a list of the ingredients needed to make 16 brownies.

Deluxe Brownies
$\frac{2}{3}$ cup butter
5 squares (1 ounce each) unsweetened chocolate
$1\frac{1}{2}$ cups sugar
2 teaspoons vanilla
2 eggs
1 cup flour

24. How much sugar is needed to make 8 brownies?
 a. $\frac{3}{4}$ cup
 b. 3 cups
 c. $\frac{2}{3}$ cup
 d. $\frac{5}{8}$ cup
 e. 1 cup

25. What is the greatest number of brownies that can be made if the baker has only 1 cup of butter?
 a. 12
 b. 16
 c. 24
 d. 28
 e. 32

26. One lap on a particular outdoor track measures a quarter of a mile around. To run a total of three and a half miles, how many complete laps must a person complete?
 a. 14
 b. 18
 c. 7
 d. 10
 e. 13

27. On Monday, a kindergarten class uses $2\frac{1}{4}$ pounds of modeling clay the first hour, $4\frac{5}{8}$ pounds of modeling clay the second hour, and $\frac{1}{2}$ pound of modeling clay the third hour. How many pounds of clay does the class use during the three hours on Monday?
 a. $6\frac{3}{8}$
 b. $6\frac{7}{8}$
 c. $7\frac{1}{4}$
 d. $7\frac{3}{8}$
 e. $7\frac{3}{4}$

CBEST PRACTICE EXAM 2

28. A floor plan is drawn to scale so that one quarter inch represents 2 feet. If a hall on the plan is 4 inches long, how long will the actual hall be when it is built?
   a. 2 feet
   b. 8 feet
   c. 16 feet
   d. 24 feet
   e. 32 feet

29. Student track team members have to buy running shoes at the full price of $84.50, but those who were also team members last term get a 15 percent discount. Those who have been team members for at least three terms get an additional 10 percent off the discounted price. How much does a student who has been a track team member at least three terms have to pay for shoes?
   a. $63.38
   b. $64.65
   c. $65.78
   d. $71.83
   e. $72.05

30. There are 176 men and 24 women serving the 9th Precinct. What percentage of the 9th Precinct's force is women?
   a. 6%
   b. 12%
   c. 14%
   d. 16%
   e. 24%

31. The basal metabolic rate (BMR) is the rate at which our body uses calories. The BMR for a man in his twenties is about 1,700 calories per day. If 204 of those calories should come from protein, about what percent of this man's diet should be protein?
   a. 1.2%
   b. 8.3%
   c. 12%
   d. 16%
   e. 18%

32. The condition known as Down syndrome occurs in about 1 in 1,500 children when the mothers are in their twenties. About what percent of all children born to mothers in their twenties are likely to have Down syndrome?
   a. 0.0067%
   b. 0.67%
   c. 6.7%
   d. 0.067%
   e. 0.00067%

33. If a population of yeast cells grows from 10 to 320 in a period of 5 hours, what is the rate of growth?
   a. It doubles its numbers every half hour.
   b. It doubles its numbers every hour.
   c. It triples its numbers every hour.
   d. It doubles its numbers every two hours.
   e. It triples its numbers every two hours.

34. A certain water pollutant is unsafe at a level of 20 ppm (parts per million). A city's water supply now contains 50 ppm of this pollutant. What percentage of improvement will make the water safe?
   a. 30%
   b. 40%
   c. 50%
   d. 60%
   e. 70%

35. An insurance policy pays 80% of the first $20,000 of a certain patient's medical expenses, 60% of the next $40,000, and 40% of the $40,000 after that. If the patient's total medical bill is $92,000, how much will the policy pay?
a. $36,800
b. $49,600
c. $52,800
d. $73,600
e. $80,000

36. If you take recyclables to whichever recycler will pay the most, what is the greatest amount of money you could get for 2,200 pounds of aluminum, 1,400 pounds of cardboard, 3,100 pounds of glass, and 900 pounds of plastic?

Re-cycler	Aluminum	Cardboard	Glass	Plastic
X	.06/pound	.03/pound	.08/pound	.02/pound
Y	.07/pound	.04/pound	.07/pound	.03/pound

a. $409
b. $440
c. $447
d. $454
e. $485

37. Water is coming into a tank three times as fast as it is going out. After one hour, the tank contains 11,400 gallons of water. How fast is the water coming in?
a. 2,850 gallons/hour
b. 3,800 gallons/hour
c. 5,700 gallons/hour
d. 11,400 gallons/hour
e. 17,100 gallons/hour

38. A train must travel 3,450 miles in six days. How many miles must it travel each day?
a. 525
b. 550
c. 600
d. 575
e. 500

39. What is another name for 20,706?
a. 200 + 70 + 6
b. 2000 + 700 + 6
c. 20,000 + 70 + 6
d. 20,000 + 700 + 6
e. 20,000 + 700 + 60

40. A dormitory now houses 30 men and allows 42 square feet of space per man. If five more men are put into this dormitory, how much less space will each man have?
a. 5 square feet
b. 6 square feet
c. 7 square feet
d. 8 square feet
e. 9 square feet

41. Ron is half as old as Sam, who is three times as old as Ted. The sum of their ages is 55. How old is Ron?
a. 5
b. 8
c. 10
d. 15
e. 30

42. A firefighter checks the gauge on a cylinder that normally contains 45 cubic feet of air and finds that the cylinder has only 10 cubic feet of air. The gauge indicates that the cylinder is
   a. $\frac{1}{5}$ full.
   b. $\frac{1}{4}$ full.
   c. $\frac{2}{9}$ full.
   d. $\frac{1}{3}$ full.
   e. $\frac{4}{5}$ full.

43. A gardener on a large estate determines that the length of garden hose needed to reach from the water spigot to a particular patch of prize-winning dragonsnaps is 175 feet. If the available garden hoses are 45 feet long, how many sections of hose, when connected together, will it take to reach the dragonsnaps?
   a. 2
   b. 3
   c. 4
   d. 5
   e. 6

44. To lower a fever of 105 degrees, ice packs are applied for 1 minute and then removed for 5 minutes before being applied again. Each application lowers the fever by half a degree. How long will it take to lower the fever to 99 degrees?
   a. 36 minutes
   b. 1 hour
   c. 1 hour and 12 minutes
   d. 1 hour and 15 minutes
   e. 1 hour and 30 minutes

45. Each sprinkler head in an sprinkler system sprays water at an average of 16 gallons per minute. If 5 sprinkler heads are flowing at the same time, how many gallons of water will be released in 10 minutes?
   a. 80
   b. 160
   c. 320
   d. 800
   e. 1650

46. Which of these is equivalent to 35°C? ($F = \frac{9}{5}C + 32$)
   a. 105 degrees F
   b. 95 degrees F
   c. 63 degrees F
   d. 19 degrees F
   e. 5.4 degrees F

47. What is the volume of a pyramid that has a rectangular base 5 feet by 3 feet and a height of 8 feet? ($V = \frac{1}{3} lwh$)
   a. 16 feet
   b. 30 feet
   c. 40 feet
   d. 80 feet
   e. 120 feet

48. How many feet of ribbon will a theatrical company need to tie off a performance area that is 34 feet long and 20 feet wide?
   a. 54
   b. 68
   c. 88
   d. 108
   e. 680

49. About how many liters of water will a 5-gallon container hold? (1 liter = 1.06 quarts)
   a. 5
   b. 11
   c. 19
   d. 20
   e. 21

50. Nationwide, in one year there were about 21,500 residential fires associated with furniture. Of these, 11,350 were caused by smoking materials. About what percent of the residential fires were smoking-related?
   a. 47%
   b. 49%
   c. 50%
   d. 51%
   e. 53%

▶ Section 3: Essay Writing

Carefully read the two essay-writing topics that follow. Plan and write two essays, one on each topic. Be sure to address all points in the topic. Allow about 30 minutes for each essay.

Topic 1

In a review of Don DeLillo's novel *White Noise*, Jayne Anne Phillips writes that the characters are people "sleepwalking through a world where 'Coke is It!' and the TV is always on." On the other hand, television is said to have brought the world to people who would not have seen much of it otherwise, that it has made possible a "global village." Write an essay in which you express your opinion of the effect of television on individuals or on nations. Include specific detail from personal experience to back up your assertions.

Topic 2

Some people say that writing can't be taught. Educators debate the subject every day, while the teachers in the trenches keep trying.

Write an essay in which you express your opinion about the matter. You may discuss any kind of writing, from basic composition to fiction. Be sure to back up your opinion with concrete examples and specific detail.

► Answers and Explanations

Section 1: Reading Comprehension

1. **a.** Choice **a** is the best choice because it is the most complete statement of the material. Choices **c** and **d** focus on small details of the passage; choice **b** is not discussed in the passage. The passage is informative, not persuasive, so choice **e** is incorrect.

2. **b.** In the context of the paragraph, this is the only possible choice. Choice **a** can be ruled out because there is no evidence that Hershey *became educated*. It is true that Hershey *was a talented person* (choice **b**), but *was talented* is not the same as having *found* something. Choice **d** is wrong because there is no evidence in paragraph 1 that Hershey called on anyone to help him. The passage talks about Hershey's hard work, but does not say he was lucky (choice **e**).

3. **b.** Because the passage states that Hershey *returned to the village where he had been born* to open his plant, and the passage also states that he was born near Derry Church, this statement must be accurate. The other choices cannot be supported. Although the writer mentions the popularity of chocolate internationally, you cannot assume that it is popular in every country (choice **a**), nor is there any indication that Milton Hershey was the first person to manufacture chocolate in the U.S. (choice **c**). Choice **d** is not discussed in the passage at all. The passage states that Hershey did not succeed in his candy-making ventures in other cities (choice **e**).

4. **b.** This is the best choice because the passage clearly shows Hershey's determination to be successful in the candy business. Although he had some failures, he could not be described as defective (choice **a**). There is nothing to indicate that he was *carefree* (choice **c**), *cautious* (choice **d**), or *greedy* (choice **e**).

5. **c.** The third paragraph states that Hershey first used chocolate for *coating his caramels*. Choice **a** can be ruled out because he didn't make cocoa or baking chocolate until a year after he began producing chocolate. Choice **b** is not in the passage. Choice **d** is incorrect because he purchased the chocolate-making equipment at the Exposition. Choice **e** is incorrect because Hershey did not try to start a town.

6. **d.** This question tests your ability to use context clues to determine the intended meaning of a word. In paragraph 3, the passage says *The Hershey Chocolate company was born in 1894 as a subsidiary of the Lancaster Caramel Company*. This indicates that a subsidiary company is one controlled by another company, choice **d**. Choices **a**, **b**, and **e** are illogical. Since the passage contains no discussion of whether any of Hershey's companies were incorporated, choice **c** can be ruled out.

7. **d.** This is an inference taken from paragraphs 3 and 4. Paragraph 3 indicates that Hershey's caramel company was in Lancaster and the chocolate company was a subsidiary. Paragraph 4 states that Hershey moved his plant in 1905, eleven years after he first got into the chocolate business. From these two facts, it is reasonable to conclude that the first chocolate business was in Lancaster.

8. **a.** This is the only choice that can be supported by the paragraph. Although tourists and caramel are mentioned in the passage (choices **b** and **e**), this is not the main purpose of the paragraph. There is a theme park in Hershey (choice **c**), but the chocolate factory still exists. Choice **d** can be ruled out because this information was given in paragraph 4.

9. **c.** This choice most nearly encompasses the passage and is reflected in the final sentence. Choice b is wrong because the passage holds out hope that we can conserve and sustain the ecology of an area. Choices a, d, and e are implied in the passage but are too narrow to be the main idea.
10. **b.** This is the only choice that reflects the idea of interaction among all members of the group mentioned in the first sentence. The other choices are only physical settings.
11. **c.** The directions indicate that the city prefers, but does not require, use of the new container. In addition, it appears the city only charges residents for additional containers.
12. **d.** The directions state the city would like households to use the new containers as their primary containers; this means other containers are allowed.
13. **a.** The final sentence states that *Nature will not mind drowning a man or a woman*, and sentence 4 speaks of Edwards' approval of God's *arbitrary will*; neither Nature nor God, as described in the passage, would notice *the fall of a sparrow*. Choice b is incorrect because Edwards has a *delightful conviction* in *God's sovereignty* (authority or power), which indicates that he believes God's judgment, no matter how arbitrary, is wise. Choices c and d are incorrect because Emerson speaks of Nature's intention as *harmony and joy*. Choice e is incorrect; both Emerson and Edwards believe God makes decisions about individuals based on the need of nature as a whole.
14. **e.** This choice says *how* the reflections of Emerson and Edwards are alike (that is, their acceptance of the arbitrary nature of Nature and God) and also speaks of the irony of the similarity between Emerson and Edwards, which is mentioned in the passage. Choice a is true, but is too general, since it does not say exactly how the two philosophers are alike. Choices b, c, and d are incorrect because they emphasize differences between the two world views, whereas the passage emphasizes similarities.
15. **d.** To be elected means to be chosen, and the passage speaks of *God's choosing according to his divine and arbitrary will, whom he would to eternal life* (i.e., to salvation). Being rejected is the opposite of being chosen or elected, so someone rejected would be damned (choice c). The other choices do not reflect an element of choice.
16. **c.** The word *horrible* most definitely contrasts to the words *exceedingly pleasant, bright, and sweet*, and the words *formerly* and *however* indicate that the sentence is describing a contrast. The other choices do not necessarily point to a contrast.
17. **e.** Although the people in the other choices might read this passage, it is not directed toward travelers, scholars, or readers (choices a, b, and c), nor is there anything in it about operating a loom (choice d). The last sentence indicates that the passage is directed toward interior decorators.
18. **b.** The blank is followed by a discussion of the shortcomings of the RDA approach. Choice a is incorrect because it does not lead into the discussion that follows regarding the RDA approach's shortcomings. Choice c is incorrect because it is contradicted by the final sentence of the passage, which states that the RDA approach remains a *useful guide*. Choice d is incorrect because its slangy style is inconsistent with the style used in the rest of the passage. Choice e is incorrect because it does not lead into the discussion which follows, and there is nothing in the passage to indicate the RDA is changing.
19. **b.** Choice b is indicated by the final sentence, which indicates that the RDA approach is useful, but has limitations, implying that a supplemental guide would be a good thing. Choice a is contra-

dicted by the final sentence of the passage. Choice c is incorrect because the passage says the RDA approach is a *useful guide*, but does NOT say it is the best guide to good nutrition. Choice d is contradicted by the next-to-last sentence of the passage. The passage states that the RDA approach is frequently used, which indicates it is not too complicated, as stated in choice e.

20. b. Choice b best reflects the writing style of the passage, which is for a general audience. Choices a and c are too informal; choice d uses jargon and choice e seems to talk down to the audience.

21. a. Either a or b are possible definitions of *speculation*, however, the passage suggests that in this case the author is referring to a theory—choice a. The other choices are vaguely similar, but are not accurate, based on the passage as a whole.

22. d. This passage is written in a style directed to a general audience; therefore, choices a, b, and e are not correct, as they are aimed toward specialized audiences. Nor is this passage in the style of a personal essay (choice c), which would contain impressions and conclusions. The articles in general circulation magazines are aimed toward wide audiences, as is this passage.

23. d. The title *Sights and History on Dublin's O'Connell Street* touches on all the specific subjects of the passage—the sights to see on this particular street and the history connected to them. Answers a and e are too general about the place described, which is a particular street in Dublin, not the whole city. Answers b and c are too specific in that they cover only the material in the first paragraph.

24. a. This choice sticks to the subject, Daniel O'Connell, announced in the sentence before it, and provides a transition to the sentence following it, a description of O'Connell's monument, by providing information about the location of the statue. Answer e provides similar content but includes a grammatical shift in subject; the shift to "we" is jarring. Answers b and c swerve off topic, and answer d essentially repeats information given elsewhere in the paragraph.

25. c. The hidden or key resource mentioned in the passage is the fine distinction between the definition of *street* and *boulevard*, which is used to win the argument with or *get the better of* tourists. Answers a, b, and e do not make sense; answer d is incorrect because there is no real fraud used in the argument in the passage.

26. d. The author offers an example of Dublin wit and mentions the *unhurried* pace of Dublin crowds. Choice a interprets the adjective *unhurried* in too pejorative a manner for the tone of the passage. Answers b and c similarly interpret the playful joke on French tourists too negatively. There is no specific information in the passage to support the view of answer e.

27. b. The context of the passage indicates that the sentences in question are pointing out an unforeseen consequence (however) and the current situation (now). The other choices would result in meanings that do not fit with the flow of information in the rest of the passage.

28. e. Choices a, b, c, and d are not supported by information in the passage. Thus, the best choice is e.

29. d. Choices a, c, and e are possible definitions of *ushered*, but do not fit in the context of the passage. Choice b is an incorrect definition. *Heralded*, choice d, is the best definition in the context.

30. a. The passage explicitly states that Charlemagne was crowned emperor in 800 and died in 814—a period of 14 years. Therefore, b, c, d, and e are mathematically incorrect.

31. b. Although all of the choices are possible definitions of *culture*, the passage is speaking of a

community of inter-related individuals—Europeans.

32. c. The missing sentence is in a portion of the passage which is discussing the long-term impacts of the Franks, therefore, **c** is the best choice. Choices **b** and **d** are written in a style appropriate to the passage, but the information is not appropriate. Choice **a** uses jargon and choice **e** is too informal.

33. c. Unprotected categories of expression are discussed on pages 225–259.

34. e. Although this information is about expression, it is not organized by the types of publications involved, choice **a**; and although the index contains court cases, it does not indicate which courts heard the cases—choice **b**—or the dates of the decisions—choice **c**. Choice **d**, the forum in which the speech took place, is an entry in the index, but does not impact its organization.

35. b. The actions in choices **a**, **c**, and **d**, come after chopping the vegetables, but not immediately. Choice **e** is actually mentioned before the direction to chop the vegetables.

36. e. See the last sentence of the passage for the correct answer, 51 percent.

37. b. The second paragraph states that the current measure identifies fewer working poor, so choice **a** is incorrect. The proposed measure does not disregard expenses for basic needs (choice **c**); it includes the value of non-cash benefits. The current measure identifies fewer people with health insurance (choice **d**). There is no indication in the passage that either measure ignores the destitute (choice **e**).

38. c. The *fellow* frightens the speaker. **a**, **b**, **d**, and **e** are not frightening.

39. a. *Tighter breathing* indicates fear, as does *zero at the bone* (one is sometimes said to be cold with fear). Also, the subject is a snake, which is generally feared animal.

40. c. In context, the speaker is discussing animals, because he follows with his contrasting attitude toward *this fellow*, meaning the snake. The other choices are all human beings.

41. b. Stanza three contains the phrase *when a boy* implying the speaker was a boy in the past and is now, therefore, an adult man.

42. e. The second sentence of the first paragraph states that probes record responses. The second paragraph says that electrodes *accumulate much data*.

43. c. The tone throughout the passage suggests the potential for microprobes. They can be permanently implanted, they have advantages over electrodes, they are promising candidates for neural prostheses, they will have great accuracy, and they are flexible.

44. e. According to the third paragraph, people who *lack* biochemicals could receive doses via prostheses. However, there is no suggestion that removing biochemicals would be viable.

45. a. The first sentence of the third paragraph says that microprobes have channels that *open the way for delivery of drugs*. Studying the brain (choice **d**) is not the initial function of channels, though it is one of the uses of the probes themselves.

46. c. The tone of the passage is enthusiastic in its recommendation of the greyhound as pet and thereby encourages people to adopt one. It does not give advice on transforming a greyhound (choice **a**). Except to say that they love to run, the passage does not spend equal time describing the greyhound as racer (choice **b**), nor does it comment on banning of greyhound racing (choice **e**). The author's tone is not objective (choice **d**), but rather enthusiastic.

47. e. See the last paragraph. The passage does not mention **b**, **c**, or **d**. Choice **a** is clearly wrong; the passage states the opposite.

48. d. Answers **a** and **c** do not include the sense of hierarchy conveyed in the phrase *to enforce social order*. Answers **b** and **e** do convey a sense of hierarchy but reverse the proper order of meanings in the context.

49. a. The question asks for what field the most men are *involved* instead of *employed*. The answer would include students, who are not necessarily salaried workers. Therefore, combining the number of students and teachers gives the largest number involved in education.

50. d. There are 200 men. 6 are in the legal profession. 6 divided by 200 is equal to 0.03 or 3%.

Section 2: Mathematics

1. e. $24,355 + $23,000 = $47,355. When this is rounded to the nearest $100, the answer is $47,400.

2. a. It would cost $7 to get three sandwiches and a piece of fruit.

3. e. The production for Lubbock is equal to the total minus the other productions: 1780 − 450 − 425 − 345 = 560.

4. e. The 3rd and 4th quarters are 54% and 16% respectively. This adds to 70%.

5. b. The average is the sum divided by the number of times Rashaard went fishing: 11 + 4 + 0 + 5 + 4 + 6 divided by 6 is 5.

6. e. An average of 90% is needed of a total of 500 points: 500 × 0.90 = 450, so 450 points are needed. Add all the other test scores together: 95 + 85 + 88 + 84 = 352. Now subtract that total from the total needed, in order to see what score the student must make to reach 90%: 450 − 352 = 98.

7. b. Yellow beans + orange beans = 12. There are 30 total beans. $\frac{12}{30}$ is reduced to $\frac{2}{5}$.

8. a. The sum of the sides equals the perimeter: 3 sides × 3 inches + 2 sides × 5 inches = 19 inches.

9. d. To find the answer do the following equation: 11 × 0.032 = 0.352.

10. a. The 90% discount is over all three items; therefore the total price is $(a + b + c) \times 0.9$. The average is the total price divided by the number of computers: $0.9 \times \frac{(a + b + c)}{3}$.

11. a. Because there are three at $0.99 and 2 at $3.49, the sum of the two numbers minus $3.49 will give the cost.

12. a. This is the same as the equation provided; each score is divided by three.

13. a. For the answer, divide $\frac{2}{3}$ by $\frac{5}{12}$, which is the same as $\frac{2}{3} \times \frac{12}{5} = \frac{24}{15} = 1\frac{3}{5}$.

14. b. 20 percent of 15 cc equals (0.20)(15) equals 3. Adding 3 to 15 gives 18 cc.

15. c. There are three steps involved in solving this problem. First, convert 4.5% to a decimal: 0.045. Multiply that by $26,000 to find out how much the salary increases. Finally, add the result ($1,170) to the original salary of $26,000 to find out the new salary, $27,170.

16. c. If 60% of the students had had flu previously, 40% had not had the disease. 40% of 220 is 88.

17. a. Divide 135 Spanish-speaking teachers by 1,125 total teachers to arrive at 0.12 or 12%.

18. c. Adding 7.8 (electrical equipment) and 7.3 (other equipment) is the way to arrive at the correct response of 15.1.

19. b. Smoking materials account for only 6.7% of the fires but for 28.9% of the deaths.

20. b. Two candy bars require 2 quarters; one package of peanuts requires 3 quarters; one can of cola requires 2 quarters—for a total of 7 quarters.

21. c. Each 9-foot wall has an area of 9 × 8 or 72 square feet. There are two such walls, so those two walls combined have an area of 72 × 2 or 144 square feet. Each 11-foot wall has an area of 11 × 8 or 88 square feet, and again there are two such walls: 88 times 2 equals 176. Finally, add 144 and 176 to get 320 square feet.

22. **e.** Use the formula provided: $\frac{9}{5}(40) + 32 = 72 + 32 = 104$.

23. **c.** Add the corrected value of the sweater ($245) to the value of the two, not three, bracelets ($730), plus the other two items ($78 and $130), for a total of $1,183.

24. **a.** The recipe is for 16 brownies. Half of that, 8, would reduce the ingredients by half. Half of $1\frac{1}{2}$ cups of sugar is $\frac{3}{4}$ cup.

25. **c.** The recipe for 16 brownies calls for $\frac{2}{3}$ cup butter. An additional $\frac{1}{3}$ cup would make 8 more brownies, for a total of 24 brownies.

26. **a.** To solve this problem, you must convert $3\frac{1}{2}$ to $\frac{7}{2}$ and then divide $\frac{7}{2}$ by $\frac{1}{4}$. The answer, $\frac{28}{2}$, is then reduced to the number 14.

27. **d.** Mixed numbers must be converted to fractions, and you must use the least common denominator of 8. $\frac{18}{8}$ plus $\frac{37}{8}$ plus $\frac{4}{8}$ equals $\frac{59}{8}$, which is $7\frac{3}{8}$ after it is reduced.

28. **e.** Four inches is equal to 16 quarter inches, which is equal to $(16)(2 \text{ feet}) = 32$ feet.

29. **b.** You can't just take 25% off the original price, because the 10% discount after three years of service is taken off the price that has already been reduced by 15%. Figure the problem in two steps: after the 15% discount the price is $71.83. 90% of that—subtracting 10%—is $64.65.

30. **b.** Add the number of men and women to get the total number of officers: 200. The number of women, 24, is 12% of 200.

31. **c.** The problem is solved by dividing 204 by 1,700. The answer, 0.12, is then converted to a percentage, 12%.

32. **d.** The simplest way to solve this problem is to divide 1 by 1,500, which is 0.0006667, and then count off two decimal places to arrive at the percentage, which is 0.06667%. Since the question asks *about what percentage*, the nearest value is 0.067%.

33. **a.** You can use trial and error to arrive at a solution to this problem. After the first hour, the number would be 20, after the second hour 40, after the third hour 80, after the fourth hour 160, and after the fifth hour 320. The other answer choices do not have the same outcome.

34. **d.** 30 ppm of the pollutant would have to be removed to bring the 500 ppm down to 20 ppm. 30 ppm represents 60% of 50 ppm.

35. **c.** You must break the 92,000 into the amounts mentioned in the policy: 92,000 = 20,000 + 40,000 + 32,000. The amount the policy will pay is (0.8)(20,000) + (0.6)(40,000) + (0.4)(32,000) = 16,000 + 24,000 + 12,800 = 52,800.

36. **d.** 2,200(0.07) = $154. $154 + 1,400(0.04) = $210. $210 + 3,100(0.08) = $458. $458 + 900(0.03) = $485.

37. **e.** 3W equals water coming in, W equals water going out. 3W − W = 11,400, which implies that W is equal to 5700 and 3W is equal to 17,100.

38. **d.** 3,450 miles divided by 6 days is equal to 575 miles.

39. **d.** Answer **a** reads 276; **b** reads 2,706; **c** reads 20,076, and **e** reads 20,760.

40. **b.** 30 men times 42 square feet of space is equal to 1260 square feet of space. 1260 square feet divided by 35 men equals 36 square feet, so each man will have 6 less square feet of space.

41. **d.** Let T equal Ted's age; S equal Sam's age, which is 3T; R equal Ron's age, which is $\frac{S}{2}$, or $\frac{3T}{2}$. The sum of the ages is 55: $\frac{3T}{2} + 3T + T = 55$. Convert the left side of the equation into fractions so you can add them: $\frac{3T}{2} + \frac{6T}{2} + \frac{2T}{2} = \frac{11T}{2}$. Now you have

$\frac{11T}{2}$ = 55. Multiply both sides by 2: 11T = 110. Divide through by 11 to get T = 10. That is Ted's age. Sam is three times Ted's age, or 30. Ron is half Sam's age, or 15 years old.

42. c. Because the answer is a fraction, the best way to solve the problem is to convert the known to a fraction: $\frac{10}{45}$ of the cylinder is full. By dividing both the numerator and the denominator by 5, you can reduce the fraction to $\frac{2}{9}$.

43. c. The answer is arrived at by first dividing 175 by 45. Since the answer is 3.89, not a whole number, the gardener needs 4 sections of hose. Three sections of hose would be too short.

44. c. The difference between 105 and 99 is 6 degrees. Application of the ice pack plus a "resting" period of 5 minutes before reapplication means that the temperature is lowered by half a degree every six minutes, or 1 degree every 12 minutes. 6 degrees times 12 minutes per degree equals 72 minutes, or 1 hour and 12 minutes.

45. d. Multiply 16 times 5 to find out how many gallons all five sprinklers will release in one minute. Then multiply the result (80 gallons per minute) by the number of minutes (10) to get 800 gallons.

46. b. Use 35 for C. F = ($\frac{9}{5}$ × 35) + 32. Therefore F = 63 + 32, or 95°F.

47. c. 5 times 3 times 8 is 120. 120 divided by 3 is 40.

48. d. There are two sides 34 feet long and two sides 20 feet long. Using the formula P = 2L + 2W will solve this problem. Therefore, you should multiply 34 times 2 and 20 times 2, and then add the results: 68 + 40 = 108.

49. c. There are four quarts to a gallon. There are therefore 20 quarts in a 5-gallon container. Divide 20 by 1.06 quarts per liter to get 18.86 liters and then round off to 19.

50. e. Division is used to arrive at a decimal, which can then be rounded to the nearest hundredth and converted to a percentage: 11,350 ÷ 21,500 = 0.5279. 0.5279 rounded to the nearest hundredth is 0.53, or 53%.

Section 3: Essay Writing

Following are the criteria for scoring CBEST essays.

A "4" essay is a coherent writing sample that addresses the assigned topic and is aimed at a specific audience. Additionally, it has the following characteristics:

- A main idea and/or a central point of view that is focused; its reasoning is sound
- Points of discussion that are clear and arranged logically
- Assertions that are supported with specific, relevant detail
- Word choice and usage that is accurate and precise
- Sentences that have complexity and variety, with clear syntax; paragraphs that are coherent (minor mechanical flaws are acceptable)
- Style and language appropriate to the assigned audience and purpose

A "3" essay is an adequate writing sample that generally addresses the assigned topic, but may neglect or only vaguely address one of the assigned tasks; it is aimed at a specific audience. Generally, it has the following additional characteristics:

- A main idea and/or a central point of view and adequate reasoning
- Organization of ideas that is effective; the meaning of the ideas is clear
- Generalizations that are adequately, though unevenly, supported

- Word choice and language usage that are adequate; mistakes exist but these do not interfere with meaning
- Some errors in sentence and paragraph structure, but not so many as to be confusing
- Word choice and style appropriate to a given audience

A "2" essay is an incompletely formed writing sample that attempts to address the topic and to communicate a message to the assigned audience but is generally incomplete or inappropriate. It has the following additional characteristics:

- A main point, but one which loses focus; reasoning that is simplistic
- Ineffective organization that causes the response to lack clarity
- Generalizations that are only partially supported; supporting details that are irrelevant or unclear
- Imprecise language usage; word choice that distracts the reader
- Mechanical errors; errors in syntax; errors in paragraphing
- Style that is monotonous or choppy

A "1" essay is an inadequately formed writing sample that only marginally addresses the topic and fails to communicate its message to, or is inappropriate to, a specific audience. Additionally, it has the following characteristics:

- General incoherence and inadequate focus, lack of a main idea or consistent point of view; illogical reasoning
- Ineffective organization and unclear meaning throughout

- Unsupported generalizations and assertions; details that are irrelevant and presented in a confusing manner
- Language use that is imprecise, with serious and distracting errors
- Many serious errors in mechanics, sentence syntax, and paragraphing

Following are examples of scored essays for Topics 1 and 2. (There are some deliberate errors in all the essays, so that you can tell how much latitude you have.)

TOPIC 1

Pass—Score = 4

I like TV. It's relaxing after a hard day, and the quotation above is correct—TV has enabled us to see places we've never gotten to go, and it has made possible a global village. But it has its dark side, too.

Take for example the case of Darrell, who, in 1989, married Sherry, a good friend of mine. Their wedding was lovely, held outdoors to the music of guitars and tamborines, on a sunlit spring day, all their friends present. I'd flown in from a thousand miles away just for the wedding, so it was a couple of years before I made it back to visit them again. By that time they'd bought a small two-bedroom house and had acquired a cat, an orange-striped, 15-pound scrapper named Chester.

But I had been in their home only hours before I realized something was wrong. During supper Darrell was cordial and seemed glad to have me there. We had pasta and wine and talked about old times. After supper, he excused himself and went into the family room and turned on the TV. Over coffee, Sherry told me he was addicted. "If there's nothing else on, he'll watch the weather channel for hours." She told me that the addiction had come on gradually. "We used to take nature walks and go to museums but not anymore."

And sure enough, the whole weekend I was visiting, Darrell spent most of the time in front of the TV. He watched good shows and bad, sit-coms and specials and old movies. The old movies kept him up til 2:00 A.M. on both Friday and Saturday nights. "They're having a Fred Astaire marathon," he explained over breakfast on Sunday. "That Fred Astaire is something else,"

A couple of years later, Sherry called me in tears to tell me she couldn't stand it anymore. "I've filed for divorce," she said. "I can't compete with Barbara Walters and that guy on the Travel Channel. I can't even compete with the dog food commercials."

I had some vacation coming from my job, so I flew back to cheer her up. By the time I got there, she and Darrell had already moved out of their house, and she just had a few things to pick up from Darrell's apartment that he had packed but decided he didn't want. He'd given Sherry a key to his apartment, because their divorce really was friendly, so we let ourselves in. The main light was a soft blue from the TV. He waved at us cheerfully, then burst into laughter. He was watching "Funniest Home Videos."

"This guys a hoot," was all he said to me after not having seen me for two years "Do you ever watch this show?"

I don't think TV is Darrell's only problem, but I do suspect its constant chatter keeps him from facing his demons. It's a passive medium—even the Explorer channel, which makes you feel you've made a trip to someplace like Shri Lanka, although you never saw how brilliant the sunlight could be in that part of the world, or feel the warm sand under your feet.

Darrell did say one last thing to Sherry as we were preparing to leave, after we'd gathered up a bag of her leftover stuff plus Chester. She leaned down to kiss him and bumped the remote. A flickering took place on the TV screen, yellow lines and text, something about an adjustment being needed.

"Oh, watch out, honey," Darrell said, grabbing the remote and punching some buttons. "You'll mess up the colors."

Marginal Pass—Score = 3

Many people say they don't watch television, and I say good for them! There is very little on TV today that is worth watching. And yet, for all that, it has an important place in society. I believe, for example, that it is an excellent teaching tool for kids who have had less than a sterling formal education in the lower grades. It's something they can relate to and something they will have in common with the other people in their class. It's something they have in common with the teacher, for that matter. And that is all-important.

Television opens a window on the world that is unique. It helps students to see more of the world than any generation before them has been able to see. With a simple flick of the switch they can look in and watch the goings-on in congress; or travel down the Ganges river or see the Scotish highlands. They can learn about other cultures, learn how to cook or build a house. They can witness events half a world away as soon as they take place.

Here is one advantage of television, as it can be used as a teaching tool. In classrooms today, especially in community colleges, for example, there are students from every strata of society, from many different social classes. Television is one thing they have in common and can bring about lively discussions and a meeting of the minds. Rich and poor alike, privileged or under privileged, all have looked through that tiny window and see wonders and horrors, current events and events long-past. And all can be used as fodder for lively class discussion, for making the subjects we're teaching come alive.

We might take pride in saying we never watch television, but we shouldn't be so quick to put it down—especially as it pertains to teaching. Television is one thing students have in common, and I think it was Winston Churchhill who said, "The only thing worse than democracy is any other form of government." I think the same can be said for television: "The only thing worse than television is no television." Sure, theres a lot on that's not worth watching, but theres also a lot that is. And to ignore it's influence is to ignore an excellent, if flawed, teaching tool.

Marginal Fail—Score = 2

I sometimes wish TV had never been invented. Especially for the younger generation, who get much of their information about the world in a distorted fashion from "the box." Of course it is entertaining after a hard day, but at the end what have you gained?

And the news gets distorted. We get our news from "a reliabel source" but who is that? Some gossip columnist in Washington or New York that has nothing to do with our real life. We get to see how rotten our politicions are and maybe thats a good thing because earlier in history they could cover it up. We get to watch them on TV and judge for ourself instead of taking someone else's word for it. So television can be a good thing if watched in moderation.

Another way TV corrups society is through advertizing. It tells us to buy, buy, buy. It gives us super models and sport's figures to tell you what to buy and where. It gives you movie stars advertising even in a TV movie away from comercials, by holding a can of Coke or other product. All of which subliminaly tells you to buy Coke. They say they even have messages flashed on the screen so on the commercial you will get up and go to the kitchen. I find myself bringing home products I never even use. The worse thing is the shows in which dificult life situatsions get solved in a half hour. You could never do it in real life but on TV it is easy. It gives us a erronous view of the world.

I think we should try to do away with it in our homes even if it is hard. After all, its your baby-sitter and advise-giver, and even your friend if you are lonely. But give it a week to be away from it and then watch intermittently. You're life will be better for it.

Fail—Score = 1

TV can be good or bad depending on how you look at it. It can be all you do if you are not careful. It can take you away from your kids if you use it as a baby sitter or when you come home from work that is all you do. Also you will never get the real story. You will never know if they are telling the truth or trying a snow job to sell you something.

I grew up with television like most peopel. It is a good thing if you try to learn from it. It probably will help in a class room discussion if the children all watch the same show. In grade school where I went we had current events and television had it's place.

One example is the news. We know if we are going to war the minute the president makes his decision. We can watch it all happening. We can know if there is a scandel in Washington. And the latest medical facts are on TV. So TV can be good in that aspect.

It can be bad to. For example the shows for teen agers. When I was a teen ager I liked them, all the music and the dancing. But now it is diferent. Drugs are spread through MTV because of the musicions who you can tell do them. And they are models for our kids.

But in some aspects TV is good and in some it is bad. I think spending time away from it will make you feel better. all the news is bad news. But you can get an education too if you just watch public TV. It is good in some aspects and bad in some.

TOPIC 2

Pass—Score = 4

I believe that writing, at least the kind of basic composition needed to be successful in college, can be taught. The most important factor in teaching a basic composition class, which usually has students who have been less than successful writers in the past, is a simple one: that the student be asked to write about something that interests her, that her writing have a context and a purpose beyond "English class," that the student be made to *want* to learn to write.

For students who have fallen behind for one reason or another—and that reason is many times a poor education in the early grades—it's difficult to see a writing class as anything but an exercise in plummeting self-esteem. Many students believe that writing well is a mystery only those "with talent" can understand, and that "English class" is just something to be gotten through, like a root canal. The first thing to teach them isn't the rules of grammar but that writing has a purpose that pertains to their lives. The teacher must appeal to their emotion as well as to their intellect.

I believe the best approach is to ask students to keep a journal in two parts. In one part, grammar and style shouldn't matter, the way they have to matter in the formal assignments that come later in the course. In this part of the journal, the student should be asked to keep track of things they encounter during the day that interest them or cause them to be happy, sad, angry, or afraid. In the second part of the journal they should keep track of subjects that make them sit up and take notice in class (or when reading an assignment for a class in which they are particularly interested), things that whet their intellect and curiosity.

For teaching grammar, the teacher can present exercises in the context of a one-page essay or story. Giving writing a context is especially important when teaching the rules of correct sentence construction. Too often in the early grades the student has been presented with dry exercises, such as to diagram the sentence, "I have a new pencil," when a small essay on an icky grub farm nearby or the behavior of wolves would

have fired their imagination, as well as their intellect, engaging the whole student.

Only appeal to emotion and intellect—and to that most primitive human characteristic, curiosity—will really succeed in engaging the whole student and making him *want* to learn to write. And he has to want to learn before anything can really be accomplished.

Marginal Pass—Score = 3

I believe writing can be taught if we work hard enough at it as teachers. The important thing is to teach students that it can be enjoyable. Years of fearing writing lie behind a lot of students, and it's one of the biggest stumbling blocks. But it can be gotten over.

Having them break up into small groups is one way to teach writing to reluctant or ill-prepared students. Have the students discuss a topic they are all interested in—say a recent TV show or an event coming up at school, then plan a paper and come back and discuss the idea with the whole class. Your next step can be to have them actually write the paper, then get into their small groups again and criticize what theyve done.

Another way for students who don't like the small groups is one on one conferences. But dont just talk about grammar or sentence structure or paragraphing, talk about the content of his paper. I did a summer internship teaching in an innter city school, and I rememmber one young man. He hated small groups so we talked privately. He had written a paper on going to a city-sponsored camping trip and seeing white-tailed deer, which was his first time. He was excited about it, and I suggested he write a paper about his experience. He did and, except for some trouble with grammar, it was an A paper, full of active verbs and telling detail!

Finally, try to get your students to read. If you have to, drag them to the community library yourself. Not only will it help their writing, it will help them in life. Only by getting them interested in the written word and by helping them to see that it matters in their everyday lives can you really reach them and set them on the path of good writing.

Yes. Writing can be taught if you are willing to take the time and do the hard work and maybe give a few extra hours. No student is hopeless. And writing is so important in today's world that its worth the extra effort.

Marginal Fail—Score = 2

I dont think writing can be taught neccesarily, although if the students are half-way motivated anything's possible. The first thing is get them interested in the subject and give them alot of writing to do in class. They may not do it if it is all outside class as many poorly prepared students hate homework. I know I did as a kid!

Writing does not come natural for most people especially in the poorer school districs. Unless they are lucky enough to have parents who read to them. That is another aspect of teaching how to write. Assign alot of reading. If you don't read you can't write, and that is lacking in alot of students backgrounds. If your students wont' read books tell them to read comic books if nothing else. Anything to get them to read.

The second thing is to have the student come in for a conference once a week. That is one way to see what is going on with them in school and at home. A lot of kids in the poorer schools have conflict at home and that is why they fail. So give them alot of praise because thats what they need.

Finaly don't' give up. It can be done. Many people born into poverty go on to do great things. You can help and you never know who you will inspire and who will remember you as the best teacher they ever had.

Fail—Score = 1

You will be able to tell I am one of the peopel that never learned to write well. I wish I had but my personal experience as a struggling writer will inspire my students, thats the most I can hope for. Writing can be taught, but you have to be ready to inspire the student. Give them assignments on subjets they like and keep after them to read. Take them to the public libary if they havnt been and introduce them to books.

Reading is one way to teach it. Maybe you're students grew up in a household without books like I did. My dad was always working and my mom to, and they didnt have time to read. So I never did. Some of my freinds were bookworms but not me.

Maybe thats the key: tell you're students they have to be bookworms! And read read read. And if they have children someday tell them to read to there children.

If you cant write people will call you dumb or stupid which hurts you're self-estem. I know from experience.

The next thing is have them come in and talk to you. You never know what is going on in there lifes that is keeping them from studying and doing there best. Maybe they have a mom that works all the time or a dad who has left the home. Be sure to teach the whole person. Also have them write about what is going on in there lives, not a dry subject like the drinking age. Have the student write about there personal experience and it will come out better. Writing can be taught if the student is motivated. So hang in there.

▶ Scoring

Again, evaluate how you did on this practice exam by scoring the three sections—Reading Comprehension, Mathematics, and Essay Writing—separately. For both Reading Comprehension and Mathematics, use the same scoring method: First find the number of questions you got right out of the 50 questions in each section, then use the table below to check your math and find percentage equivalents for several possible scores.

Number of questions right	Approximate percentage
50	100%
46	92%
43	86%
39	78%
35	70%
32	64%
28	56%
25	50%

If you achieve a score of at least 70% on both the Reading Comprehension section and the Mathematics section, you will most likely pass those portions of the CBEST. (Remember that the scores are converted from raw scores to scaled scores, so the actual number you receive on the real CBEST will *not* be "70"; however, a percentage will work for the purpose of finding out if you passed the practice exams.) In addition, as mentioned in previous chapters, you must receive a passing score on the Essay Writing section of the CBEST, which will be evaluated by specially trained readers. The criteria are outlined in detail in the Answers section above, but generally the essays are scored as follows:

4 = Pass (an excellent and well-formed essay)

3 = Marginal Pass (an average and adequately formed essay)

2 = Marginal Fail (a partially formed but substandard essay)

1 = Fail (an inadequately formed essay)

To see how you did on your essays for this third and final practice exam, be sure to give them and the scoring criteria to a teacher and ask him or her to score your essays for you.

You have probably seen improvement between your first practice exam score and this one; but if you didn't improve as much as you'd like, following are some options for you to consider:

- **If you scored below 60%,** you should seriously consider whether you're ready for the CBEST at this time. A good idea would be to take some brush-up courses, either at a university or community college nearby or through correspondence, in the areas you feel less sure of. If you don't have time for a course, you might try private tutoring.

- **If your score is in the 60 to 70% range,** you need to work as hard as you can to improve your skills. The LearningExpress books *Reading Comprehension Success in 20 Minutes a Day* and *Practical Math Success in 20 Minutes a Day* or other books from your public library will undoubtedly help. Also, reread and pay close attention to all the advice in Chapters 2 and 4 of this book in order to improve your score. It might also be helpful to ask friends and family to make up mock test questions and quiz you on them.

- **If your score is between 70 and 80%,** you could still benefit from additional work by going back to Chapter 4 and by brushing up your reading, math, and writing skills before the exam.

- **If you scored above 80%,** that's great! This kind of score should make it easy for you to pass the real CBEST. Don't lose your edge, though; keep studying right up to the day before the exam.

There's an ancient joke that goes like this: In New York City, a man stops a second man on the street and asks, "How do I get to Carnegie Hall?" The second man answers, "Practice."

The key to success in almost any pursuit is to prepare for all you're worth. By taking the practice exams in this book, you've made yourself better prepared than other people who may be taking the exam with you. You've diagnosed where your strengths and weaknesses lie and learned how to deal with the various kinds of questions that will appear on the test. So go into the exam with confidence, knowing that you're ready and equipped to do your best.

APPENDIX

How to Use the CD-ROM

So you think you're ready for your exam? Here's a great way to build confidence and know you are ready: using LearningExpress's Academic Skills Tester AutoExam CD-ROM software included inside the back cover of this book. This disk can be used with any PC running Windows 3.1 through Windows ME. (Sorry, it doesn't work with Macintosh.) The following description represents a typical "walk through" the software.

To install the program:

1. Insert the CD-ROM into your CD-ROM drive. The CD should run automatically. If it does not, proceed to step 2.

2. From Windows, select **Start**, then choose **Run.**

3. Type D:/Setup.

4. Click **OK.**

The screens that appear subsequently will walk you right through the installation procedure.

HOW TO USE THE CD-ROM

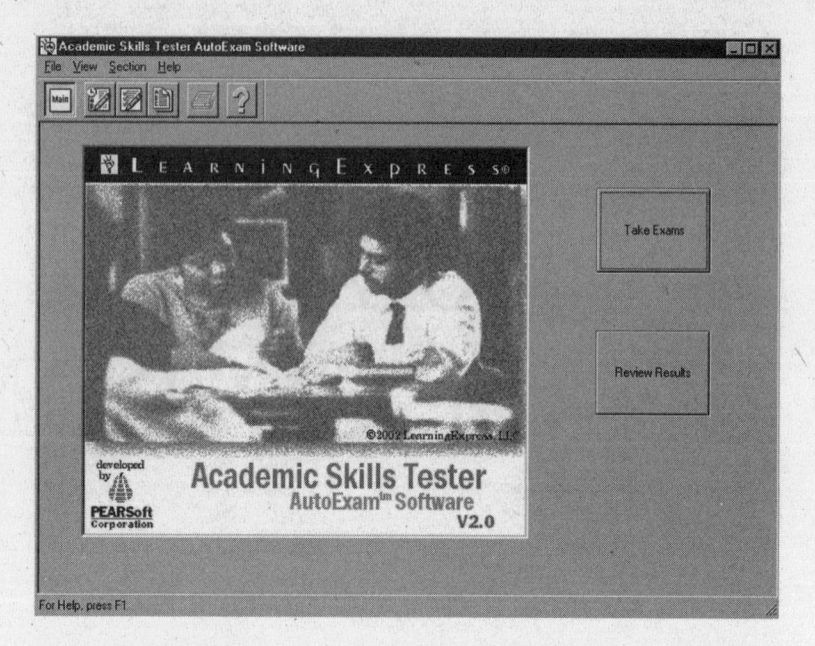

From the Main Menu, select **Take Exams.** (You can use **Review Exam Results** after you have taken at least one exam, in order to see your scores.)

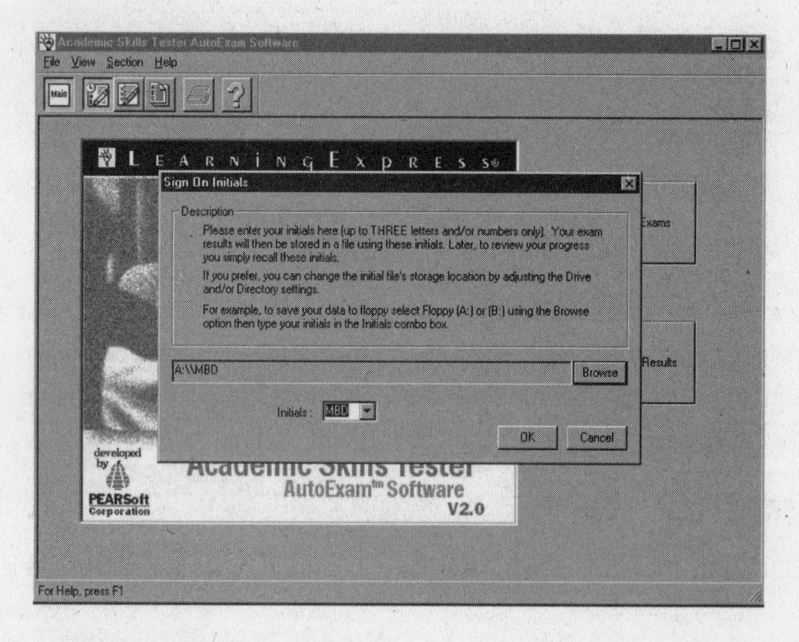

Now enter your initials. This allows you a chance to record your progress and review your performance for as many simulated exams as you'd like. Notice that you can also change the drive where your exam results are stored. If you want to save to a floppy drive, for instance, click on the "Browse" button and then choose the letter of your floppy drive.

HOW TO USE THE CD-ROM

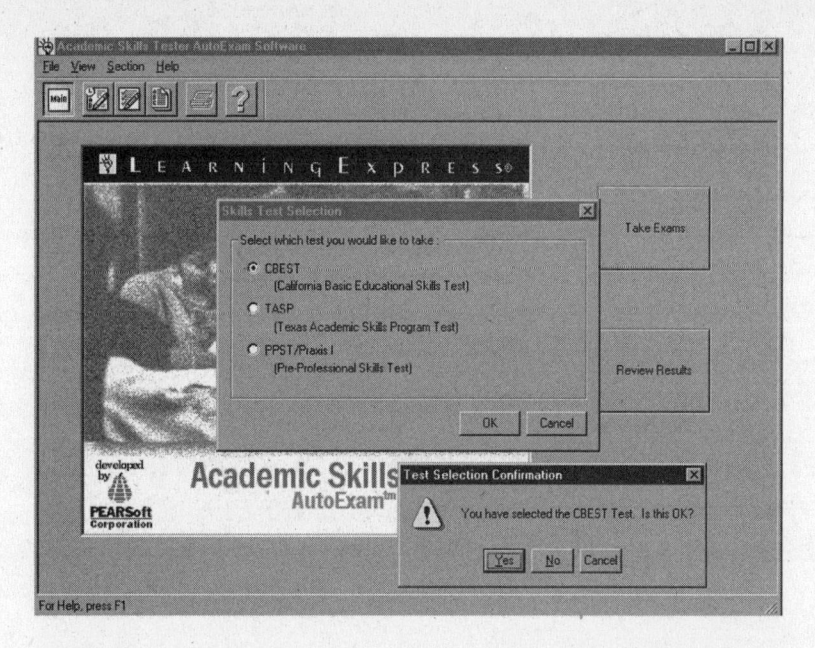

Now, since this CD-ROM supports three different academic exams, you need to select your exam of interest. Let's try CBEST, the California Basic Education Skills Test, as shown above.

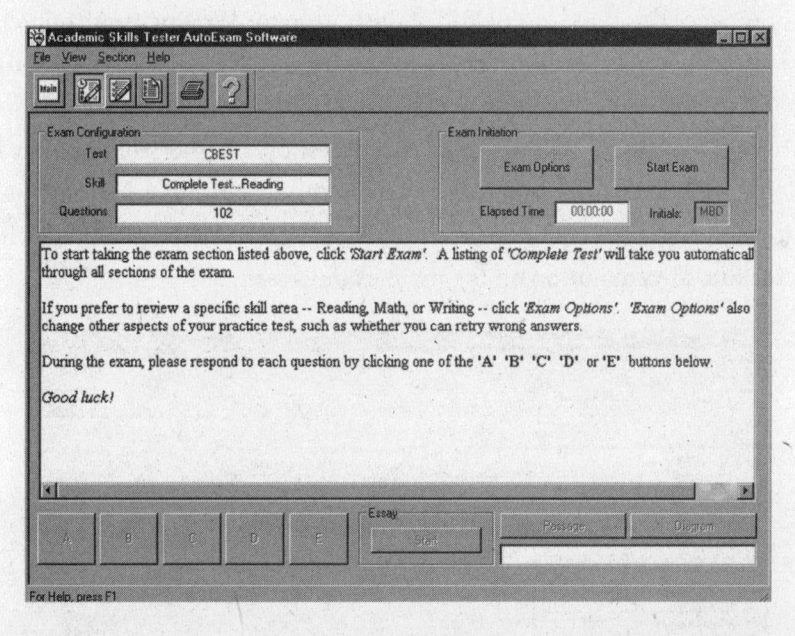

Now you're into the **Take Exams** section, as shown above. You can choose **Start Exam** to start taking your test, or **Exam Options.** The next screen shows you what your **Exam Options** are.

HOW TO USE THE CD-ROM

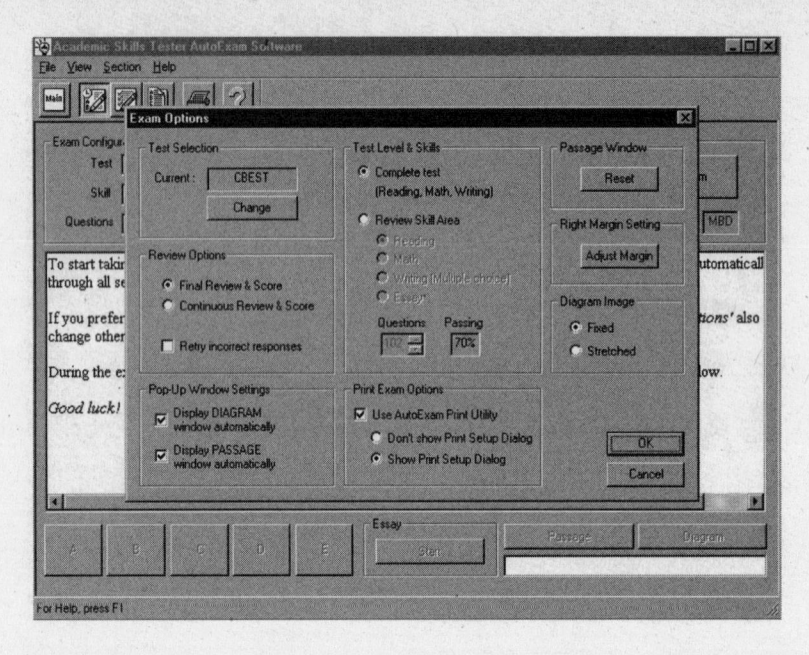

Choosing **Exam Options** gives you plenty of options to help you fine tune your rough spots. How about a little math to warm up? Click **Review Skill Area,** and then the **Math** option. Choose the number of questions you want to review right now. Since this is a sample CBEST, the button for **Writing (multiple-choice)** is gray; CBEST doesn't have multiple-choice writing questions. If you are taking a PPST or TASP, the **Writing (multiple-choice)** button will be active. On the left you can choose whether to wait until you've finished to see how you did (**Final Review & Score**) or have the computer tell you after each question whether your answer is right (**Continuous Review & Score**). Choose **Retry incorrect responses** to get a second chance at questions you answer wrong. (This option works best with **Review Skill Area** rather than **Complete Test**.) When you finish choosing your options, click **OK**. Then click the **Start Exam** button on the main exam screen.

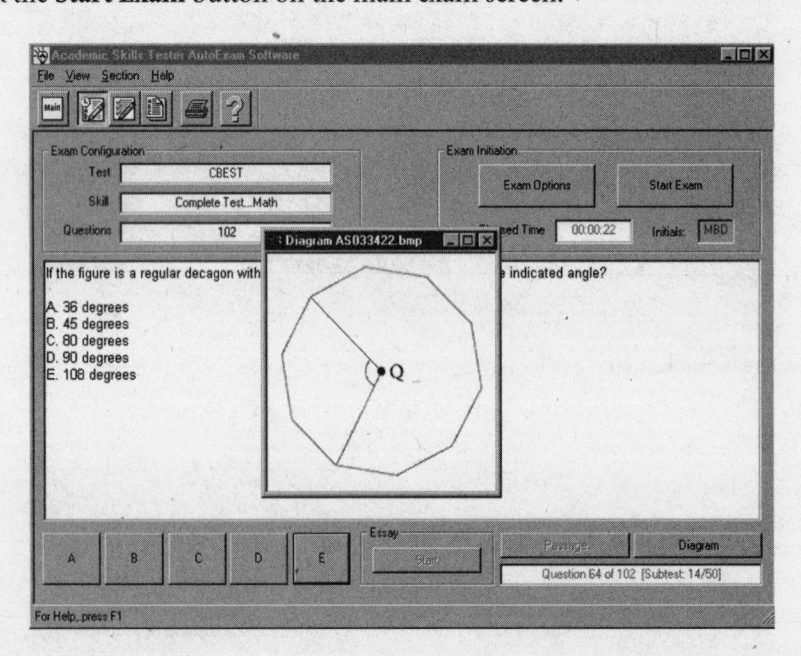

HOW TO USE THE CD-ROM

As you can see, diagrams are displayed any time a math problem calls for one. You can move the diagram window (or a passage for reading questions) by clicking on the bar at the top of the window and dragging to where you want it. You can also minimize the diagram window by clicking on the left box in the right corner. You can get the diagram back any time by clicking the **Diagram** button.

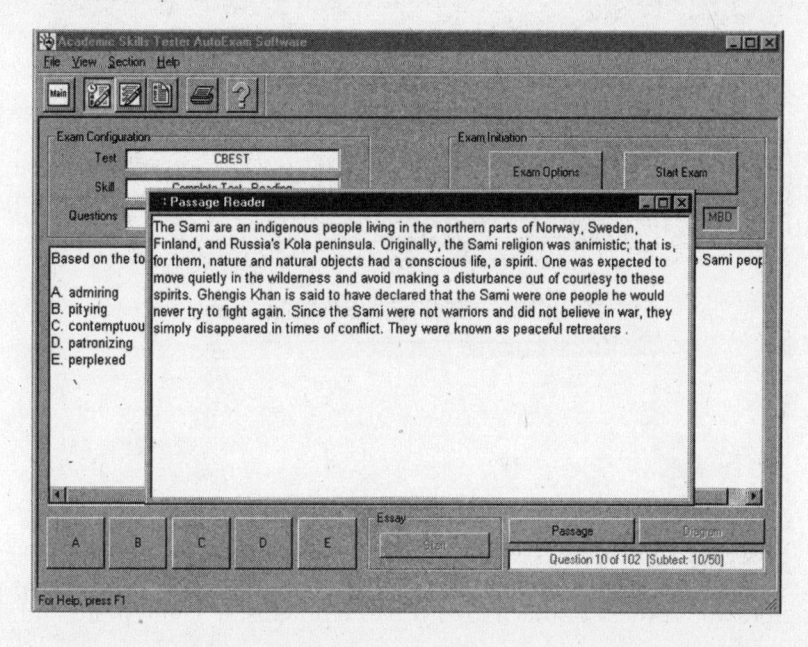

Once you've responded to all ten of the questions, go back to **Exam Options** and select a **Reading** exam; then click on **Start Exam.** AutoExam makes it easy by displaying the reading passage in its own window, which always "rides on top" of the exam window, as seen above. You can scroll through the reading passage using the scroll bar on the right, or minimize the passage so you see only the question window. To get the passage back, click the **Passage** button.

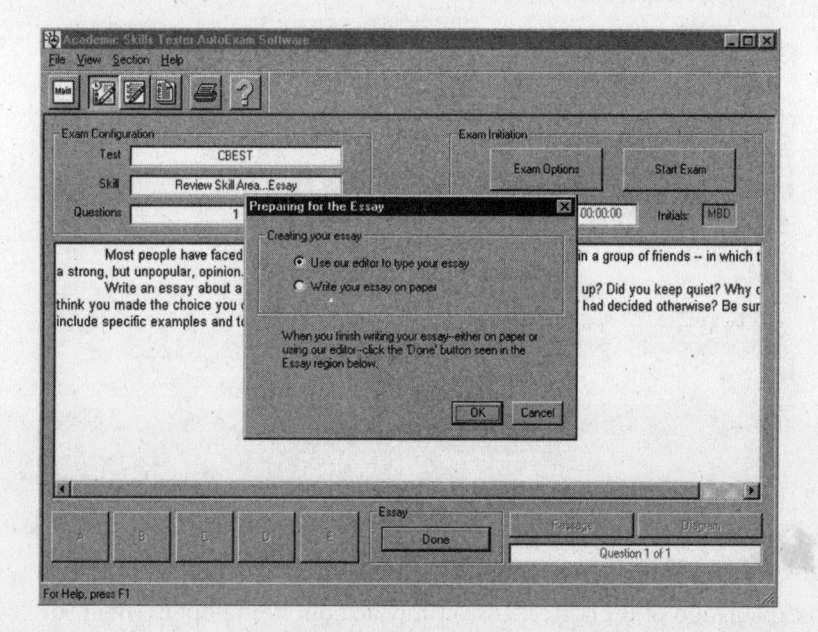

Don't forget about an essay or two for some good practice. Once again, click the **Exam Options** button, select the Essay setting, click **Start Exam,** and you're on your way again. You have the option of writing out your essay by hand or using AutoExam's built-in editor.

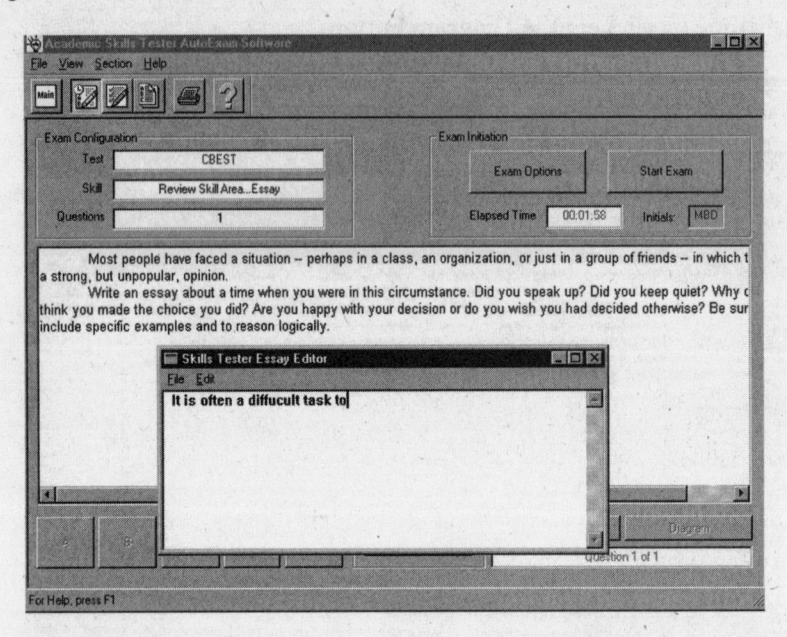

This editor is a simple word processor that allows you to type, erase, cut and paste, and save. When you finish writing your essay—by hand or on screen—click **Done.**

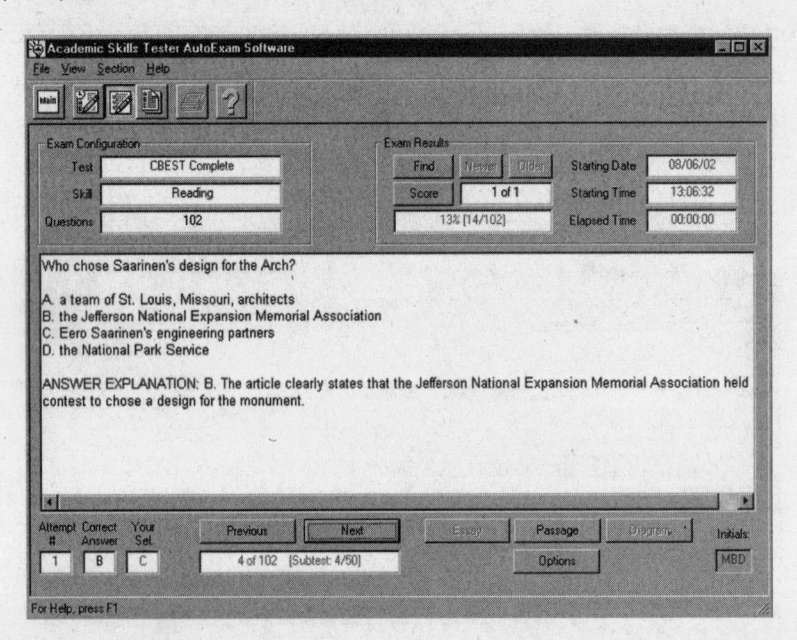

After you have had a good dose of exams, why not check your progress? Simply click the **Review Exams** menu button (as seen on the first screen) and you can review your progress in detail and check your score. You can see how many questions you got right and how long each section took you, and review individual questions. Note that you can choose to have an explanation of the correct answer for each question pop up when you review that question.

HOW TO USE THE CD-ROM

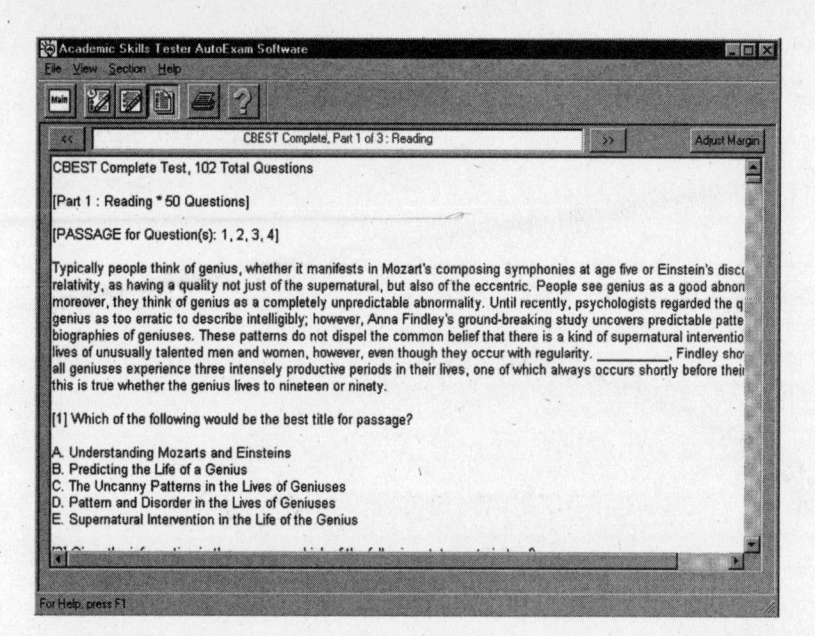

What's that? No time to work at the computer? Click the **Print Exams** menu bar button and you'll have a full-screen review of an exam that you can print out, as shown above. Then take it with you to the game.

For technical support, call (212) 995-2566.

Master the Basics... Fast!

If you need to improve your basic skills to move ahead either at work or in the classroom, then our LearningExpress books are designed to help anyone master the skills essential for success. It features 20 easy lessons to help build confidence and skill fast. This series includes real world examples—**WHAT YOU REALLY NEED TO SUCCEED.**

Easy to Use & Understand

All of these books:

- Give quick and easy instruction
- Provides compelling, interactive exercises
- Share practical tips and valuable advise that can be put to use immediately
- Includes extensive lists of resources for continued learning

Write Better Essays
208 pages • 8 1/2 x 11 • paper
$13.95 • ISBN 1-57685-309-8

The Secrets of Taking Any Test, 2e
208 pages • 7 x 10 • paper
$14.95 • ISBN 1-57685-307-1

Read Better, Read More, 2e
208 pages • 7 x 10 • paper
$14.95 • ISBN 1-57685-336-5

Math Essentials, 2e
208 pages • 7 x 10 • paper
$14.95 • ISBN 1-57685-305-5

How To Study, 2e
208 pages • 7 x 10 • paper
$14.95 • ISBN 1-57685-308-X

Grammar Essentials, 2e
208 pages • 7 x 10 • paper
$14.95 • ISBN 1-57685-306-3

Improve Your Writing For Work, 2e
208 pages • 7 x 10 • paper
$14.95 • ISBN 1-57685-337-3

To Order: Call 1-888-551-5627

Also available at your local bookstore. Prices subject to change without notice.
LearningExpress • 900 Broadway, Suite 604 • New York, New York 10003

LearningExpress®

LearnATest.com™